ENVIRONMENTAL MANAGEMENT IN HOSPITALITY

ENVIRONMENTAL MANAGEMENT IN HOSPITALITY

M. C. METTI

ANMOL PUBLICATIONS PVT. LTD.
NEW DELHI - 110 002 (INDIA)

ANMOL PUBLICATIONS PVT. LTD.

H.O.: 4374/4B, Ansari Road, Darya Ganj,
New Delhi-110 002 (India)
Ph.: 23278000, 23261597

B.O.: No. 1015, Ist Main Road, BSK IIIrd Stage
IIIrd Phase, IIIrd Block
Bangalore - 560 085 (India)
Visit us at: www.anmolpublications.com

Environmental Management in Hospitality

ISBN 978-81-261-3245-4

PRINTED IN INDIA

Printed at Mehra Offset Press, Delhi.

Contents

Preface

"Environmental Management in Hospitality" is designed to provide interactive discussion among class members and the instructor as they discuss problems, risks, opportunities, and alternatives related to each case study. The cases are real-life stories of positive and negative situations that managers have experienced in relating to the environment within the hospitality arena.

They are designed to help students develop professional characteristics that can be inherent in their futures as hospitality managers. While for many hospitality companies interest in the sector started with environmental management issues, the focus has now widened to include social and economic impacts, more broadly defined as Corporate Responsibility.

The cases are organized by segment and include situations in restaurants, hotels, country clubs, business and industry, healthcare, university/college/public school food services, and other facilities. The cases include both domestic and global hospitality operations with opportunities to explore a diverse workforce.

Author

Chapter 1

Introduction

HOSPITALITY DIRECTIONS

The hospitality sector has adopted numerous strategies, approaches and measures in response to the challenge of sustainable development. The sector has particularly used environmental management systems and tools to demonstrate commitment to an environmentally friendly work ethic. Many multinational and independent hotel companies have introduced environmental management practices at the property level. These include:

- Environmental management systems and tools
- Education, awareness creation, training and information dissemination
- Voluntary initiatives
- Multi-stakeholder communication and consultation
- Environmental reporting
- Implementation of the Rio principles

Ideally, the framework for this involves defining an environmental policy and building a management system to measure environmental impacts and compliance with the policy and local regulations, as well as documenting the system's performance for inspection and auditing purposes. Such environmental management systems (EMS) help businesses to evaluate manages and reduces their negative environmental impacts by providing a methodology to integrate environment management into business operations in a systematic manner.

Connected Thinking

Businesses are increasingly being asked to shoulder responsibility for their social, ethical and environmental impacts, with this pressure particularly keenly felt in consumer-facing industries. While for many hospitality companies interest in the sector started with environmental management issues, the focus has now widened to include social and economic impacts, more broadly defined as Corporate Responsibility.

The travel industry of course drives demand for hotel accommodation and between 1950 and 2000 the number of journeys taken by international tourists, including business travellers, increased nearly 28 fold. This year alone 840million tourist arrivals are forecast globally, and by 2020 the figure could reach 1,580 million.

Fears that numbers of this size are unlikely to be sustainable have led to calls for less air travel and for more personal and Corporate Responsibility. However, despite some progress, Jonathon Porritt, Chair of the UK Sustainable Development Commission, recently commented on the travel industry:

> "The industry cannot begin to claim that it's even remotely responsible. Our collective efforts to date are hopelessly inadequate".

In January 2006, PricewaterhouseCoopers undertook new research into 14 of Europe's leading hotel groups, accounting for some 1.5 million rooms globally. We tested these hotel companies against 11 key components of Corporate Responsibility to assess the relevance of Corporate Responsibility to their businesses, the expectations of key stakeholders, and how well the sector is performing. This article presents the results of this research and also assesses some of the future challenges the sector must tackle. Overall, our research shows that:

- Some progress has been made, but the sector lags behind other European industries in responding to Corporate Responsibility challenges;
- Because of the complexity of the sector it is not easy for hotel companies, and others in the industry value chain, to respond too many of the issues without engaging with their business partners;
- Long term, there is a clear business advantage for those who get their Corporate Responsibility response right but real risks for those who don't.

> "The industry creates buildings full of air conditioning and there's no comment on how waste is being disposed of. For an 'eco' agenda to be meaningful, hoteliers have to look at the repercussions of what they're doing from the beginning. Yes, a large number of hotels now have light-saving devices. They ask us to hang up our towels. But that's not enough. Let's be honest: these are often just mechanisms for the hotelier to manage costs".

Mark Banning-Taylor, owner of upscale hotel and lodge development, Moonlight Head, Australia.

While consumer awareness of Corporate Responsibility in the hospitality industry is still in its inception, consumers are becoming more active in directing their spending towards goods and services that meet their ethical expectations and boycotting companies and brands which they view as exploitative. This is particularly apparent in the clothing and grocery sectors.

Corporate Responsibility

Over the past few years, a wide range of stakeholders have become increasingly interested in the social, ethical and environmental performance of the hospitality industry, including the media, investors and rating agencies, consumers, employees, governments and non- governmental organisations (NGOs):

The media is paying ever-greater attention to sustainability issues. Much of this interest has previously focused on the retail sector, for example, with headline-grabbing statements on issues such as child labour. Such exposes have had a considerable impact and in some cases have led to boycotting of certain consumer brands with a consequent impact on shareholder value. The hospitality sector cannot shy away from these issues any more than the retail sector can. Current headlines are focusing on topics such as climate change, the impact of global travel, worker exploitation, binge drinking and obesity. This media attention has amplified the need for companies in the sector to not only establish systems and controls to monitor supplier performance, but also to develop reporting mechanisms to demonstrate to external audiences what actions they are taking to ensure high standards of Corporate Responsibility.

Governments across Europe are also taking an increasing interest in Corporate Responsibility, although they are not currently a key driver for change in the sector. Initiatives in place include, for example, at the EU level, the European Commission's White Paper on Corporate Social Responsibility, which contains guidance on labour standards.

Many corporate investment companies are now screening their investments according to a range of social and environmental criteria. Additionally, rating indices such as FTSE4Good and the Dow Jones Sustainability Indices (DJSI) include ratings on hospitality companies on the basis of their performance in this area. For example, the DJSI has an assessment category covering "hotels, restaurants, bars and recreational services". As of September 2005, DJSI had identified Accor, Compass Group, McDonald's, Sodexho and Starbucks as sustainability leaders. The Socially Responsible Investment (SRI) market is expected to expand significantly in the next decade with a greater scrutiny of performance in this area.

A November 2005 report on Responsible Tourism from First Choice, based on more than 1,000 people questioned by market research firm Mintel, found that a quarter of respondents were concerned about the impact of tourism on the environment of the countries they visited and 28 per cent were prepared to pay a small supplement to offset the carbon emissions of their flights. One in five said that it was important that their visit benefited local communities. More than half said they would be happy to take more public transport to explore on holiday (54 per cent), half said they would recycle on holiday (50 per cent), and four out of 10 said they would accept local drinks if this meant fewer imports (44 per cent). Other suggestions included:

- Reducing the changes of towels and bedlinen (34 per cent)
- Buying locally produced souvenirs (32 per cent)
- Borrowing brochures from travel agents to avoid wastage (30 per cent)
- Accepting a smaller range of food in hotel buffets to reduce wastage (20 per cent)
- Reducing the number of holidays taken (14 per cent)
- Spending a couple of hours to help with local projects such as beach cleaning (11 per cent)
- Paying more for a holiday so a higher proportion can benefit the local community (11 per cent).

First Choice Mainstream Sector managing director Dermot Blastland commented on the findings that:

> "We and other travel companies need to make it as easy as possible for people to do the right thing while they are away. It also means we need to show our customers how, with their help we can make a positive difference and preserve holiday destinations for future generations".

Increasing numbers of travel companies appear to be responding to consumer concerns. Several mainstream companies now include information or advice about ethical, social or environmental issues in their brochures, and niche companies specialising in 'eco-friendly' or 'responsible' travel have sprung up in recent years. For example, Earth, a London-based travel company focusing on luxury properties. The company has made a soft environmental impact, by being small and respectful of the landscape and local culture. Amanresorts follow ecologically sympathetic architectural principles and tend to be small and sensitive developments.

Additionally, the travel industry is starting to respond. British Airways has recently launched a scheme where its customers can choose to offset the carbon dioxide emissions created during their flights. Customers can pay via a link from the airline's website for the cost of the emissions created by their journey. For example, a return flight to Madrid will cost £5 and a return flight to Johannesburg will cost £13.30.

The money raised will be used by an organisation called Climate Care to invest in sustainable energy projects that tackle global warming by reducing carbon dioxide levels. Climate Care's projects include a scheme in South Africa that has distributed 50,000 energy efficient lamps this year via school groups as part of an environmental awareness campaign. In India, Climate Care's support means schools are able to use stoves that run on renewable energy briquettes made from crop waste rather than liquid petroleum gas. Customers can offset their carbon emissions via the booking confirmation form when they book British Airways flights.

Responsible Organisations

Employees are increasingly demanding assurances from their employers regarding the management of a broad range of Corporate Responsibility issues. Employee concern is the most commonly cited reason for companies producing Corporate Responsibility reports. This is supported by research by the Work Foundation and the Virtuous Circle Ltd, 'Achieving High Performance: CSR at the heart of business', which found a strong positive correlation between companies that are seen to take their responsibilities towards society seriously and those seen as a good employer to work for.

NGOs are increasingly looking at the practices of the hospitality industry. Although such organisations do not have any direct power to force change in the sector, the publicity that NGO campaigns can generate is an important driver of business behaviour. In the summer of 2004, Tourism Concern started a campaign looking at working conditions in the tourism sector. They conducted research in five popular holiday destinations - Bali, Mexico, the Dominican Republic, Egypt, and the Canary Islands. The research revealed examples of exploitative labour conditions.

These included over-dependence on tips, long working hours, unpaid overtime, stress, lack of secure contracts, poor training and almost no promotion opportunities for locally employed people. Their research also found that tour operators often use their considerable purchasing power to force down prices in much the same way as supermarkets do when imposing price cuts on farmers.

The result is invariably cost-cutting and longer hours for the lowest paid workers. Those who suffer most are the socially weaker and less skilled staff members, a high proportion of whom are women. In response to this research, Tourism Concern is now calling on all tour operators to 'audit' labour standards across the tourism supply chain. The industry is currently considering its Europe Edition response to this specific campaign. Additionally, Federation of Tour Operators (FTO) members last year signed a statement of commitment to sustainable development and management of tourism. The statement commits members to making a positive contribution to the natural and cultural environment and to generate benefits for host communities. Members are committed in the future to following the FTO Integrated Responsible Tourism Programme, which is currently under development.

Challenges Facing the Hospitality Industry

Irrespective of wherever individual hospitality companies have got to in their thinking on Corporate Responsibility, the issue is clearly here to stay, indeed with issues such as climate change coming further to the forefront in 2006, many are likely to become more pressing. In the hospitality industry, it will affect daily activities including location and site decisions, employment issues, management of the supply chain, and customer treatment and management. Sustainable tourism is about preserving popular destinations, the environment and its resources. We have got to get it right for this generation and beyond.

Within the hotel and travel sector, various initiatives and standards have been established to try to better define what Corporate Responsibility means for the sector. Such initiatives include the International Tourism Partnership and the International Eco-tourism Society. In addition, various award programmes now exist to recognise good performance in Corporate Responsibility in the sector. For example:

- International Hotel & Restaurant Association's Environmental Award: launched in 1990 and conducted with the UNEP, the United Nation's Environment Programme and sponsored by American Express. Judges include Conservation International, Green Globe 21 and ITP. The award recognises the efforts being made to 'green' the hotel industry from within.
- British Airways Tourism for Tomorrow awards launched in 1991 by British Airways and, since 2004, under the auspices of World Travel and Tourism Council (WTTC), Tourism for Tomorrow recognises and promotes best practice in travel and tourism development around the world.
- Conservation International & National Geographic Traveller: Traveller magazine and Conservation International together launched the 2004 World Legacy Awards, a global campaign to promote environmentally, culturally, and socially responsible tourism practices across a wider spectrum of the

tourism industry, with the goal of "protecting the Earth's natural and cultural heritage".

- Conde Nast Traveller's Ecotourism Awards: These awards have been set up to recognise properties, tour operators, and destinations committed to preserving the local environment, assisting and employing the people who live there, and educating the guests who visit. Organisations can nominate themselves for entry to the awards, after which a panel of industry judges vote on the finalists.

What do stakeholders expect from companies who are serious about addressing Corporate Responsibility? Leading companies follow the same broad principles, although these may differ in their application and emphasis. First, stakeholders, be they staff, customers, shareholders or the community at large, expect to see commitment from the top of an organisation - this means leadership and advocacy. If employees, communities and customers do not actually see repeated evidence of this commitment, then the organisation will lack credibility.

"My priorities for 2005 are to continue our focus on generating shareholder value through further disposals of hotel assets, returning additional funds to shareholders, and retaining and enhancing our powerful brand positions and infrastructures. We will also maintain our focus on Corporate Social Responsibility, where we seek to be an industry leader." - Andrew Cosslett, CEO of IHG.

They view their contribution and buy-in as essential in assessing environmental, social and economic dimensions of hospitality management, and in balancing short-term priorities against long term needs.

The ITP is a programme of The Prince of Wales International Business Leaders Forum (IBLF) and exists to inspire and provide global leadership for responsible business in hotels, travel and tourism. The initiative builds on the success of the International Hotels Environment Initiative

(IHEI) launched in 1992. Organisations including airlines, car hire companies and tour operators through to existing hotel chain members and non government organisations (NGO) all work together within ITP to promote responsible practical actions that ensure sustainable solutions. Partners are drawn together to work on specific projects to drive actions and awareness in areas that affect responsible travel and tourism. The ITP also assists hotel, travel and tourism companies define and build a leadership role in responsible business by contributing to policy dialogues, pioneering new approaches to changing business and development agendas and by providing practical business solutions.

The ITP has developed "BenchmarkHotel" - an environmental benchmarking tool designed to help hotels around the world improve their environmental performance.

The International Eco-tourism Society (TIES)

TIES was founded in 1990 and is the largest and oldest ecotourism organisation in the world dedicated to generating and disseminating information about ecotourism. It currently has members in more than 70 countries. The organisation membership includes academics, consultants, conservation professionals and organizations, governments, architects, tour operators, lodge owners and managers, general development experts, and ecotourists. TIES provides guidelines and standards, training, technical assistance, research and publications to foster sound ecotourism development.

This is a very tricky process for a company to get right. All too often, "engagement" is a one-way dialogue, with the company telling stakeholders the decisions that it has made. This risks engendering alienation and, potentially, opposition from stakeholders who feel insulted rather than consulted. Effective engagement, by contrast, is invaluable in shaping corporate strategy, understanding upcoming risks and opportunities, and providing a suitable response and feedback. It is best practice, for example, to refer directly to stakeholder concerns and corresponding actions in corporate reports.

Publishing your Corporate Responsibility strategy and defining priorities for action is also a key part of best practice. Corporate commitments should then be enshrined in "policy" - which could be a formal sustainability policy, code of practice or some guiding principles. This policy should be effectively communicated and implemented, for example through objectives and performance targets/indicators. It should be monitored through appropriate control processes and management systems, such as the ISO 14001 environmental management standard.

Performance indicators should be determined, with regular reports disclosing performance. Best practice is to have these reports assured by an independent third party. Corporate Responsibility is still a relatively new concept for the hospitality industry. However, by taking action now and reporting to stakeholders on progress made, forward- looking companies do have the opportunity to gain a leadership position in this respect. Adopting such a leadership position would have corresponding potential long term beneficial impacts on critical business areas such as customer and staff recruitment and retention, ultimately translating into shareholder value.

In order to look at how the industry is currently responding to the Corporate Responsibility agenda, PricewaterhouseCoopers conducted new research into the Corporate Responsibility activities of Europe's 14 largest publicly listed hotel companies in January 2004.

Together these hotels accounted for more than 1.5 million hotel rooms across the world in 2004. Our research examined how each company was responding on 11 key components of Corporate Responsibility, such as their overall level of disclosure, policies in place, management systems and stakeholder engagement. The research was based solely on publicly available information, for example, through company websites, investor briefings and annual reports. This research builds on previous work by PwC in 2001 to examine the implementation of environmental policies in European hotels.

PwC's research found that 10 out of 14 of Europe's leading hotel companies provided at least some information relating to Corporate Responsibility in their published information. For example, Accor's website contains an interactive web-based Corporate Responsibility report.

Research results: how well are Europe's leading 14 hotel groups responding to the Corporate Responsibility agenda? Accor's website contains interactive sections on its responsibilities towards shareholders, For example, while most companies did have Corporate Responsibility, environmental or social polices in place, only three of the 14 companies stated that they had conducted a Corporate Responsibility risk assessment. Additionally, only four of the companies had made a clear link between their Corporate Responsibility activities and business strategies. This lack of risk assessment and connection with broader business strategy could mean that many of these companies are not currently deriving real business benefits from their Corporate Responsibility activities.

Environmental Policy

In terms of policy disclosure, nine out of the 14 companies had environmental policies in place. Accor, Hilton Group and Whitbread all disclosed a significant amount of information on their environmental performance.

- Hilton Group reported on the use of the Hilton Environmental Reporting tool (HER) and staff training (15,000 staff to date). Hilton group also publicly report their target of a 10 per cent reduction in utility consumption across the UK and Ireland by 2006
- Accor publicly disclosed that, in 2004, 26 properties were awarded ISO14001 certification. Significant disclosure was also provided in areas such as water and energy consumption, waste, biodiversity, and environmental building design
- Whitbread published a stand alone environment report, which received third party assurance. The report contained considerable disclosure on

environmental performance, e.g. reductions in C02 emissions, water, energy consumption, and recycling was also provided.

Whitbread refer to their Environment Management System (EMS) in their report. Detailed information on how Accor sees its responsibilities towards customers, employees, suppliers, the environment, local communities and shareholders. Likewise, Hilton Group plc has published a detailed "Responsible Business" report for the last three years. This report contains information on Hilton's vision and core values, corporate governance and key Corporate Responsibility issues, defined as people, equal opportunities and diversity, human rights, health and safety, environment, business practice, customers, products and services, business partners and supply chain and communities/charities.

For companies that did not produce standalone Corporate Responsibility reports, disclosure was usually focused on case study examples of particular developments or initiatives that were initiated with Corporate Responsibility in mind. These ranged from employee volunteering schemes, to monitoring working conditions across the supply chain, to providing details of community impacts in terms of working with local people to provide employment opportunities. These examples demonstrate how, to some extent, all hotel companies are actively considering Corporate Responsibility in their operations, and in doing so, are focusing on the full range of issues – not simply environment, health and safety.

Once we dug below the surface, we found the organisations we benchmarked had markedly different levels of Corporate Responsibility activity. In terms of disclosure on 'social' areas of Corporate Responsibility, ten out of the 14 companies benchmarked publish information on policies in this regard. Areas covered by many included:

- People issues
- Diversity
- Equal opportunities

- Community/charitable donations

However, fewer companies reported their activities in emerging issues such as:

- Human rights and
- Supplier management

One exception to this was Intercontinental Hotels Group (IHG), who have publicly stated their commitment to the Universal Declaration on Human Rights and the International Labour Organisation's (ILO's) core conventions. Another notable exception was Accor's significant disclosure on its programme in place to monitor the social and ethical performance of its key suppliers.

However, where applicable, none of the hotels covered within the survey disclosed any significant information on the environmental or social performance of their franchised hotels. Rather, the sector is currently focusing on the activities of directly owned and managed properties. Looking to the future, it is likely that stakeholders will expect the sector to also disclose the performance of franchised hotels. In addition, it would be prudent for companies to include coverage of these franchised properties in Corporate Responsibility programmes as franchised hotels do have the ability to cause significant reputation and brand damage if found lacking in sensitive Corporate Responsibility issues, such as child labour and minimum wage payments.

In terms of Corporate Responsibility board sponsorship, the research found that only 4 of the 14 companies publicly articulated a board level commitment to Corporate Responsibility. Such board level sponsorship is critical to Corporate Responsibility programmes being taken seriously by external audiences. IHG is a good example of a company that has made a clear, board-level, commitment to Corporate Responsibility:

"We need to build an IHG culture. A culture that's focussed on driving returns for our owners and on supporting each other in a more collaborative way. Part of the culture will be about raising our commitment still further to helping the communities in which we operate. As an organisation we will increase our commitment to Corporate Social Responsibility and ensure that we are industry leading in this area. Not just because it helps to drive the culture which it does, but because it increasingly helps attract talented people to the business." - Andrew Cosslett CEO IHG.

Looking at the implementation of management systems to actively monitor and control elements of Corporate Responsibility such as environment, health and safety, only five organisations claimed to have established management systems, and three more were in the process of developing them.

One company that does disclose details of its Corporate Responsibility management systems are Rezidor SAS, which has an established Responsible Business (RB) programme. The programme focuses on three key areas: taking Responsibility for the health and safety of employees and guests, respecting social and ethical issues in the company, as well as in the community, and reducing negative impacts on the environment. The operational responsibility for the RB programme lies with the Hotel Managers, who are supported by the RB co-coordinators at each hotel. In 2003, a regional structure was added, supporting the hotels at a regional level and providing a liaison between the hotels and the Corporate Director of Environmental and Social Affairs. The local RB action plans guide the hotels in what measures and actions they will implement during the year to improve performance.

Six companies within the benchmark provided details of their stakeholder engagement plans and a further two provided limited details with a commitment to future activity in this area. However, even for these six companies that did disclose information on engagement, the level of disclosure was limited. It is increasingly expected that companies will publicly disclose who they believe their key stakeholders are and what activities/processes they have in place to engage with these key stakeholder groups. The hotel industry is significantly behind other sectors in this area, for example, British Telecom has a highly established process of stakeholder engagement.

Looking at disclosure on actual performance, just four of the 14 organisations were able to publish meaningful data on Corporate Responsibility type parametres (e.g. health and safety, resource use, waste production, community consultation); while four more produced some limited data. For example, the Hilton Group plc reported in its most recent Corporate Responsibility report that 'team member satisfaction scores have increased across the world by up to 7 per cent from 2003, averaging at 75 per cent.' Hilton was also the only company in the survey to have third party assurance over their reported information on Corporate Responsibility, although three other companies did provide assurance in some limited areas.

What conclusion should we draw from this information? Perhaps the majority of hotel companies are focusing on Corporate Responsibility, but not publicly talking about it? Or, alternatively that they recognise that Corporate Responsibility is important but have not fully implemented the necessary processes or controls throughout their business. Alternatively, there could be a more complex explanation. Perhaps the industry's current response results from the complex value chain and business partner relationships in the hospitality sector generally.

Individual companies may not always be responsible for the direct buying relationship with the customer, often being dependent on other companies up and down the value chain in terms of Corporate Responsibility related impacts. Whatever the explanation, it is clear that progress has been made in terms of implementing environmental policies for many in the sector since PricewaterhouseCoopers examined this issue of Hospitality Directions. However, the sector is behind other European industries, e.g. the retail sector, in terms of Corporate Responsibility reporting, and faces a challenging agenda to catch up and respond effectively to the concerns of stakeholders.

Indeed, in the 2004 Business in the Community Corporate Responsibilty Index, of the top 100 quoted companies from a Corporate Responsibilty perspective, only four came from the leisure and hotels sector. By comparison, a sector such as Banks and Utilities had 11 apiece. However, this could partly be explained by relatively few hotel companies being quoted on the FTSE 100 and FTSE 250.

Looking Towards the Future

Many companies in the hospitality industry are currently not making the most of the Corporate Responsibility agenda. While it can easily appear to business as a threat and a recipe for extra burdens, the reality is that Corporate Responsibility related issues present real business opportunities. In a recently published report by the leading global business organisation, the World Business Council for Sustainable Development, "From Challenge to Opportunity: the role of business in tomorrow's society", business leaders in a number of major companies have produced a model for tomorrow's global business. It is based on recognising and capturing the opportunities that are presented by societal and environmental concerns.

By focusing on the issue strategically, companies which address Corporate Responsibility are likely to achieve better community relationships, save money through operational efficiencies and differentiate themselves as responsible and accountable companies. Transparent and accountable behaviour helps to build stakeholder trust and enhance corporate reputation, both long-term drivers of value. Other sectors such as the European retail, telecommunications, pharmaceutical and extractive industries have already started to yield such benefits through established Corporate Responsibility programmes.

There are several steps that the hospitality industry will have to take to embed Corporate Responsibility into the way it does business day-to-day. The most immediate steps include instituting the right policies, processes, and systems for monitoring and reporting performance. Additionally, for such Corporate Responsibility programmes to be credible, it is important to ensure the following:

- A serious commitment to Corporate Responsibility is shown from the top of the organisation;
- Stakeholders are actively involved in decision making;
- Corporate Responsibility strategy is published, with defined priorities for action;
- Corporate commitments are enshrined in policy; and
- Performance indicators are determined, with regular reports disclosing performance.

Overall, the biggest challenge for the sector will be to win over the 'hearts and minds' and thus the behaviour of the company. This is a longer term and more complex process, and will demand cross industry collaboration, but is essential for Corporate Responsibility to really 'stick'. Many leading hospitality companies have made a start, but achieving maximum value from Corporate Responsibility will be far from simple. It will require a clear sense of direction, a commitment from the organisation, robust planning and strong implementation to deliver.

"All this talk about jumping on the green bandwagon has died down. Being 'green' is no longer fashionable or glamorous, it is a fact of life. Now considered by all industries to have a direct impact on profitability, it has been absorbed in business practice. Having left the glamour and excitement, we are now at stage two – the detail of implementation." - David Henderson, Former Marketing Manager of Plysu Containers, UK

Environment Management System (EMS)

An environment management system (EMS) helps businesses to evaluate, manage and reduce their environment impacts by providing a methodology to integrate environment management into business operations in a systematic manner. A typical EMS consists of the following actions:

- Conduct a preliminary environment review to identify all resource inputs and waste outputs;
- Establish an environment policy;
- Establish environment objectives/targets;
- Implement EMS through an environment management programme;
- Establish EMS procedures in all departments and divisions;
- Establish environment performance monitoring and data collection procedures;
- Internal environment communication, delegation and training;
- Environment-related communication to visitors;
- Conduct an EMS audit;
- Compare actual performance against objectives/targets;
- Review objectives/targets for continual improvement;
- Report on environment performance to employees, customers, stakeholders and the wider public.

The Origins of EMS

EMS was developed on the following bases:

- Compliance and Due Diligence Auditing: Compliance audits were developed in the 1970's in response to the costly fines companies were incurring due to non-compliance with environment legislation. Due diligence or pre-acquisition audits are conducted to identify the environment issues of sites and businesses before they can be considered for investment or takeover.
- Total Quality Management: EMS is based on the TQM process: plan do check act.

The Benefits of EMS

- EMS enables tourism businesses to comply with, and even exceed, environment legislation.
- EMS lowers costs by reducing resource use, improving operating efficiency, lowering waste output and avoiding non-compliance fines.
- EMS makes a property a safer and healthier environment for employees and visitors. Work related accidents, occupational illnesses and related absenteeism can therefore be reduced.
- Along with the growth of public environment awareness, tourists are demanding 'greener' services. EMS enables businesses to meet this demand. The growth of tourism eco-labels and environment awards is a strong indication of the growing response of tourists to environmentally responsible services.
- Banks and insurance companies now require information on environment performance when making lending and coverage decisions. In 1997, UNEP brokered the Statement by Financial Institutions on Environment and Sustainable Development, a commitment by 104 signatories to improve environment management and adopt industry best practice in credit risk management, reduction of energy and materials use and waste management. The signatories include a range of financial institutions: commercial and investment banks, venture capitalists, asset managers and multilateral development banks. As a spin-off from this initiative, over 70 insurance companies from 25 countries have come together under UNEP to form UNEP Insurance Industry Initiative for the Environment.
- Corporate social responsibility is a growing agenda. Companies are no longer judged by their profit alone and face mounting pressure to participate in

improving the quality of life of their customers, employees and the wider society within which they operate. EMS is the first critical step in this direction.

Assign Environment Responsibility

In any business, responsibility for a task must be assigned to someone to ensure that it is performed and completed. Responsibility for EMS can be assigned to one employee or to a group. Most tourism businesses appoint an 'environment champion', supported by an environment management team. The environment management team should include representatives from top management and from all departments: this will ensure that the environment burdens of the entire business are identified and included in the EMS.

The environment champion and management team should have the skills to:

- Appreciate the importance of EMS;
- Understand legislative requirements and the implications of non- compliance;
- Appreciate the technicalities of EMS so that priority actions can be identified;
- Implement EMS, which includes gathering information, conducting interviews, data analysis and report writing.

There is always the choice of using external consultants, especially at the early stages when adequate expertise may not be available in-house. While external consultants may facilitate the identification and implementation of cost-effective improvements, their services can be quite expensive, especially for a small business. External consultants must work closely with employees to provide training and build in-house expertise. An environment status review is similar to a SWOT analysis. It identifies the environment-related strengths, weakness, opportunities and threats of a business by assessing:

- How and where resources are used;
- How and where waste is generated;

- Which codes and standards are being violated in daily business practices.

The Environment Status Review involves data collection, interviews, inspection, observation, and review of existing documents and records on resource/materials use and waste output. The objective is to gather baseline data to:

- Establish environment management objectives and targets;
- Identify the best areas to start EMS that will bring both business and environment benefits.

It is best to begin with the documentary evidence and supplement this information with data gathered through interviews, observation and inspection.EMS in a hospitality business is based on nine action areas:

- Reduce water use;
- Reduce waste water output;
- Reduce energy use;
- Reduce waste;
- Purchase environmentally-preferable products;
- Lower emissions, including ozone-depleting substances;
- Improve indoor air quality;
- Reduce noise;
- Monitor and document environment performance.

A series of fact sheets and environment status review checklists for each of the above areas are given below. (The fact sheets contain important background information for an environment review). Neither the fact sheets nor the review checklists are fully comprehensive; they have been developed to demonstrate the type of background data and issues that should be considered in an environment status review.

Water Fact Sheet

- Water can account for a significant part of purchasing costs in hospitality businesses.

- Most businesses are supplied with water by utility companies who purify the water before distribution. Some businesses (especially in rural areas) may draw supplies directly from surface waters (rivers, streams etc.) or aquifers. In this case, water purification may need to be conducted on-site.
- The various uses of water in hospitality businesses are:
  - Hot and cold water for bathrooms, kitchen and laundry;
  - Hot and cold water for toilets;
  - Cold and hot water for HVAC;
  - Cold water for drinking;
  - Cold water for fire fighting.
- In most businesses, drinking water is drawn from the mains, whilst non-drinking water is drawn from storage tanks.
- Over 50% of water is used in guestrooms and kitchens. Other major users are laundries and public toilets.
- Hot water is held in, and distributed from, hot-water storage tanks. In larger facilities, separate boilers and storage tanks may be used to heat and hold water supplies at different temperatures. An alternative is to use location-specific water heaters to increase temperatures as required.
- Much energy is needed to heat and store hot water, and lowering hot water consumption will reduce water-heating costs.
- Different degrees of hot water are required for different purposes. Typical water heating thresholds for hospitality businesses are:
  - Guest rooms 50°C
  - Laundry 40-80°C
  - Kitchens 60°C
- Wastewater should be directed to sewage treatment plants for treatment before discharge. Yet large

volumes of wastewater are discharged without treatment in both industrialised and non-industrialised countries.

- Water treatment is expensive, and is usually charged by volume discharged.
- Biological treatment ponds could be set up if no municipal sewer is available.

Is water use being monitored? How much hot and cold water is used on the main property, in the swimming pool and in the garden every month/year? Have efforts been made to save water? What are the sources of water supply? Are water quality standards being met? Are there signs of corrosion, high levels of scale or other deposits, or pH increase, indicating that water quality needs to be improved? What is water consumption cost as a proportion of operating costs? Are employees encouraged to save water during daily work routines? Are guests invited to save water? How often is the water distribution system checked for leaks, pressure control malfunctions and other inefficiencies? Have separate departments been sub-metreed to monitor the water consumption of each? Is there adequate turnover in water storage tanks to prevent the forming of bacteria? Is wastewater treated before discharge? Have water purchasing and waste water discharge costs risen over the last 3 years?

Energy Factsheet

- Energy accounts for the largest share of operating costs in tourism facilities.
- Energy is used for lighting, heating and cooling, ventilation, and powering appliances.
- Most tourism businesses draw their electric energy from the national grid, whose power is generated from various sources: fossil fuels such as fuel oil and coal, hydropower, nuclear power, natural gas; and renewable sources such as solar, wind, bio-fuels and geothermal energy.

- Apart from grid electricity, hospitality businesses use a range of other fuel and energy sources for water and space heating and cooking. These include fuel oil, natural gas or propane, solar and wind power, bio-fuels and geothermal energy.
- What area of a hospitality business is the most energy-intensive? The answer depends on building configurations, climate conditions, heating and cooling requirements, levels of occupancy and activity, the energy sources used, and the energy-efficiency of appliances.
- While some activities may require high amounts of energy, associated costs may be relatively low. Apart from pricing distortions, this could be due to the high energy-efficiency of equipment or the high calorific value of the fuel used. The UK Department of the Environment, Transport and the Region's Energy Efficiency Best Practice Programme, provided the following estimates on energy intensity and costs based on energy consumption data from hospitality facilities in the UK.
- Energy management considerations differ in hot and cold climates. In hot climates air-conditioning is used to reduce temperatures and humidity, while in cold climates, heating systems are required to increase temperature and control ventilation and humidity.
- Degree-day thresholds provide guidance to property managers on heating and cooling levels. They differ from country to country. Comparing outside temperatures with the degree-day threshold will indicate the levels to which buildings have to be heated or cooled. Degree-day thresholds are published ahead of time in energy and property management literature.
- When carrying out energy audits it may be necessary to convert quantities of fuel into units of energy. 'Input value' means the energy being converted in the

power/heat generation process. These input values must therefore be multiplied by the energy efficiency of the appliance to obtain the actual output of energy. Accurate data of the exact calorific values of fuels and the efficiency of equipment can be obtained from suppliers.

Estimates of Energy Intensity and Costs

- It will also be necessary to convert values from watt-hours to joules or vice versa. The calculation is:

  1 kilo watt-hour (kWh) = 3,600 kilojoules (kJ) or 3.6 megajoules (MJ)
- Emissions from different fuels should be taken into account. The UK Department of the Environment, Transport and the Regions provides the following estimates:
- The potential savings linked to energy efficiency are significant. Repair and good housekeeping measures will reduce energy costs by 10%. Retrofit and refurbishment options bring savings of 30% or more.

Waste Factsheet

Waste disposal is a major economic and environment challenge facing all societies.

- Waste generated by hospitality businesses include:
  - Paper and cardboard items such as stationery, disposable items and packaging;
  - Aluminium products such as beverage cans and tins;
  - Plastic items such as packaging, containers and disposable items;
  - Organic waste such as food waste and garden trimmings;
  - Hazardous waste such as batteries, solvents, paints and anti-fouling agents;
  - Building materials and furniture;

  - Oils and fat;
  - End-of-life appliances and furniture.
- Municipal waste (which includes the above) is recycled, incinerated or land filled. In most countries, most waste goes for landfill.
- Landfill sites have significant environment impacts. In an effort to reduce landfill volumes, many countries are enforcing landfill taxes and legislation to discourage new sites. Simultaneously, efforts are being made to increase the recycling of paper, plastic and aluminium wastes. The incineration of waste with heat recovery is also being promoted, though to lesser extent.
- For tourism businesses, the revenue gains through the sale of reusable and recyclable wastes can greatly offset the costs of waste separation, bailing and compacting.
- The waste management hierarchy is:
  - Avoid;
  - Reduce;
  - Reuse;
  - Recycle;
  - Recover.
- Based on material use and recycling statistics from the US:
  - Recycling one aluminium can saves enough energy to run a TV for 3 hours;
  - Recycling one glass bottle saves enough energy to light a 100-watt bulb for 4 hours;
  - Every 3 weeks, Americans dispose of an amount of used motor oil equivalent to the Exxon Valdez oil spill;
  - Recycling one tonne of paper saves 1,400-kilowatt hours of energy, enough to heat an average American home for 6 months.

The first step in preparation for a preliminary waste status review is to compile an inventory of all materials disposed of by the business. The following should then be considered:

How much waste is generated under the main waste categories: paper, plastic, aluminium, organic (kitchen and garden) and hazardous, every month/year? Which departments generate high volumes of waste? How much is known about waste disposal methods? Have initiatives been taken to separate waste? Is organic waste separated from other waste? Have initiatives been taken to reduce waste? What are waste disposal charges as a proportion of operating costs? Have waste disposal charges increased over the last 3 years? Are there items in the waste stream that have never been used? Has a waste audit been conducted?

Purchasing Factsheet

- The hospitality industry is a large buyer of consumer goods and services and can, therefore, have a significant influence on suppliers and contractors. On average, 26 five-star hotels purchase the same volume of goods as 1,200 families.
- Environmentally-preferable products include:
  - Products made entirely or partly with recycled materials;
  - Materials with reduced toxicity - e.g. water-based paints and non-solvent cleaners;
  - Products manufactured through cleaner production processes - e.g. unbleached paper;
  - Products that are more durable and last longer;
  - Products that require less energy during manufacture and use;
  - Reusable or recyclable products;
  - Products with reduced packaging - most packaging ends up in the waste stream less than 9 months after manufacture;
  - Environmentally certified products;

- Products manufactured locally not requiring long-distance transportation.

- The use of environmentally-preferable products can be a valuable showcase for corporate environment commitment.
- Environment-conscious purchasing practices avoid and reduce waste. For example, buying items with less packaging reduces packaging waste.
- Changing purchasing practices should be undertaken in close collaboration with suppliers to ensure that the most cost-effective and environmentally-preferable alternative is selected.

Emissions and Indoor Environment Factsheet

- Emissions from tourism facilities include:
  - Combustion gases (carbon dioxide, nitrous oxide, hydrocarbons) from fossil fuel and gas-operated boilers, stoves and generators;
  - CFCs from refrigeration and air-conditioning equipment;
  - Halons in fire-extinguishing equipment;
  - Vapours from dry cleaning solvents;
- Vehicle emissions.

- Indoor environment quality is of great importance to the comfort and well-being of occupants. Most people living and working in cities spend 90% of their time indoors.
- Indoor air quality depends on the activities and emissions within the building and the pollutants brought into it from the air outside. Common sources of indoor air quality contamination include:
  - Combustion gases from stoves, boilers and other combustion equipment;
  - Tobacco smoke;
  - VOC vapours from cleaning solvents, paints, varnishes, photocopy emissions and pesticides;

- Asbestos fibres;
- Ozone brought in from the outside;
- Dust and particles;
- CFCs from refrigeration and air-conditioning equipment;
- Radon released from building materials.

- Poor indoor air quality can induce adverse health effects, from headaches and nausea to respiratory irritations and allergic reactions. Long-term exposure (in the case of hospitality employees) can induce more serious illnesses.
- The best-known indoor environment-related health issue is 'sick building syndrome', associated with continual exposure to fumes from paints, adhesives, varnishes, and chemical emissions from photocopiers, furnishings and fabrics. The World Health Organisation (WHO) estimates that 30% of new and refurbished buildings have registered complaints of sick building syndrome symptoms: headaches, dizziness, rashes, asthma, and allergies.
- Adequate ventilation is critical in improving indoor air quality. Fresh air is needed to renew oxygen, remove micro-organisms, vapours and odours, as well as excess heat and moisture.
- Most small hotels are likely to use mechanical ventilation systems, while the use of integrated heat, light and ventilation systems is both more efficient and more feasible for larger properties.

Noise Factsheet

- Noise pollution can be defined as undesirable sound that is disturbing, annoying and which may be detrimental to human health.
- Undesirable noise can include music, traffic, crowds, and workplace-related noise from machines and appliances.

- Noise is measured in decibels (dB), which follow a logarithmic scale. Therefore even a small increase in decibels means a large increase in the magnitude of the sound. For example, a sound of 30dB is ten times greater in intensity than 20dB, and a hundred times greater than 10dB.
- The frequency of noise is measured in Hertz (Hz).
- Vibration is a major source of noise transmission.
- Continuous exposure to intensities of noise can have adverse health effects:
  - Noise levels between 70dB-12dB can induce migraines, circulatory disturbances, high blood pressure and ulcers;
  - Noise levels between 10dB and 120dB can cause loss of hearing;
  - Noise levels above 130dB can cause direct damage to the ear;
- High levels of noise in hospitality businesses can reduce the value of the property and lead to the loss of business. It also affects employee productivity and causes conflicts with neighbouring businesses and homes.
- Areas that generate the most noise in hospitality businesses are mechanical rooms with fans, compressors, boilers and generators, kitchens, laundries, delivery and waste output areas including compactors, garages, discotheques and function rooms, lobby areas and bars.
- The most noise-sensitive areas in hospitality properties are guestrooms, meeting and conference rooms, and offices.

It is useful for a hospitality business to gain an insight into potential guest response to the impending environment effort:

- Have any guests inquired about the business's environment policy?

- Have tour operators and travel agents inquired about the businesses' environmental policy?
- Do competitors have an environment policy?

As part of the environment status review, a short guest survey could be conducted to evaluate visitor interest in environment issues and environmentally responsible service providers.

The Environment Status

To fully analyse and appreciate the data gathered through the environment status review, it should be compiled into an environment status report. This report should include:

- Volume of costs of water and energy used;
- Volumes and charges of waste disposal;
- Inventory of all materials purchased;
- Levels of compliance;
- Environment improvement activities already in place;
- Management and operation procedures that could facilitate/obstruct EMS implementation;
- Local initiatives that could facilitate EMS implementation - for example voluntary industry partnerships on the environment, eco-labelling schemes, loans or grants for environment improvement, environment help-lines, EMS literature produced by the national environment agency or local authorities, etc;
- Employee interest in the impending EMS;
- Potential visitor response to the impending EMS;
- Time spent on the review;
- Sources of information, including interviews and observations;
- Recommendations on EMS objectives and targets.

Environment Legislation

A full review of relevant environment legislation needs to be undertaken at the same time as the environment status review. The environment status report will identify areas where legislation is being violated. It also helps to be aware of impending legislation, since the EMS can then be planned to meet and exceed the new requirements.

The environment status report should provide the information needed for establishing EMS objectives and targets. The objectives should specify environment goals, and the targets should indicate the level of improvement to be attained. For example:

Activities that are highly resource-intensive, generate large quantities of waste and emissions, violate legislation, are poor environment practice, and pose health hazards to employees and guests, should be given priority. Objectives and targets should be established with input from all departments and approved by top management.

Objectives and targets must be realistic and achievable from a business and environment perspective. An over-ambitious target can discourage action; reduce enthusiasm and interest, while an under-ambitious one will not provide a sense of achievement and impetus for continuous improvement.

Establish the Environment Policy

The environment policy is a public statement of a company's environmental commitment and responsibility. It declares how the business is responding to environment challenges, and establishes the overall framework for achieving objectives and targets. It also validates the EMS. The policy should be developed on the basis of the findings of the environment status review and the objectives and targets established. It must have top management support. The policy statements of five businesses are reproduced below.

Bass Group's Environment Policy

With major hotel and leisure retailing activities around the world, Bass Recognises that it faces a wide range of environmental responsibilities. Bass is committed to a policy of seeking continual improvement in environmental matters. Group companies have introduced environmental management programmes, which will deliver regulatory compliance in each country, commercial efficiency and good environment citizenship programmes. These programmes are an integral part of the proper management of group business and will help provide a safe and healthy environment for employees, contractors, customers and neighbours. Bass will ensure that group companies:

- Undertake a thorough risk and hazard analysis;
- Are sensitive to environment issues and consider their potential impact on all new projects and developments;
- Implement their company environment policies;
- Have management accountability and responsibility for environment matters;
- Develop management programmes and set quantified targets where appropriate;
- Monitor and report on performance on a regular basis;
- Communicate with those affected by their actions, and train and involve employees at appropriate levels and function within the organisation.

Hotel's Environment Policy

Golden Tulip and Tulip Inn Management Hotels focus on offering a high standard of services and products. Part of our policy is to promote the well-being of all parties concerned, as well as reduce health risks to our staff, guests and society at large, both now and in the future. We conduct a proactive environment policy, called 'Golden Tulip Goes Greener', to reduce our environment load as much as possible. We do this without loss of comfort for our guests. We also maintain optimum safety for our staff, guests and other parties concerned without losing sight of sound business management. Golden Tulip and Tulip Inn Management Hotels oblige themselves to:

- Conduct a proactive environment policy in all hotel departments and offices;
- Meet environment requirements, rules and regulations;
- Optimise use of energy, water and materials;
- Limit waste, and recycle when possible;
- Limit the use of harmful materials;
- Stimulate suppliers and guests to contribute to reducing the environment load;
- Share knowledge and experience with other companies in the hospitality industry;
- Provide hotel staff with the information and means to reach the Green Objectives;
- Measure the level of implementation on a regular basis;
- Evaluate and adjust the measures taken that should lead to an acceptable environment load;
- Unceasingly introduce improvements to the Green Programme.

Nestlé's Commitment to Environmentally-preferable Business Practices

Nestlé respects the environment, supports sustainable development and is committed to environmentally sound business practices throughout the world. To fulfil this commitment, Nestle:

- Integrates environmental principles, programmes and practices into each business;
- Strives for the continuous improvement of its environmental performance through application of the Nestlé Environmental Management System (NEMS);

- Complies with applicable environmental legislation. Where none exist, Nestlé's own internal rules are applied;
- Provides appropriate information, communication and training to build internal and external understanding concerning the Company's environmental commitment.

Hotel Nikko's Environment Policy

Hotel Nikko, Hongkong, is an environmentally-conscious hotel which not only aims to provide quality services for its guests, but is also committed to taking appropriate measures for pollution prevention and resources conservation. To fulfil the requirements of ISO14001 Standard, the environmental policy statement for Hotel Nikko Hongkong is as follows:

- The hotel is committed to complying with all local environmental legislation and continuously seeks to improve its environmental performance;
- The hotel's management and staff understand and support the Environment Policy and are committed to continuous improvement of environmental performance by identifying ways to minimise both wastage of natural resources and pollution to the environment;
- The 'Green Innovator Award' will be presented to employees who devise the most innovative and practical environment improvement initiatives. These initiatives will be reviewed and included in the environment management programme;
- The hotel will continuously identify ways to minimise waste arriving at source and develop and implement resource and waste management strategies that conform to its 6R policy - Reduce, Reuse, Replace, Repair, Refill and Recycle. The hotel will also adopt best environmental practices to control and minimise all wastewater discharges;

- The hotel will identify and implement practices to optimise energy and water usage without affecting the quality of services provided to guests;
- The hotel will take appropriate measures to eliminate environmental, occupational and health risks and is prepared to respond to emergencies at all times;
- The hotel will support purchasing initiatives that are committed to sustainable environmental development, and continuously seek environmentally-friendly products and services that represent genuine value for money. The hotel will encourage and influence its suppliers to take part in the environment protection initiatives, to understand its purchasing policy, and to provide products and services that have the minimum adverse impact on the environment;
- The hotel will carry out regular internal programmes of education and training to enhance environment awareness amongst staff. The hotel will also actively participate in external environmental activities, as well as various training and development programmes, to broaden its horizon;
- The hotel will share its environment experience with other organisations in the community, raise the interests of its stakeholders by explaining the hotel's environment philosophy, and seek their co-operation in improving their own attitude towards environment concerns.

The Orchid Mumbai, India Hotel's Environment Policy

We at The Orchid, Asia's first five star, certified Ecotel hotel, commit ourselves towards continually Improving our Environmental Management in the hospitality industry, so as to remain leaders by:

- Optimising the use of resources such as energy, perishable food products, water, paint and paper;
- Striving to go beyond the applicable environmental laws and other requirements;

- Enhancing the practice of waste management, which is to reduce, reuse and recycle;
- Implementing environmental awareness of our suppliers, team members, guests and the local community;
- Providing a hygienic and safe working environment in the hotel;
- Increasing and maintaining the green cover.

The review covered 4 areas:

1. *An examination of existing environment practices and procedures:* This was done through a 78-point questionnaire/checklist covering corporate issues, management structure, staff awareness, training processes, public relations, investment, office/classroom/workshop-based activities, energy use and sources, water use and effluent discharge, waste minimisation and disposal, travel and transport, estate maintenance, major and minor works, and monitoring performance targets.
2. *A review of relevant environment legislation and regulatory requirements:* Activities already regulated by the local authorities' planning and development system and already enforced health and safety regulations were not included. The legislative areas reviewed were transport, airborne emissions, energy use, waste disposal and water use.
3. *An evaluation and registration of significant environment effects:* Although only sparse information was available, a register of effects (which records data on environment effects - resource inputs and waste outputs) was begun for atmospheric emissions, effluent discharge, waste and energy use.
4. *Observed regulatory non-compliance:* On the basis of this review, PCFE was able to set realistic environment objectives and targets, establish a formal environment

policy and develop a 90-activity environment management programme.

Implementing the Environment Management Programme

An environment management programme is needed to implement the EMS. It is the mechanism through which environment objectives and targets are achieved and the environment policy realised. An environment management programme works to integrate environment action - reducing resource use and waste output - into business activity through identifying the specific procedures and technological improvements that need to be incorporated into existing practices and operations. (An environment management programme is referred to as an 'environment action plan' in some sources.)

It helps to start by drawing up an activity plan, so that a complete overview of the environment management programme can be seen at a glance, perhaps in the form of a table.

An environment management programme for hospitality facilities typically consists of the following action areas:

- Reducing water use and wastewater output;
- Lowering energy consumption;
- Reducing waste output;
- Purchasing environment-preferable products;
- Lowering emissions, including of ozone-depleting substances;
- Improving the indoor environment;
- Lowering noise;
- Internal communication, delegation and training;
- Environment communication to guests;
- Monitoring and documenting progress.

A range of environment management options for each of the above action areas will now be discussed. It will help to bear in mind these considerations:

- What procedural or process changes might be needed for environment improvement?
- What technology could be used to facilitate environment management?
- What changes will increase efficiency?
- What improvements will require substantial capital investment?
- Will better training help address some of the issues?

Water management in hospitality facilities includes:

- Maintaining water quality;
- Managing water storage and distribution works;
- Reducing water use;
- Reducing wastewater output;
- Purifying water for swimming-pools;
- Monitoring water consumption;
- Reusing treated wastewater;
- Maintaining water supply quality.

Most countries have water quality standards, and ensuring compliance with them is important. The WHO and the EU have their own standards, which can be referred to for additional guidance. The most common indicators of poor water quality are: suspended solids, discolouring due to corrosion, rising pH levels, excessive hardness, high mineral content and bacterial contamination, especially legionnella pneumophilia. Any change in water quality should be brought to the attention of the water supply company/authority. A quick review of the on-site water storage and distribution works should then be conducted to find out if the source of the contamination is on or off the property.

Managing Water Storage and Distribution Works

- Ensure a frequent turnover of water to avoid the build-up of bacteria such as legionnella pneumophilia;
- Storage tank openings should be covered and

protected from dust, pests, and other sources of contamination;

- Inlet and outlet valves should be placed to avoid the build-up of stagnant water;
- Tanks should be cleaned every six months, and exterior and interior scale build-up removed;
- Tanks should be regularly checked for leaks.

Water Distribution

- Ensure regular maintenance to avoid leaks, spills and back siphonage between drinking and non-drinking supplies;
- Vacuum breakers and calibrated systems can be used to control flow, reduce pressure and optimise cost savings;
- Maintain and upgrade insulation on hot water tanks and pipes.

Reducing Water Use

- Repair leaks and dripping pipes;
- Run washing machines and dishwashers only when fully loaded;
- When watering gardens, direct flow to the roots of plants;
- Place plastic containers filled with water in toilet cisterns to reduce flush water volume;
- Encourage employees to save water;
- Collect rainwater for watering gardens and other non-drinking uses;
- Avoid rinsing under running taps: use buckets or bowls instead;
- Place tent cards in bathrooms inviting guests to save water;
- Invite guests to reuse their towels and linen.

Repair and Retrofit Options for Reducing Water Use

- Place volume reducers in toilet cisterns;
- Install hot and cold water mixers in all outlets;
- Install pressure flush valves on toilets and urinals. This can reduce flush water by 30-50%;
- Retrofit taps and showers with aerators. This can reduce water volume by 35%;
- Install photoelectric cells in public washstands;
- Install chemically purified urinals that do not use water.
- Replace baths with showers;
- Fit low-flow showerheads and toilets.

Purification of Water in Swimming Pools

There are several environment-preferable techniques used to purify swimming pool water that do not use chlorine or other chemicals. One such technique is ionisation, the release of metallic ions (usually copper and silver) into the water. Before release, low-voltage electricity is passed through electrodes to generate positive and negative ions. They kill algae, bacteria, and other micro-organisms. A small amount of chlorine (or other oxidiser such as bromine) is however needed to eliminate water-clouding elements such as suntan oil and dust, which are not affected by ions. Ionisation reduces chlorine use by almost 80%, and eliminates eye-sting and beaching effects.

Another technique involves ozone, which has been used for many years in industrial water purification and wastewater treatment plants throughout the world. Ozone is a very reactive form of oxygen which can destroy a variety of liquid waste materials, toxins, micro-organisms such as viruses, bacteria, spores, and some chemical impurities. Ozone can be created through:

- The UV, or photochemical method, which passes air through UV lamps, the UV rays turning the oxygen molecules into ozone, just as in the stratosphere;

- High-voltage electricity being passed through dry air in a vacuum.

The ozone obtained is then introduced into the water via a compressor or similar device. Also gaining ground is pool water purification by UVC radiation lamps, which radiate UV energy at 240-280 nanometres per second. The light is absorbed by the DNA of bacteria, moulds, viruses and yeast, which then leads to a change in the genetic material so that they are no longer able to multiply. Some chlorine (about 10% of conventional quantities) is then needed to provide residual bacterial control. A second benefit of this method is that UVC light has a photochemical effect, which can destroy chloramines and other by-products of chlorine. 'Free' chlorine is then released back into the water to perform its intended task of disinfection. Not only are water quality and atmospheric conditions considerably improved, but also much less chlorine has to be added to provide the residual bacterial control.

Monitoring Water Consumption

Since water is directly linked to the level of occupancy/ activity, it is best to monitor and benchmark water use on the basis of guest nights or visitor numbers. Water metres are essential for the monitoring of water use. Different areas of the business could be sub-metreed for the collection of more specific data. Comparing water use over the years and benchmarking with other facilities of similar size and standing can provide valuable information for improved water management and increased savings on water and energy costs. When benchmarking with other properties it must be remembered that water use will vary greatly depending on the size of the property, services offered, level of activity and climatic conditions.

Reuse of Treated Wastewater

It is good environment and business practice to collect and reuse rainwater for irrigation and other non-drinking uses.

Water collection tanks can be installed on the roof or at ground level. If the water is to be used in-house it may require a minimum level of treatment. It is possible to supplement non-drinking water needs by treating and reusing wastewater. The first consideration in wastewater reuse is to distinguish between 'grey' and 'black' water. Grey water is wastewater from bathrooms, laundries and kitchens; black water is wastewater from toilets. Black water contains pathogens and almost ten times more nitrogen than grey water, and therefore needs to go through a two- or three-stage biological treatment process beforeit can be reused.

Grey water treatment is less intensive and can be safely conducted on-site. The treated water can be used for irrigation, toilet flushing and other non-drinking uses. Over the last ten years, many national water supply and plumbing regulations have been modified to accommodate the reuse of grey water. They are most easily incorporated in the initial design process of a building, as separate drains and septic tanks have to be built. In the case of existing buildings, retrofitting drainage systems may be expensive, and a cost-benefit analysis must be conducted to determine if the effort is worthwhile.

The level to which grey water needs to be treated depends on the level of biological oxygen demand, or BOD, of the wastewater and the purpose for which it will be reused. The BOD level is the level of oxygen extracted from the water by bacteria when pollutants decompose. The more organic materials there are in wastewater, the more oxygen is needed for pollutant decomposition.

In most hospitality businesses, grey water can be reused for irrigation or flushing toilets, and in this case it may be enough to pass the wastewater through a sand filter. To maximise sand filter efficiency, it is important to minimise the suspended solids in the wastewater. Bathroom, laundry and kitchen outlets should therefore be fitted with filters, and additional grease traps should be added to kitchen outlets. But if grey water is to be used for drinking, it must go through a complete biological treatment process:

- Preliminary filtration process to remove grit and large suspended solids;
- Preliminary sedimentation process during which 55% of suspended solids are allowed to settle and are subsequently removed from the wastewater;
- Biological treatment process, either activated sludge or a percolating filter to oxidise the effluent, and reduce BOD;
- Secondary sedimentation process to remove all suspended matter and render the effluent suitable for reuse.

The treatment of wastewater should not be undertaken without the services of wastewater treatment specialists. Plumbing codes and discharge regulations should also be consulted.

Examples of Good Practice

At the Cama Rajputna Club Resort, Rajasthan, India, ten to twenty thousand litres of grey water are first passed through a gravel and sand filter bed and then used for watering the garden. Water use and water bills have further decreased by changing towels and bed linen every three days. At the Steigenberger Kurhaus Hotel, Amsterdam, Netherlands, a calibrated water pressure control system together with water-saving pressure nozzles on washbasins, sinks, and toilet cisterns is bringing substantial water savings. The new dishwasher unit is programmed to reuse water from the previous wash. A wastewater treatment works has been installed at the Taj Residency, Indore, India, through which 40,000 litres of wastewater are treated and reused every day. The treated water is used to water the garden. Further water conservation was made possible by changing watering times from during the day to dawn and dusk. Losses from evaporation, which used to account for 8,000 litres per day, are thus reduced.

The Hong Kong Hotel, Hong Kong has reduced water consumption by 20% by installing aerators in bathroom outlets and eliminating the use of running water for cleaning. In Canadian Pacific Hotel and Resorts hotels, water outlets and distribution pipes are regularly checked for leaks, aerators are installed in taps, low-flow showerheads and low-volume cisterns are used in bathrooms, and photoelectric-cell-operated toilets and washbasins are used in public facilities. At one of the chain's hotels, the Hotel Vancouver, a solution based on baking soda and salt is used to purify swimming-pool water. This has reduced chemical use and associated costs, and made handling and disposal easier.

Environment Management Programme for Energy

Energy efficiency not only reduces fuel and electricity bills, it also increases the overall comfort of the property. Energy management may be divided into two main areas:

- Maintenance or good housekeeping options;
- Repair, retrofit and refurbishment options.

Maintenance or 'Good Housekeeping' Options

- Loft insulation can help prevent condensation and mould, and can reduce heating bills by almost 20%. Insulation materials include mineral wool and brown cellulose fibres. A thickness of 15 to 20 cm should be ensured for maximum energy efficiency. As insulation makes the loft area colder, hot water tanks and pipes in this area must also be insulated.
- Shut down power in sections of the building that is not in use. This can be done through the use of Building Management Systems (BEMS), discussed later in this section.
- Insulate all hot water tanks, pipes and boilers.
- Seal gaps in walls, windows, doors, roofs and floor to control heating/cooling loss and penetrating damp.
- Make visitors aware of the importance of energy conservation. Invite them to switch off equipment and lights when not required.

- Match the size of the appliances to demand requirements. Oversized or undersized equipment wastes energy.
- Train staff to use less hot water and to save energy by switching off equipment when not needed.
- In the kitchen, match pan size to hot plate/burner size. Defrost food at room temperature and not in hot water.
- Maintain hot water in taps at 50°C.
- Use translucent lampshades to optimise light output.
- Open and close curtains to maximise and minimise heat gain as required.
- Ensure timers and controllers are set according to the degree-day thresholds and levels of activity inside the property.
- Ensure boilers and chillers are regularly serviced to maximise efficiency.
- Do not place furniture in front of heating or cooling units.
- Radiators and air-conditioning units should be placed below windows to prevent down-draughts; curtains should therefore not be allowed to drape over them.
- Select the most energy-efficient cycles and fully load washing machines and dishwashers before use.

Repair, Retrofit and Refurbishment Options

A number of repair, retrofit and refurbishment options are presented below:

- Automatic load-shedding control systems;
- Controls for heating and hot water;
- Double-glazing;
- Sealing and stripping;
- Controlled ventilation;
- Low energy lighting;

- Covering and coatings;
- Heat recovery;
- Building Energy Management Systems (BEMS);
- Combined heat and power;
- Replacing old equipment;
- Renewable energy options;
- Wall, roof, and floor insulation.

Automatic Load-Shedding Control Systems

Most electricity suppliers require that hospitality businesses pay a maximum demand tariff based on peak demand loads. This is designed to discourage users from having large peaks and falls in their energy demand patterns. To reduce peak demand loads and tariffs, it is first necessary to investigate the causes of loading and to check if the use of some appliances can be avoided during peak periods. Automatic load-control systems continuously monitor electricity use.

When demand rises to the maximum threshold, they automatically switch off the appliances programmed into the system. They also allow the user to choose which appliances get switched off first. Large hospitality businesses have found that automatic load-shedding control systems can greatly reduce peak demand loads and bring significant cost savings.

Controls for Heating and Hot Water

The right controls are crucial for the efficient operation of hot water and heating/cooling systems. These include:

- Room thermostats, which switch-off boilers when rooms are heated to a set temperature;
- Programmer and timer switches, which switch off space and water heating at required times;
- Zone controls, allowing one or more zones to be controlled separately
- Hot water cylinder thermostats to switch off boilers when water is heated to a given temperature;

- A thermostatic radio valve fitted onto a radiator and used in conjunction with the room thermostat system or boiler energy control system; it works by reducing water flow into the radiator when the thermostat reaches the set temperature;
- Storage water controls, used for storage or combination heaters: they include such features as automatic thermostats (to control heat storage and output according to peak demand loads and tariffs windows), convector-control room temperature thermostats, and external timers.

A complete heating and cooling control package can usually be installed at any time, but installation costs can be substantially reduced if it is done during refurbishment. Based on energy savings alone, the pay-back time for double-glazing replacement windows is 4 to 7 years. The most important feature in reducing heat loss is not the thickness of the glass, but the space between the layers of glass, which should be around 20 mm. Low-emissivity glasses will further reduce heat loss.

In the case of windows already installed, secondary glazing usually made of glass in plastic or aluminium frames is a cost-effective option. Wood and PVC frames are better insulators than aluminium. Trickle vents to ensure adequate ventilation should accompany replacement windows. Badly fitted doors and windows are a major source of heating and cooling loss, but are cheap and easy to repair. Sealing and stripping materials include silicon strips, blade seals, brush piles and fillers, and rubber, PVC and aluminium seals.

It is especially important to maintain adequate ventilation where flued (fuel and gas) appliances are in use, since adequate air must keep entering the area to allow fires to burn safely. If trickle vents are not fitted, the upper part of windows should not be sealed.

Controlled Ventilation

While sealing and stripping is important, so too is controlled ventilation. Adequate ventilation is important to reduce condensation and the resulting damp, and to ensure that odours, carbon dioxide and stale air are removed and good indoor air quality is maintained. There are several types of controlled ventilation suitable for hospitality buildings:

- Background ventilation systems such as trickle vents;
- Rapid ventilation systems such as extractor fans;
- Ducted systems including heat recovery.

Low-Energy Lighting

Low-energy lighting is easy to install and can reduce energy costs by 10-15%. Low-energy lamps include compact fluorescent (CLFs), fluorescent tubes, and tungsten halogens.

CLFs last about 8 times longer than tungsten halogen lamps and use about 25% less energy for the same light output. Tungsten halogen lamps are about 50% more efficient than standard lamps and last twice as long. All energy-efficient lighting offers the advantage of dimmer switches, which allow control of light output.

Coverings and Coatings

In warmer climates, weatherproof coverings should be finished off with sun-reflecting paints to reduce solar heat gain. Similarly, pale shades used for decorating exteriors and interiors reduce heat gain and increase light reflection.

Heat Recovery

Hospitality properties can achieve substantial savings by recovering sensible and latent heat from kitchen, laundry and swimming-pool exhaust systems, boiler flues, and condensed heat recovery. This heat can be channelled back for space or water heating. Heat recovery requires the installation of heat exchangers to separate the heat from its source (water, gas or combustion products) and transfer it to where it can be reused – the water or space heating system. The most cost-effective heat-recovery systems for hospitality businesses are usually sensible heat exchangers such as run-around coils and thermal wheels.

The feasibility of heat recovery depends on:

- The temperature of the waste heat in the air or water;
- Where the waste heat is to be used, which should be closely connected to the source of the waste heat;
- Purchasing and operating costs of the heat-exchange unit: the cost of the heat recovered should be higher than the purchasing and operation of the heat-exchange unit.

Sensible heat is the heat associated with a change in temperature. Latent heat is associated with a change in state such as from liquid to gas.

Building Energy Management Systems (BEMS)

BEMS are computer-based energy-management systems which provide for the integrated control of thermostats, boilers, and zone controllers, each zone having its own heating, cooling and lighting units. They therefore enable different areas of a property to be controlled separately and even shut down when not in use.

Combined Heat and Power (CHP)

CHP systems generate electricity and channel the heat generated in the process (normally regarded as waste) to use for water or space heating. As both electricity and heat are generated at the same time, the efficiency of CHP systems can be as high as 80-90%. CHP is most suited to properties that require water and space heating for longer periods of the year. The UK Department of the Environment, Transport and the Regions reports that around 17% of total CHP installations in the UK are in hotels.

Replace Older Equipment

Older boilers and chillers are more energy-intensive than newer models. Replacing equipment over 15 years old will reduce energy bills by 10-15%. If equipment is less than 10 years old, investing in controls may prove more economical.

Renewable energy is a source of energy that can be produced at the same rate as or faster than it is consumed, and therefore does not deplete natural resources. Renewable energy technology for tourism and hospitality includes solar water heating, photovoltaics (PV), mini-hydro systems, wind turbines, bio-fuels and geothermal heat pumps.

Wall, Roof and Floor Insulation

Around 80% of cooling and heating is lost through external walls. In conjunction with heating/cooling controls, wall insulation also reduces condensation and damp. Many recycled and more environmentally-preferable insulating materials are available and should be given preference. Formaldehyde should be avoided. The types and methods of roof insulation depend on the roof pitch (sloping or flat), boulders, eves, rafters, weatherproof coverings, etc.

The most commonly used insulation materials are plastic (mainly polystyrene) and mineral wool. Floor insulation is best done when floors are being replaced or extensions built. If insulation is laid above existing floors, care should be taken that the extra thickness does not affect existing fittings and skirtings. Floor insulation is especially useful to reduce heating and cooling losses in buildings with suspended wooden floors. Insulation materials include mineral wool, polystyrene and foam glass.

Examples of Good Practice

Through power factor correction and the installation of a load-shedding system, the Hotel Inter-Continental in Sydney, Australia, is achieving savings in electricity costs of A$27,000 a year. A BEMS is used to control and monitor all chillers, boilers, steam generators and hot-water tanks. 70% of the hot water requirements of the Welcome Group Mughal Sheraton Hotel in Agra, India, is obtained through solar water heaters. Energy-efficient compact fluorescent lamps are fitted in guestrooms and public areas, and infrared sensors automatically switch off lights when rooms are vacant. As a result of an environment status review on energy, The

Renaissance Jamaica Grand Resort, Ocho Rios, Jamaica, has replaced its old chillers with new CFC-free equipment with 0.50kw/tonne energy-efficiency. The cooling towers have also been upgraded. The hotel is reviewing the feasibility of CHP.

Canadian Pacific Hotels and Resorts lowered water heating costs by insulating hot-water pipes and tanks, and regularly monitoring boiler thermostats. Some properties use solar water heaters to provide hot water for swimming pools. Energy-management measures which collectively reduce energy costs by 20-25% per annum, at the Taj Residency, Indore, India, include:

- Timers on office air-conditioners to switch off units for 15 minutes every 45 minutes;
- BEMS and link panels to turn power on and off in guest rooms;
- Solar water heaters;
- Waste heat from air-conditioning units recovered and reused for water heating;
- Sun-control films on glass panes to reduce solar gain and air-conditioning loads;
- Roofs and outer walls of the rooms on the top floor, which are exposed to direct sunlight for long periods, embodied with 50mm of insulation to reduce heat gain.

Environment Management Programme for Waste

Reducing and reusing waste is one of the easiest areas for environment improvement and therefore one of the best areas to start. The preliminary environment status review requires a list of all waste generated by the business. This can now be used to identify products that can be:

- Replaced with alternatives which avoid waste or generate less;
- Reused for the same or another purpose;
- Sorted and collected for recycling under municipal waste recycling schemes;
- Used for longer.

A checklist on waste management for hospitality facilities is given below. It follows the order of the waste management hierarchy:

1. Avoid
2. Reduce
3. Reuse
4. Recycle

How can the Separation of Waste be Easily Incorporated into Hospitality Operations?

- Place separate waste containers in rooms and invite guests to use the containers as labelled;
- Ask guests to sort out waste such as batteries for separate collection and disposal;
- Install housekeeping carts with separate waste containers;
- Place separate waste containers in kitchens, other F&B outlets, housekeeping and administration areas;
- Place bulk containers for separate waste in an appropriate back office area;
- Train employees in all departments to separate waste.

In the case of hazardous waste such as solvents, pool chemicals, paints, chemical pesticides and other such products, the local authority's disposal stipulations should be followed. Hygiene and food safety codes provide guidance for food and packaging waste disposal, which will facilitate waste management.

Some Facts About Composting Composting is the use of micro-organisms to break down organic waste (vegetable clippings, leaves, seeds, skins, shells, rinds, garden waste, etc) into inorganic form, which can then be used to improve the nutrient and water retention capacity of soil. Composting techniques range from simple backyard heaps to in-vessel systems. As composting waste is wet, backyards heaps need to be layered with dry bulking materials such as wood, sawdust, hay, leaves or shredded paper. Commercial compost activators can also be used. A small amount of nitrogen fertiliser can be added to increase energy content and speed up decomposition. Compost heaps need to be kept moist and thoroughly mixed to ensure waste breaks down rapidly. An unturned pile will become anaerobic (lack oxygen) and smell.

In-vessel systems allow waste to be composted in enclosed vessels, reducing composting time to less than 30 days. As the composting takes place in enclosed vessels, they can be installed indoors (in kitchens and corridors, for example) or outside without the problems of smell, space or leakage. These systems have loading and screening devices, computerised or mechanical aeration systems, and mixers to turn the piles. Most composting systems recommend that only 15% of the waste heap consist of meat; in-vessel systems have partly overcome this disadvantage.

Preparation of Waste for Recycling

If waste is to be successfully prepared and used for recycling, it must be uniformly sorted and cleaned, and free from bottle-caps, food, metal, plastic, etc. Compactors can be used to reduce waste volume. This lowers the space required to collect and store waste and increases its value as a recyclable material: But compactors can be expensive and are only worthwhile in large properties with significant waste volume. Plastic and paper waste usually needs to be baled and compacted before collection for recycling. Advice needs to be obtained from local and/or municipal waste collection and recycling schemes on the preparation of waste, use of compactors, baling specifications, and the market price for recyclables.

Revenue from recycling waste depends on the type and volume of waste separated and made available for collection, the local market for recycled products, and local policies on the recycling of post-consumer waste. For best returns, the waste must be sorted and contamination-free. Working closely with recycling dealers will enable effective sorting and collection plans to be developed and returns to be optimised.

All recyclables need to be sorted, cleaned, and baled before collection from commercial sites, homes and businesses. They then have to be transported to material handling facilities where they are further sorted, cleaned, and crushed (or pulped in the case of paper) before they can go to manufacturing sites for reuse. The transport involved in recycling increases if people drive to waste collection points to dispose of their waste. These processes and transport requirements can consume large amounts of water, power, fossil fuels and other materials, and emit wastes and emissions.

The answer requires detailed environment, life-cycle and economic studies and will vary with each recyclable material. Consideration must also be given to the entire organisation, profitability, and growth prospects of the recycling market in question. Some recent and controversial studies in the UK and the US show that for paper and plastic, incineration with energy recovery can be a better business and environment-preferable alternative than recycling; the parametres are too numerous to discuss here. But it should not be forgotten that incineration plants are very capital-intensive to build and operate, and even state-of-the- art incinerators can emit harmful gases, including dioxins. Another argument against incineration with energy recovery is that it drives down incentives for waste reduction.

The other waste disposal option is landfill, which has significant environment impacts. In an effort to reduce landfill waste volumes, landfill levies and taxes have risen significantly over recent years and legislation aimed at restricting the building of new landfill sites is being enforced in many countries. In the light of these trends, recycling is expected to gain new ground in the future. As large generators of post-consumer waste, the hospitality industry has a key role to play in increasing recycling volumes and the market for recyclable products.

Examples of Good Practice

At the Trouville Hotel, Restaurant and Conference Centrein Hornbaek, Denmark, waste is separated as follows: organic waste, paper and board, coloured and non-coloured glass, returnable bottles, aluminium, and packaging material. Plastic materials are reused and do not enter the waste stream.

- Organic waste is frozen and sold for conversion into animal food;
- Paper and board are compacted and sold for recycling;
- Packaging materials are returned to suppliers;
- Glass is deposited at the nearest recycling collection point;
- Returnable bottles are sold for reuse.

The Trouville has also discontinued the use of disposable items. Shampoo and bath and shower gel are provided in refillable wall-mounted dispensers; glasses have replaced disposable plastic mugs. The use of individual packages of butter, marmalade, honey, cream etc., has been discontinued. Most brochures are printed on recycled paper. The Trouville is a holder of the 'Green Key', the Danish national eco-label for environmentally-preferable hospitality facilities. The Cama Rajputana Resort, Rajastan, India, composts all food, kitchen and garden waste through 'vermicomposting', the use of specially-bred worms to break down waste into compost. The hotel operates its own vermiculture laboratory that produces worms for composting on-site as well as for the local community. The resort is also working towards using the biogas generated during the breakdown of waste for cooking.

Along with waste management, purchasing is an easy and visible area to start environment action. Using environmentally-preferable products demonstrates a company's environment commitment to employees, visitors and suppliers, and helps avoid and reduce waste. The purchasing inventory compiled during the environment status review indicates the best place to start. Excessive packaging is neither economical nor environment-suitable. However, a minimum level of packaging must be maintained to protect goods from contamination, prevent damage and spoilage, and facilitate transport, storage and end use. If a reduction in packaging results in increased product damage and spoilage, the effort is pointless. Food safety, hygiene codes and local packaging legislation will provide additional guidance on the minimum levels and types of packaging that need to be maintained.

The purchasing policy has been a central element in the EMS of the Hotel Inter-Continental, Sydney. Environment sensitivity, energy-efficiency, durability, price and quality are primary considerations. Suppliers are asked to reduce packaging, and to keep suggesting 'greener' alternatives as they arrive on the market. They are also asked to respond to the Hotel Supply Questionnaire about their products and commitment to environment responsibility. As part of its award-winning EMS, the Sanga Saby Hotel, Study and Conference Centre, Svartsjo, Sweden, buys exclusively Swedish. Food is purchased from agricultural co-operatives. Transport distance being an vital element in purchasing, preference is given to locally grown and manufactured products.

Emissions from hospitality facilities are mainly emissions from vehicles and from the burning of fossil fuels used for space and water heating and cooking. Regular maintenance checks should be conducted on boilers and generators. Filters and scrubbers should be fitted to exhaust fans, and be regularly cleaned and maintained. Local legislation on emission standards should be consulted before control devices are installed. The use of vehicles, boilers and generators that can operate on ethanol blends and bio diesel should also be considered.

Some Facts About Bio-Fuels

The use of 85%-ethanol-blended fuels has been shown to reduce greenhouse gas emissions by 30-36%. A 10%-ethanol blend results in a 25-30% reduction in carbon monoxide emissions (by promoting a more complete combustion of the fuel) and a 6-10% net reduction of CO2. In addition, as ethanol oxygenates the fuel, there is a roughly 7% decrease in exhaust VOCs emitted from low-level ethanol-blended fuels compared with fossil fuels. In high-level blends, the potential for exhaust VOC reduction is 30% or more.

At the WelcomeGroup Mughal Sheraton, Agra, India, carbon monoxide and sulphur dioxide emissions from boilers are purified through scrubbers before being released. All fossil-fuel-operated equipment is maintained in good working condition to minimise carbon dioxide emissions. The Sanga Saby Hotel, Study and Conference Centre, Svartsjo, Sweden, in association with the Swedish Ethanol Foundation, acquired the first rape methyl ester fuelled car in 1995. Today,all vehicles, tractors, boilers and some of the lawn mowers operate on rapeseed oil (the other lawn-mowers are powered by PV).

Indoor air pollutants include combustion gases such as carbon dioxide, nitrous oxides and hydrocarbons, tobacco smoke, VOCs, asbestos, ozone, dust and particles, CFCs and radon. The worldwide ban on the manufacture of CFCs came into effect in 1999. The phasing-out of CFCs and other ozone-depleting substances used in the hospitality business merits detailed consideration, and is discussed in the following sub-section of this unit. Detailed information on the management of ozone-depleting substances in the hospitality industry can be found in the UNEP DTIE publication, entitled How the Hotel Industry can Help Protect the Ozone Layer, in 1998. Indoor environment quality depends on specific pollutants and their levels of concentration inside the building. Monitoring air quality will give the most accurate picture of the types and concentration of pollutants in the air. This requires specialist help and equipment that may not be available in-house.

Monitoring must be conducted over a long period to enable a range of data to be collected. A single monitoring attempt will not give a correct estimate of air quality, for pollution levels will vary at different times of the day and year, being influenced by weather conditions, activity levels and the air quality of the outside environment.

The first step is to regulate the changeover of air according to the number of occupants, concentration of pollutants in the air, level of activity and climate conditions. In a typical hotel in a moderate climate one change of air per hour is suitable for bedrooms, 5 per hour for offices, reception and lobby, and up to 20 per hour in kitchens, laundries and garages.

Exterior sections of the ventilating system should be kept clean and free of obstructions to airflow. This is vital to ensure that stale air does not re-circulate back into the ventilation system. Boilers, stoves and generators should be kept in good repair and vents and filters should be cleaned regularly. Filter replacement should be carried out according to the manufacturer's instructions.

Employee and guest complaints about indoor air quality can be recorded and studied over time to identify regular patterns or sources. For example, if more complaints come from people spending time in newly decorated areas, it could mean a problem with VOC emissions from building materials. If employees working in areas near busy garages and roads report dizziness, it could be caused by continued exposure to higher levels of carbon monoxide and carbon dioxide.

The Tampere Hall Concert and Conference Centre, Tampere, Finland, adjusts air-conditioning during concerts and meetings according to load levels. Staff responsible for air-conditioning circulates in the halls with carbon dioxide metres and increase or decrease air-conditioning as required. At the Maurya Sheraton Hotel and Towers, New Delhi, India, 'ozoniers' are installed in guest rooms to improve indoor air quality. These devices (sometimes referred to as 'aranisers') energise the oxygen in the air. Energised oxygen accelerates the breakdown of odours, pollutants and many other harmful substances.

As long as the halons in a fire extinguisher remain contained in the extinguisher and are not discharged, they do not contribute to the depletion of the ozone layer. Equipment should therefore be checked for leaks. Once the contents have been discharged or the extinguishers become redundant, they should be replaced with zero-ODS alternatives, which include dry carbon dioxide powder and foam appliances. Halons in redundant equipment can be recycled at halon banks. National ozone units can provide information on halon recycling in each country. When replacing extinguishers it is important to consider optimising fire-extinguishing capacity. Employee and guest safety should never be compromised.

With aerosols and foams, it is best to switch to zero-ODS alternatives as soon as current stocks have been used. Zero-ODS alternatives include natural fibre-based materials to replace foams, and pump-action or refillable spray cans to replace aerosols. If an environment management programme is to be successful, employees must be motivated and trained to integrate reducing resource use and waste into daily operating procedures. In tourism and hospitality, it is the employees who are in contact with the customer, who create the experience, and who deliver the service.

If they are well informed and motivated to achieve environment objectives, this will reflect in their working practices and improve service quality. Employees are also the hospitality industry's biggest public relations instruments. They are the best placed to inform visitors of the business's environment policies. This will in turn enhance corporate image and reputation. Well-trained employees can identify problem areas and suggest improvements more effectively than external consultants and managers.

The environment status review can be used to inform employees of the company's environment commitment and that an environment management programme is in the pipeline. Once the environment policy has been established, it should be communicated to all staff, posted on notice boards, enclosed in internal newsletters, and announced at staff meetings. An informal meeting might be organised to mark the launch of the environment effort. Delegation and training become critical during implementation of the environment programme. Environment responsibility should be integrated at all levels and in all job descriptions. Delegation is best done within the formal management hierarchy and existing reporting lines.

The environment champion and the management team should serve as the central co-ordination unit. The environment management team should include a representative from each department, with responsibility for ensuring that the environment management programme is implemented in that department.

Establishing departmental environment performance targets facilitates delegation of responsibility. For example, F & B departments could be required to reduce packaging waste by 20%, and housekeeping to reduce the use of toxic cleaners by 40%. On-the-job training, supported by training instruction sheets in the case of complex technical work, is most suitable for integrating environment action into hospitality.

Senior management should show leadership. Small actions such as switching off lights, using both sides of office paper and separating waste are good ways to demonstrate that environment management is a serious effort and has company commitment. Networking is important. Businesses should participate in local environment initiatives such as round tables, industry partnerships, tree planting and wildlife conservation initiatives.

It is also good to subscribe to a few business and environment journals. This helps the environment champion and the management team to gain a deeper understanding of environment issues and how other businesses handle them. As the environment management programme gets underway, employees should be kept informed of progress, with reports and monitoring sheets posted up, announced at staff meetings, and featured in internal newsletters. This will help reinforce responsibility and motivation. Employee morale may increase as staff come to realise they are working for a business that is concerned about working comfort, safety and environment improvement. Participation in the environment management programme should be a criterion for performance evaluation. 'Good environment ideas' and 'outstanding environment contributions' could be rewarded with prizes. Some hotels organize.

The Taj Group of Hotels, India, has developed an in-house environment 'train the trainers' programme. Department heads and all senior-level staff are trained for two days on conducting environment awareness, resource consumption, waste reduction and environment performance monitoring classes for all staff in their respective units. Resource consumption training includes water and energy auditing procedures, cost-benefit analysis, benchmarking against international standards, energy and water conservation strategies, and building employee awareness on water and energy conservation. Training in waste reduction is based on the '3 Rs'–reduce, reuse, and recycle.

The rationale of this programme is that increased environment awareness will raise commitment, enthusiasm, and participation in the EMS. Senior staff are encouraged to attend the environment leadership-training programme conducted by the Indian Institute of Hotel Management. The EcoTaj Environment Information Centre in Bangalore, India, has an EMS and conservation library and resource centre for the use of all employees. An in-house environment magazine is circulated to all units and employees.

All new employees undergo an environment-training programme as part of their induction. There is little point in implementing an excellent environment action plan if clients are not told about it. Guest communication is critical to optimise the business benefits of the EMS. The preliminary environment status review provides initial insight into the environment awareness and demands of clients. If a business works with travel agents and tour operators who have environment policies, and if competitors have begun to work on EMS, it is likely that visitors will be receptive to environmentally responsible services. But even when environment action is not widespread, a business can enhance its corporate image by becoming a pioneer in environment action.

A business should never indulge in 'green-wash' or false environment claims. Care must be taken not to blow achievements out of proportion. If the business has a major environment impact, it is best not to draw attention to it before rectifying action is in place. There are many groups interested in the environment performance of businesses, including environment groups, non-government organisations, regulators, and competitors. While transparency is important, false green claims are always found out: this can seriously damage the reputation and credibility of the business.

A standardised environment-monitoring format helps standardise data-collection and record-keeping across the company. The following is an example of a monitoring format used for documenting water and energy consumption.

The best evidence of good implementation is the level of environment improvement. Other evidence can be found in resource and material use records, data sheets on waste and emissions, training instruction sheets, visitor comments, fines imposed. A corporate environment report communicates to all stakeholders the company's environment performance over a given period. It is a key indicator of the business's environment commitment and an important tool for building dialogue and communication with local communities, legislators and non-government organisations. Corporate environment reports detail the results of the EMS. They also catalyse environment action across the company, validate the efforts of environment managers and increase support for environment improvement. The environment management programme was discussed under the action areas:

water and wastewater, energy, waste, purchasing environmentally-preferable products, emissions, indoor air quality, noise, internal communication and training, visitor communication, and monitoring and documenting the progress of the environment management programme. These actions will now be briefly recapitulated as department checklists.

The headquarters of the group are in London, UK, with regional offices in Atlanta for the Americas, Hong Kong for Asia Pacific, and Windsor for Europe/Middle East/Africa. Each region has an environment team leader who reports to the Vice-Chairman of BHR. The vice-chairman is the company sponsor of the BHR Environment Initiative, and as such represents BHR on the Bass PLC Environment Working Group. One of BHR's worldwide environment initiatives is the Conserving for Tomorrow programme. With over 1,100 participating hotels worldwide, it focuses on energy and water conservation and offers guests the opportunity to reuse towels and sheets during multiple-night stays.

Towels and linens are washed every three days. Based on the number of participating hotels, the programme is estimated to save 7,038,000 gallons of water and 46,920 gallons of detergent every month, in addition to the energy savings from using less hot water. BHR conducts on-going guest surveys to measure consumer perception of the towels and linen programme: response has been very favourable. The lighting programme also calls for a reduction in mercury lighting, which reduces not only environment impact but disposal costs as well.

Green Teams and Environment

The corporate environment effort began in late 1997 with a bottom-up approach: Green Teams and Environment Champions were appointed in all Golden Tulip-owned hotels and inns in the Netherlands. The members of the Green Teams are volunteers from all levels of hotel staff. Most co-ordinators are employees with a high level of social awareness and an overall appreciation of environment issues. While they are well placed to identify practical and low-cost good housekeeping improvements, it was found they did not have the overall business perspective needed to integrate environment management into business operations and to 'sell' the needs and benefits of environment management along the management hierarchy. To address this issue, the Golden Tulip Business School has developed an in-house training pack for Environment Co-ordinators and Green Team members on:

- Obtaining the active participation of general managers in environment management;
- Creating and maintaining environment-oriented enthusiasm among colleagues and employees.

The objective was to begin action with no-cost and low-cost good housekeeping and repair activities and move on to more capital-intensive improvements at a later stage. Action therefore began in a phased effort, with a new environment action area being introduced every month. The action areas implemented to date are water, waste, energy and chemicals. Newsletters introducing and discussing each environment action area were distributed to all employees-

> "For us in the hospitality business, environment management is imperative for continued business success. We began environment action in a practical and hands-on manner, and used this experience to establish a corporate environment policy. We are now working on improving environment performance with increased support from top management and an effective environment policy behind us. For Golden Tulip Hotels, environment action is not a marketing tool, but a business and social responsibility. We are not planning to market our environment performance until fully-fledged environment-management programmes are up and running, and valid performance data is available."

This section introduces cleaner production, eco-efficiency, industrial ecology and life-cycle assessment, which will provide the reader with a greater appreciation of the EMS philosophy.

Cleaner Production

While traditional environment action has focused on cleaning up waste and pollution after it has been created, cleaner production aims to avoid the generation of waste and pollution in the first place. Strategies for cleaner production include:

- Reducing the use of raw materials and energy;
- Reducing the use of toxic raw materials;
- Reducing toxic waste output;
- Reducing environment impacts during the lifecycle of products and services - from raw material extraction to manufacturing, production, storage, distribution, consumption and recycling and/or final disposal. In economic terms, cleaner production means reducing material and energy use and related costs, auditing, adopting more efficient production processes, lowering waste volumes and disposal costs, eliminating clean-up costs, fines and charges, and producing higher quality goods and services. Cleaner production is the continuous application of integrated preventive strategies applied to processes, products and services to increase efficiency and reduce risks to humans and the environment.

Eco-Efficiency

Eco-efficiency is about doing more with less -using the same or a lesser amount of materials and energy to deliver a higher quality or quantity of goods and services. The World Business Council for Sustainable Development (WBCSD) provides the following definition:

Eco-efficiency is reached by the delivery of competitively priced goods and services that satisfy human needs and bring quality to life, which progressively reduces ecological impacts and resource intensity throughout the life cycle, to a level that is at least in line with the earth's carrying capacity.

Industrial Ecology (Systems Thinking)

Industrial ecology refers to business operations that mimic the natural ecosystem, where an industrial system is managed like an ecosystem - a continuous and sequential flow of materials, energy and information. The two major concepts of industrial ecology are sealing the material cycle and dematerialisation:

- Sealing the material cycle means carrying out production in closed-circuits, in the same way as an ecosystem. For example, through photosynthesis plants produce carbohydrates. These feed herbivores, which then fall prey to carnivores, whose waste is, in turn, food for detritus organisms. Similarly, industries could reuse waste as raw material and reuse or recycle end products after they have been consumed. In this way materials and waste would move round in closed circuits.
- Ecosystems have built-in methods for optimising the use of materials and energy. Similarly, dematerialisation is about doing more with less: optimising the use of raw materials and extending the service life of end products. An additional benefit in extending service life is that it creates new job opportunities, especially in maintenance and repair.

Industrial Ecology in Practice

One of the best examples of industrial ecology in practice is the case of the Danish town Kalundborg. Kalundborg has four main industries:

- Asnaes Power Station, a coal-fired plant;
- Novo Nordisk, producing enzymes and pharmaceuticals;
- Gyproc, a plasterboard manufacturer;
- Statoil, an oil refinery.

The evolving industrial ecosystem works as follows:

- Asnaes produces steam and heat while generating electricity, and sends some of its steam to Statoil and Novo Nordisk. Statoil, which gets 40% of its steam requirements from Asnaes, uses the steam to heat pipes and tanks. Novo Nordisk gets 100% of the steam it needs from Asnaes, and uses it as a source of heat and pressure.
- Asnaes also pipes excess heat to local fish farms and some homes. Plans are underway to expand this to all homes in Kalundborg by 2005. This process of heat and steam recycling has raised the efficiency of coal burning from 40% to over 90%.
- Asnaes' waste steam and the by-product gypsum (produced in the scrubbers which reduce sulphur dioxide emissions) are used by Gyproc to make plasterboard. The remaining gypsum is sent to local cement producers.
- At the Statoil Refinery, flue gas is created as a by-product of oil refining. The gas first goes through a de-sulphurisation process. The hot, liquid sulphur captured is sold to the Kemira Acid Plant in Jutland.

Statoil's sulphur-free flue gas goes to Asnaes and Gyproc, instead of being burned off. Asnaes thus saves 30,000 tonnes of coal a year. Statoil's flue gas meets nearly 95% of Gyproc's gas needs.

- Novo Nordisk gives its nitrogen-rich sludge to local farmers via pipeline or truck. This is reported to save each farmer about US$50,000 a year in fertiliser costs.
- This evolving symbiotic scheme is also being extended to water use.

Life Cycle Assessment

Life Cycle Assessment (LCA) is a method of assessing the environment impacts of a product or service during its life cycle - extraction, processing, manufacturing, transport and distribution, consumption, maintenance, reuse and recycling, and final disposal. It is a quantitative and scientific analysis, designed to generate objective information about environment impacts. Economic and social issues only enter the picture once the scientific analysis is complete.

LCA can be used to:

- Develop new products and services;
- Improve manufacturing/service delivery;
- Provide consumers with credible information on the environment aspects of products/services;
- Develop environment-preferable purchasing policies;
- Improve the quality of existing products and services.

Specialised life cycle analysis software, together with methodology improvements and increased data availability, is making LCA easier to carry out. LCA methodology consists of four main stages.

Case Study: The LCA of a Vending Machine

An LCA was conducted on a fully automated hot drink dispensing machine for tea, coffee and chocolate. The LCA findings showed that:

- The energy consumption was highest for the production and transport of the ingredients and for the use and servicing of the machine;
- 70% of the energy used during the lifetime of the machine was to maintain it on stand-by;
- The majority of waste and emissions came from the use and servicing of the machine;
- The material input for the ingredients (tea, coffee, chocolate, hot water, milk, and sugar) was 10 times greater than the material input in the manufacture of the dispensing machine.

These findings were used to implement the following improvements:

- The ingredients in the machines were replaced with more environmentally-preferable alternatives;

- The ingredient containers were enlarged;
- Daily servicing was reduced to weekly servicing;
- The hot water tank was insulated.

Ingredient and energy use was reduced by over 10%. As servicing costs were also substantially reduced, the price of the hot drinks dispensed could be lowered.

- Businesses have realised that if they are to remain profitable and competitive, they must integrate environment management into daily processes and practices.
- National legislation that makes EMS and environment reporting mandatory is on the rise. Taxes on emissions and waste are adding momentum to EMS implementation. Non-compliance will be punishable with heavier fines and even imprisonment.
- Increased environment expertise, together with more efficient and cleaner technologies, will greatly facilitate environment improvement.
- EMS will also move from piecemeal improvements to reducing the overall impacts of production and processes. Eco-efficiency, cleaner production and industrial ecology will move from being noteworthy but isolated achievements to common practice.
- EMS goals are fast evolving from environment management to sustainable development. Companies will not only have to reduce resources and waste, but also take steps to improve social welfare and the quality of life in the societies in which they operate. Corporate social responsibility involves good management, better pay and benefits, health and safety in the workplace, training, non discrimination, indigenous rights, avoiding child labour, and transparency in product and service procurement.
- The market and immediate stakeholders are demanding greater transparency. Companies have to

not simply carry out environment management efforts, but report on environment performance with independent verification of performance data.

- There will be greater transparency on corporate lobbying activities, and the role of companies in influencing public policy on sustainable development.
- In tourism, leading airlines, airports, tour operators, hotels, and visitor attractions are working on EMS. There is still much scope for improvement - especially in small and medium-sized businesses that constitute a large part of the industry.

Develop and Implement EMS in a Hospitality Business

Ask hotels and restaurants in the region if they would be interested in having a group of students develop an EMS for their business. This will provide a hands-on practical project for several groups of students (5 to 6 students per group), and help local businesses improve environment performance. The first group of students would visit the property, interview the management and employees, and:

- Conduct a preliminary environment review (including research on level of compliance, fines and charges, costs of resource use and waste disposal);
- Analyse the findings of the review;
- Develop an environment policy;
- Establish environment objectives and targets;
- Develop a baseline environment management programme.

A group of students from the next semester could:

- Help the business finalise the environment management programme
- Implement the programme;
- Set up regular performance monitoring practices;
- Analyse environment progress.

A group of students from the semester after that could:

- Carry out an environment audit;
- Assess the findings of the audit;
- Make recommendations on further improvements, revise targets and objects for continual improvement;
- Investigate how to maintain enthusiasm about the environment within the business.

Develop an EMS training programme for the management and employees of a small hotel or restaurant in the region. The exercise should involve site visits, a short preliminary environment review and interviews with management and employees. Make a presentation describing the programme. (Managers of the hotel/restaurant could be present during the presentation). Consider the environment management concepts and tools, cleaner production, eco-efficiency, industrial ecology, and life-cycle analysis. Devise examples of the application of each of these concepts in a hospitality business. Make a presentation of your examples.

Critically discuss the following statements. Your answer should be about 1,500 words long. 'Whose responsibility is environment quality? The tourism industries, the hospitality businesses, the tourist's, the supplier's, or all?' 'Tourism and hospitality trade associations can be veryeffective in promoting EMS in the industry.' 'EMS is equally important for small to medium-sized businesses and large companies.'

Develop and carry out an environment status review of your hotel school or the hotel and hospitality department (if it is part of a larger college or university). Based on the findings of the review:

- Create an environment policy for the school or department;
- Establish environment objectives and targets;
- Develop an environment-management checklist.

What EMS steps and wider sustainable tourism actions could be taken in the Egyptian Museum in Cairo and in Egypt as a whole to improve conservation and environment protection? Egypt has more antiquities and tourists than it can cope with. Stopping the latter from destroying the former is its biggest challenge.

Many countries would envy Egypt's predicament. With the possible exception of Italy, no place in the world contains such a colossal stash of antiquities. Trouble is, Egypt enjoys only a small fraction of Italy's wealth. Just coping with what has already been found (let alone with the artefacts that keep pouring out of Egypt's bottomless archaeological motherlode, or with the hordes of tourists who want to see the stuff, or with the constant threat of encroachment on sites) is an increasingly onerous burden on the government and museum authorities. At the Egyptian Museum in Cairo, the numbers are awesome. With more than 120,000 ancient objects on display, and even more crammed in the basement, the century-old building is stretched far beyond capacity.

Despite costly renovations completed last year, the hall containing the gold of Tutankhamun packs in such a crush of visitors it is beginning to resemble Grand Central Station at rush hour. Over the next decade the numbers are expected to rise from 2m to 8m a year. Controversial plans for a mega-museum have been mooted, but its construction remains a distant prospect. In the field meanwhile, each week produces exciting new finds, creating yet more pressure on bulging storerooms, as well as on the time and budgets of those

Ewho analyse, catalogue and restore artefacts. "The last thing we need is more mummies," groans one archaeologist, faced with the recent discovery of a desert cemetery that Egyptian experts believe holds as many as 10,000 graves from the Greco-Roman period. Only a few choice pieces, some with gilded facemasks, will be displayed near the site in the oasis of Bahariya, a little over 300km southwest of Cairo. The rest will have to be reburied. Rainer Stadelman, who is retiring as director of Cairo's German Archaeological Institute after four decades in Egypt, explains that you can dig practically anywhere and find something. "More than 3,000 years of high civilisation – and I'm only talking about Ancient Egypt – gives an enormous wealth of antiquities," he says.

Although nothing quite so flush with loot as Tutankhamun's tomb has been unearthed in the past ten years, recent discoveries have greatly enriched the science of Egyptology. At Abydos, 400km south of Cairo, a German team excavating a royal cemetery from the middle of the fourth millennium BC believes it has found the world's oldest readable writing. Inscriptions on ivory labels attached to oil jars show that officials of the First Dynasty used primitive hieroglyphs to record where the jars came from. Overturning the theory that Egypt adapted the art from Mesopotamia, the phonetic symbols put back the 'invention' of writing by two or three centuries, to around 3,300 BC.

Across the Nile at Akhmim, Egyptian archaeologists are beginning to uncover a temple precinct that may prove as large as the temple of Karnak at Luxor. This would make the site rank next to Angkor Wat and the Vatican as one of the world's biggest religious complexes – only many centuries older. The Akhmim site has already produced an exquisite 14-metre-high limestone statue of Ramses II's daughter, Merit-Amun.

In Luxor's Valley of the Kings, Kent Weeks, an American archaeologist, continues to explore a vast underground funerary complex dating from the reign of Ramses II (1304-1237 BC). With more than 200 rooms uncovered since excavation started in 1995, the purpose of this mysterious warren of chambers remains unknown. Theories range widely: perhaps it was a tomb for all of Ramses' 52 sons, perhaps a model representing stages of the afterworld.

Other recent finds include an intact pyramid capstone (at Dahshur), a tomb belonging to Tutankhamun's nurse that is decorated with beautiful relief carvings (at Sakkara), a cemetery devoted to the workers who built the pyramids (at Giza), fortresses in the Sinai Peninsula dating from 1500 BC, and a palace in the Delta decorated with Minoan paintings that prove there was a close trading relationship between Egypt and the ancient Cretan civilisation.

Leaving aside Ancient Egypt, finds from later periods are just as alluring. Divers off Alexandria have uncovered sculptures from the famous Ptolemaic lighthouse as well as Greco-Roman ports and palaces. The site where Napoleon's flagship, L'Orient, was sunk by Lord Nelson in 1798, with an estimated 10m gold francs of treasure aboard, has also been found. Far out in the desert, meanwhile, an Italian team has just finished restoring a chapel in the Coptic monastery of St Anthony. The stunning 13th-century frescoes on its walls, completely obscured by soot until three years ago, now rank among the most brilliant examples of Eastern Christian art.

All this work costs money. With Egypt's own resources severely strained, and with 20-odd foreign missions facing cutbacks, archaeologists must increasingly scout for their own backing. Rival French teams in Alexandria have each sought corporate sponsorship. Both have signed away exclusive rights for television coverage of their finds. To support his work in the Valley of the Kings, Mr. Weeks is obliged to spend half his time in pursuit of private funding. Egypt's own Supreme Council for Antiquities is beginning to go commercial. Earlier this year, its officials obligingly staged the 'discovery' of a tomb by the Giza pyramids for Fox Television. The US network paid US$60,000 for the privilege. National Geographic recently coughed up US$30,000 for exclusive film rights to the cache of mummies at Bahariya.

These sums are paltry compared with the task at hand, however. Much of the site at Akhmim, for example, lies beneath a village and a modern cemetery. Relocating them will cost as much as $10m. The budget for dismantling and rebuilding the 2,500-year-old Temple of Hibis at the oasis of Kharga, which is threatened by rising groundwater, is a hefty $6m. This is only one of hundreds of monuments —including some 200 medieval buildings in the centre of Cairo — that need urgent attention.

Fixing the Temple of Hibis is likely to exhaust funds earmarked for work in Egypt's oasis regions. Too bad, because these remote areas have lately produced remarkable finds:

some recent desert discoveries include a Sixth-Dynasty governor's palace that proves early Egyptian occupation of the oases, a gold crown from the Ptolemaic period, and a surprising cache of Greek papyri, among them unique scriptures from the Manichaean religion that vied with early Christianity.

More pressing perhaps is that many desert sites need protection from treasure hunters. At an abandoned Roman fortress town 40km from Kharga, scavengers last year used backhoes to rip open cemetreies, leaving a macabre scattering of discarded mummy parts. At a nearby site that can be reached only by four-wheel drive vehicles, a desert guide recently caught a group of American tourists red-handed. They were using metal detectors and air compressors to sift through the ruins for booty.

Yet the damage from pilfering pales in comparison with the organised menace of mass tourism. At sites such as the Valley of the Kings or Sakkara, thousands of visitors mill about each day in cramped tombs that were designed for one occupant's afterlife. The deterioration of the paintings and reliefs on their walls is plain to see. Even the apparently indestructible pyramids of Giza are suffering. With each visitor who descends to their inner chambers exhaling some 20 grams of clammy water vapour, cracks have begun to appear. The antiquities service now works the great structures in shifts, closing one each year for rest and recuperation. Sadly, this solution cannot work for monuments that are more unique or more delicate. "Tourism is already a catastrophe," says Mr. Stadelmann, who like most Egyptologists is understandably worried about the future. "But we have to admit that without tourism there would be no public interest, and without that there would be no money for our work." He is right, but as tourist numbers grow, Egypt is going to have to find a better balance between showing off its heritage and preserving it.

The Eland Safari Lodge is located on the outskirts of a major game reserve, somewhere in Central Africa. It operates 83 rooms, two indoor restaurants, a garden bar and restaurant, a lounge bar, a swimming pool, and a pool bar. The back office areas consist of administrative offices, kitchen, storerooms, a cold room, and maintenance rooms. The average length of stay is 4-6 days. Over 70% of guests are from overseas. The Eland Safari Lodge also operates a safari (wild life viewing) service 'Savannah Calling'. The welcome and information desk is located next to the Lodge's reception, and this enables guests to confirm bookings directly upon arrival.

Savannah Calling operates 5 open-roof, four-wheel drive vehicles, which seat 7 passengers, and 3 open-roof, 16-seat minibuses. The service employs 6 full-time game rangers. During the peak seasons 3 to 4 additional wildlife enthusiasts are hired to work as ranger-chauffeurs. Savannah Calling operates a programme of 4 game drives a day - at dawn, late afternoon, dusk and night. Each drive lasts around 2 1/2hours.

The surrounding landscape is typical of the savannah bush: dryland vegetation and grass plains interspersed with wooded areas, ponds, and the occasional small lake. There are two monsoon seasons per annum. However, over recent years, the monsoons have not been regular and annual rainfall has halved. The Park originally covered 1,700 square kilometres but today incorporates 1,500 square kilometres.

- Increasing pressure for agricultural land from the local population living in the buffer zones;
- The lack of adequate funds to maintain 1,700 square kilometres as a protected area.

Resident wildlife species include over 300 species of birds, elephant, wildebeest, rhino, hippopotamus, zebra, giraffe, antelope species such as gazelle, topi and eland, crocodile, fox, hyena, and the big predator cats - lion, leopard and cheetah. The local population lives around the buffer zones of the Park, and continue to rely on the Park's ecosystems for fuel and building materials such as peat and grass. They are also allowed to hunt 'permitted species' for meat.

The nearest large town, Pembroek, is 250 kilometres north of the Park - five or six hours by road. The capital city is 400 kilometres west of the Park. There are 2 flights a week from the capital to a small airport located around 100 kilometres north of the Park.

Water and Wastewater

- Despite prevailing droughts and water shortages, no water conservation measures have been taken at the Lodge. Towels and linen are changed daily and gardens and lawn are watered throughout the day. All rooms are equipped with large baths - no provisions are made for showers. The interior floors and windows are mopped and exteriors are spray-washed every day. The swimming pool is refilled twice a week during peak season and chlorine is used as a purifying agent. Many cold and hot water taps and toilet cisterns in guestrooms, back office and F&B outlets leak continuously.

  Water pressure at tap is not regulated. Hoses and sprinklers used to water the garden do not fit the water outlet, and here again there is significant water loss.

- Fresh water to the Lodge is usually supplied through a small diversion from the nearby river Nila, after purification in a water supply purification plant. Prevailing droughts have, however, drastically reduced the river water level, and water is now being supplied from the aquifer that lies directly beneath the park. Park authorities are concerned that the water levels of the aquifer are decreasing. The aquifer is critical to the maintenance of the Park's entire ecosystem, supplies the natural ponds and lakes that serve as waterholes for the animals, and provides water (through boreholes) to the local population.

- The wastewater from the Lodge is said to be treated at the wastewater treatment plant that serves the town of Pembroek. However, local citizen groups have reported that the wastewater ends up without treatment in the River Nila - the outfall being only a few kilometres upstream from the water supply diversion to the Lodge.

Energy

- Hot water, maintained at 70°C at tap, is provided by fuel-operated boilers. All other equipment operates on electricity, obtained partly from the national grid, and partly from the Lodge's own noisy and expensive diesel generators located onsite. Grid electricity is generated through hydropower. Peak tariffs are charged for power use between 08.00 and 10.30 and 17.00 and 20.00 hours.
- The garden restaurant operates a nightly barbecue dinner where coal and wood are used for torches and cooking.
- Prevailing droughts and low water levels across the country are now causing grid electricity shortages. The grid supply is interrupted from 23.00 to 05.00 hours at night and from 13.00 to 16.00 hours during the day. At these times, the Lodge makes maximum use of its diesel generators to produce electricity.
- Incandescent bulbs are used for lighting in all areas of the hotel, except the back offices and kitchens where fluorescent tubes are installed. Lights in public areas and corridors are left on throughout the day and at night.
- All guestrooms are equipped with single-unit air-conditioners. However, the thermostats of most units do not function, and therefore when turned on they only work at full capacity. Guests often have to open the windows as the rooms get 'too cold'. Most units are also noisy and leak water produced by condensation.
- No other areas of the hotel are air-conditioned. Ceiling fans operate day and night in public areas and restaurants.

- It is usual practice for the kitchen stoves to be turned on at the beginning of the day and left on the whole day until the dinner service is complete.
- There appear to be significant quantities of flash steam escaping from the boilers.
- The refrigeration system in the cold rooms is often out of service.
- Stoves, boilers and washing machines are over 10 years old. Dishes are washed by hand in tubs and buckets.
- There is no awareness of energy saving, how to lower energy use, renewable energy, or of equipment maintenance and monitoring. Little help is available from the national electricity company.

Waste

- No waste is separated and all waste including food, kitchen, and garden is sent for land filling. Old linen and uniforms are included in the waste stream.
- Owing to problems with refrigeration in the cold rooms, leftover food from the breakfast and barbecue buffets is not reused. Significant quantities of food are therefore wasted.
- Paper napkins and tumblers, cocktail sticks, paper cups and glass holders are the main sources of disposable waste. Plastic waste includes packaging, food and cleaning products and chemical product containers. All beverages are purchased in glass bottles, which can be returned on a deposit refund scheme. However, no separate sorting system is in place and glass bottles are also sent for land filling.
- Items with longer shelf life such as dry food, tins, stationery, office supplies and cleaning supplies etc. are bought in bulk.
- There were some attempts to compost kitchen and garden waste. However, owing to poor maintenance

and the contamination of the compost heap (by plastic, glass, animal fats and meats included in the compost), it began to attract rodents and birds, and gave rise to unpleasant odours. The effort was therefore abandoned.

- A significant volume of paper is used in the back office.
- No attempts have been made to reduce or reuse waste. There are two recycling companies based near the airport, but they have not been contacted for information on and assistance with the collection of waste for recycling.

Purchasing

- All items, including fresh produce, are sourced directly from the capital city 400 km away and transported by truck twice a week. No attempts have been made to source goods locally or use the produce of local farmers, expect for game meat.
- Despite the availability of a good selection of nationally-produced alcoholic and non-alcoholic beverages, preference is given to imported products from Europe, the USA or South Africa.
- Chemical cleaners, non-degradable detergents and pesticides are freely used all over the property.
- Stationery is printed on imported bleached gloss paper.
- Even though some purchases are made in bulk, they include substantial volumes of packaging, which is sent for land filling with the rest of the Lodge's waste.
- There is no awareness of how to purchase environmentally-preferable products, except for buying in bulk.

Emission

- All the air-conditioners, refrigerators and the cold room use CFC-11 as a refrigerant. During repair, significant amounts of refrigerant are allowed to escape. The fire extinguishers contain halon. Insecticides and air fresheners are purchased in aerosol spray cans. Foam is regularly used as packaging.

- All Savannah Calling's vehicles operate on diesel. Owing to poor maintenance, the engines are noisy and give out copious exhaust fumes.
- The lobby, public areas and back office are all designed as open verandas, so the Lodge's management is confident that indoor air quality is not an issue. However, the kitchen and laundry exhaust fans are in poor working condition and there is no ventilation in the boiler room.
- Overall environment awareness is low to non-existent. Management does agree that 'the environment is important', and that 'it is good to recycle', but have no further environment expertise.
- The Park authorities require that only licensed game rangers - those that successfully complete the recommended series of ecology, conservation and communication courses - conduct safari tours. There is also a special license for ranger-chauffeurs. However, the Lodge has not verified if any of the rangers and chauffeurs employed by Savannah Calling hold the required licence.
- It is further reported that rangers and chauffeurs are very willing to drive off-road to get close to animals for better photographs and even chase and track down bigger species when large tips are imminent.
- The Park has put together one brief wildlife information leaflet on resident and migratory species, the only information available to guests. The leaflet contains only scant information and needs to be upgraded.

- The Lodge has just began talks with the Park authorities on a series of management-related problems including conflicts of interest with local communities, poaching, costly administrative delays, poor environment and visitor management, lack of funds and the gradual degradation of the Park's ecosystem. The Lodge's management and the Park authorities are working on how the Lodge could contribute towards increasing conservation funds, ensuring game ranger licensing, increasing visitor management and implementing EMS.
- The Lodge has no direct contact with the local communities living in the buffer zones, except for the purchase of game meat. A handful of people living in the buffer zone villages work as housekeeping staff and kitchen hands. The rest of the employees are from Pembroek and its suburbs. They are provided with employee housing next to the hotel.

Chapter 2

Environmental Externalities

UNIDIRECTIONAL EXTERNALITY

It is well known that economic externalities can lead to outcomes which are not Pareto-efficient. Pollution is a negative externality, since the emissions of one country have an adverse effect on the well-being of others. In the absence of any corrective measures, each country will tend to pollute too much, since it does not internalize the cost that such pollution imposes on other countries. Corrective measures include command and control, taxes or tradable permits. Command and control or permits directly limit emissions, while the additional cost imposed by taxes causes reductions in emissions.

There is another approach which can potentially correct the inefficiency, when one recognizes that there is a time dimension to real economies. A country can be threatened with a future punishment if its emissions are too high. The threat can overcome a country's temptation to emit at a level which is inefficient, providing that the punishment is sufficiently severe. A punishment is severe if it has a low actual payoff, and if countries do not discount the future too heavily, which is commonly referred to as being patient. If there is too much discounting, then the severity of the low future payoff is mitigated. There are two assumptions implicit in such a solution. First, it must be possible to monitor the actions of each country. Of course such monitoring is also required in order to implement the other corrective measures mentioned above. Second, the threatened punishment must be credible, that is, it must itself be an equilibrium of the game.

The Folk theorem, which applies to infinitely repeated games, addresses the issue of credibility. Friedman showed that a threat of a static Nash equilibrium forever after any deviation from an equilibrium path gives players – I am grateful to the editors for very careful and helpful comments, and also to Henk Folmer for suggesting the topic.

The Nash threat is credible since it involves each player choosing a best response to the other. McMillan (1979) used this idea to show that an efficient amount of a public good could be provided in an infinitely repeated game. Pollution abatement is a public good. Maler(1993) and Barrett (1994) discuss such a supergame solution for international environmental externalities.

Barrett suggests that Nash threats may not be credible since countries would have an incentive to renegotiate away from such an inefficient punishment outcome, if they were actually called upon to enforce it. This is an important possibility. Unfortunately, there is not a consensus amongst game theorists concerning a notion of renegotiation-proofness. Different notions have been proposed by Farrell and Maskin (1989) and Pearce (1987). Farrell and Maskin's notion of weak renegotiation-proofness requires that the continuation payoffs after any histories in the game cannot be Pareto-ranked. Pearce calls an equilibrium renegotiation-proof if its lowest continuation payoff (after any history) is required in order to provide incentives to conform with the equilibrium or, in other words, if a less severe punishment would not be sufficient to support the equilibrium.

Renegotiation is a delicate issue. In an efficient equilibrium of a deterministic game, the players would not actually have to carry out the punishment. They merely need to believe that the punishment would be carried out if they were to deviate.

It is in their interests to believe this, since it is the threat that gives them an incentive to cooperate.

The Folk theorem was strengthened by Fudenberg and Maskin , who showed that there are more severe threats than reversion to Nash for ever. Abreu gave a nice characterization of the worst symmetric punishment for oligopoly games in terms of a 'stick and carrot'. That is, there is one bad period followed by a good future. The prospect of a good future gives the players an incentive to go along with the single punishment period. A punishment with only a single bad period is somewhat more credible than one that is infinitely long. It is also more severe than Nash in oligopoly games. The reason for this is that the 'stick and carrot' punishment allows for different behaviour depending on whether players accept their punishment. The Nash punishment does not permit such flexibility.

However, the worst punishment in other games may not have the 'stick and carrot' structure. For example, the worst punishment in a prisoners' dilemma game is the static Nash equilibrium for ever. It is of interest to know the structure of the worst punishment in games with environmental externalities. Section 4 gives an example of such a game where the worst symmetric equilibrium does have the 'stick and carrot' structure. It also shows that countries do not have to be very patient in order for a Pareto-efficient outcome to be equilibrium.

Sections 2 and 3 discuss the folk theorem for repeated environmental games with two countries. Section 2 is concerned with a unidirectional externality; section 3 with bidirectional externalities. These sections emphasize that the main issue concerning international environmental externalities need not be efficiency, but rather equity. No taxes or permits are required in order to achieve an efficient outcome. What is required instead is good monitoring of emissions, and a meeting of all affected parties, such as the Montreal Protocol, to agree on one of the much efficient equilibrium which is equitable. The debate at such meetings must of necessity be intense, since in matters of equity, any gain for one country is at the expense of another.

There is an obvious deficiency in repeated game models of environmental externalities, namely that most pollutants accumulate over time. Thus it is not the same game that is repeated. In addition, a stock of abatement capital may accumulate and/or preferences and technology may change over time. Section 5 contains a review of dynamic environmental game models. There are some exciting recent developments, which show that efficient equilibria exist in certain games. Some of these equilibria rely on threats similar to those in repeated games. Thus it is useful first to understand the simpler class of repeated games.

This section considers a simple infinitely repeated game with two countries. In each period the upwind (or upstream) country chooses its level of emissions. The downwind (or downstream) country is adversely affected by the emissions. Emissions do not accumulate over time. We consider two models. In the first, it is not possible for the downwind country to make any monetary transfers to the upwind country. Although unrealistic, this simple model shows that an externality need not lead to inefficiency. The second model adds realism by allowing for monetary transfers between the two countries.

We shall show that the static Nash equilibrium in the game with money transfers is not efficient, and discuss the many efficient outcomes. Any of these can be realized as a subgame-perfect equilibrium of an infinitely repeated game if the countries can monitor each other while they maximize their present value payoffs, providing that they are sufficiently patient. This shows that the main problem when there is a unidirectional externality in a repeated game is not inefficiency, but rather the establishment of an agreement concerning which of the many efficient outcomes is equitable.

Without Monetary Transfers

This model is deliberately simple and naäve. However, it illustrates the efficiency and equity aspects of international externalities quite clearly. Suppose that the utility of the upwind country when it chooses a level of emissions x is u(x). Suppose also that u(x) achieves a maximum for some unique level of emissions x^*. The emissions affect the downwind country. This country may have mitigation measures available to reduce the impact of the emissions. Let v(x) be the utility of the downwind country when it applies these mitigation measures optimally. Assume that v is strictly decreasing in x.

In a static (and rather degenerate) game the upwind country chooses its level of emissions, and the downwind country receives them. In equilibrium, the upwind country will choose the level of emissions x^*. Notice that this outcome is Pareto-efficient! Any other level of emissions will make the upwind country worse off.

Of course, there are also other Pareto-efficient outcomes in which the upwind country emits less than x^*. Whether any of these other outcomes is more desirable is a matter of equity, and not of efficiency. Unfortunately, any discussion of equity is inevitably controversial, since it involves trading off the well-being of one country for that of the other.

We mention briefly that none of these other Pareto-efficient outcomes can be achieved by a subgame-perfect equilibrium of a supergame, even if the countries are patient. According to the folk theorem, any feasible outcome which is individually rational, that is, at least as good as the security level, can be achieved by a subgame perfect equilibrium if the players are sufficiently patient. In this unrealistically simple model the security level of the upwind country is u(x), since the downwind country cannot affect the utility of the upwind country. Thus there is a unique feasible and individually rational outcome, with emissions of x.

Clearly the restrictive assumptions of this model lead to an unrealistic conclusion that there is no inefficiency when there is a unidirectional externality. We now turn to a more realistic model in which the downwind country can compensate the upwind country for reducing its emissions. In this case, the static equilibrium is not efficient.

With Monetary Transfers

Consider almost the same model as before, but with one change. Suppose that each country also gets utility from some other good, which we will call money. Let M be the aggregate amount of money, and let ω_1 and ω_2 be the money endowments of the upwind and downwind countries respectively. The utility functions of the two countries are now $u(v, m_{1)}$ and $v(x, m_{2)}$, where m_i is the amount of money for country i =1, 2. Assume that

i. both it and v are strictly increasing in money,

ii. v is strictly decreasing in x,

iii. for any given m_1 there is a unique best level of emissions for the upwind country $x^* (m_{1)}$,

iv. the utility functions of each country are strictly concave, and

v. there is a maximum possible level of emissions, X.

In a static game, the upwind country decides on its level of emissions, and simultaneously each country decides how much money to give to the other. There is a unique Nash equilibrium, in which neither country makes any transfers to the other, and the upwind country chooses a level of emissions $x (\omega_{1)}$.

This outcome is not Pareto-efficient, since both countries could be better off if the downwind country compensated the upwind country for reducing its emissions. The horizontal axis represents money, with m_1 measured from the left axis. The width of the axis is M. Thus m_2 is measured from the right axis. The point labelled co represents the money endowment of each country. Emissions are measured on the vertical axis. The figure shows indifference curves for each country. The indifference curves for the upwind country are shaped like the letter 'C', since for any fixed amount of money its utility at first rises as emissions increase from zero, but then falls as emissions exceed the optimal level. The utility of the upwind country increases to the right. The other indifference curves are for the downwind country, whose utility increases to the southwest. These indifference curves always slope down, since utility is assumed to be strictly increasing in money and strictly decreasing in emissions.

At the static Nash equilibrium, labelled N, the upwind country chooses its level of emissions to maximize its utility given its monetary endowment ω_1. This outcome is not efficient because the upwind country's indifference curve is vertical at this point, whereas that of the downwind country is not. Point A shows a Pareto-superior outcome at which the downwind country pays the upwind country to reduce its emissions. The downwind country is just as well off at A as at the Nash equilibrium, while the upwind country is better off. Point B shows another Pareto-efficient outcome in which the upwind country is again compensated for reducing its emissions, but all gains accrue to the downwind country.

Notice that the downwind country is worse off at A, B or N compared to the situation with no emissions (point O). The outcome with no emissions is itself not efficient. The point P corresponds to an efficient outcome in which the downwind country is compensated by the upwind country for accepting some pollution. At point P the upwind country is worse off than at the static Nash equilibrium, reflecting the fact that it pays for the right to pollute. Point P is consistent with the polluter pays principle, since the downwind country is just as well off at P as at O.

Point T is another efficient outcome that satisfies the polluter pays principle. It is the outcome that would be achieved by an efficient Pigouvian tax, with proceeds going to the downwind country. The figure is drawn with a lower level of emissions under the tax than at point P. This need not be the case, but the downwind country will always be at least as well off if it receives the proceeds of the tax as at P. That is, among all efficient points which satisfy the polluter pays principle, point P is the worst for the downwind country.

The static Nash equilibrium is in the interior of the utility possibility set, since it is not Pareto-efficient. Points A and B are both Pareto-superior to the static Nash equilibrium. Points P and T are also efficient, but give the upwind country a lower utility than it gets in the Nash equilibrium. Point M is the minmax point. The upwind country's minmax utility is its Nash equilibrium utility, since the worst action that the downwind country can impose on the upwind country is not to give it any money. However, the minmax utility of the downwind country is below its Nash utility, since the upwind country can 'punish' the downwind country by emitting its maximum level of emissions, X.

According to the Folk theorem, any outcome in the region BME can be achieved by a subgame-perfect equilibrium, if the countries are sufficiently patient. Thus any of the efficient outcomes on the frontier BE can be achieved by an equilibrium. The inefficient static Nash outcome is also equilibrium in the supergame. However, if the countries can meet to coordinate on an equilibrium, then there is no reason why they would choose such an inefficient one. The negotiations at such a meeting will not be trivial, since they will be over equity. However, it is important to note that the environmental externality need not lead to any inefficiency.

It is worth commenting on the structure of an efficient agreement. Given that the utility functions are strictly concave, the utility possibility frontier is strictly convex. Thus any outcome on the frontier BE must be stationary, that is, the same in every period. Each country will have an incentive to deviate from this stationary outcome. The upwind country can increase its utility by emitting more, and the downwind country can increase its utility by paying the upwind country a smaller amount (possibly zero). However, if either of the countries deviates from the efficient outcome, then there is a credible (subgame-perfect) punishment which will be imposed. The threat of this punishment deters a country from deviating.

Such a threat is an elegant way of correcting for the potential inefficiency due to an environmental externality. In this deterministic model, the threat need never be carried out, because the countries will not deviate. Efficiency is achieved without taxes or permits! There is a need for perfect monitoring of the country's actions, so that any deviation would be detected. The set of equilibria is smaller if monitoring is less effective. However, the monitoring requirements are no more stringent than they would be under a system of taxes or permits. Both tax and permit schemes also require monitoring of the actual emissions.There is an equity issue which cannot be addressed by a threat of punishment. The highest utility which can be achieved by the downwind country in a subgame-perfect equilibrium is at point B, which is lower than its utility if there is no pollution (point P, which gives the downwind country the same utility as point O;). Thus implicitly the upwind country has the right to pollute by virtue of geographical and/or meteorological conditions.

Naturally this will seem quite reasonable to the upwind country, but less so to the downwind one!Some of the equilibria seem particularly inequitable, for example, point E. In this equilibrium the upwind country receives a large payment from the downwind country. This extortion is supported by the threat of a large emission if the downwind country does not make the payment. In effect, the ability to pollute at a high level allows the upwind country to extract resources from the downwind country. Although this outcome is Paretoefficient, it seems to violate notions of morality. It illustrates the fact that although Pareto-efficiency may be a necessary condition for a desirable outcome, it is by no means sufficient.There are two remaining issues concerning these supergame equilibria: (i) how patient do the countries have to be for efficient outcomes to be an equilibrium, and (ii) would they carry out the punishments if called upon to do so? These are reasonable concerns, which will be addressed in section 4. We first consider the case of bilateral externalities.

Bilateral Externalities

Consider now an economy with two countries, each of which chooses its own level of emissions. The emissions of each country impose a negative externality on the other. Let x and y be the emissions of the two countries, and let u(x, y) be the utility of the country which emits x and v(x, y) the utility of the country which emits y. Assume that:

i. Both u and v are strictly concave in (x, y),

ii. u is strictly decreasing in y, and v is strictly decreasing in x, that is, $u_y < 0$ and $v_x < O$, where subscripts denote partial derivatives,

This section considers the issues of (i) how patient the countries must be for the results of the Folk theorem to apply, and (ii) the nature of the worst punishment, that is, the subgame-perfect equilibrium with the lowest payoff. These must be considered together since the deterrence which is provided by the threat of a future punishment depends both on the severity of the punishment and on the countries' rates of time preference. It would be desirable to present results for general games.

Learning about Global Warming

Two of the central policy questions that arise in the climate change debate are how to secure international cooperation to reduce emissions of greenhouse gases, and how to respond to the considerable uncertainty about both the extent of any possible climate change and any resulting damages in different parts of the world. The possibility that better scientific information in the future will reduce uncertainty leads to the suggestion that action to curb greenhouse gas emissions be delayed, while concern about the possible irreversible accumulation of greenhouse gases leads to the suggestion that such delay could be costly.

To date much of the analysis of these two policy questions has proceeded independently. Thus there is a substantia literature1 which uses dynamic game theory either to compare cooperative and noncooperative time paths for emissions of greenhouse gases, or to design international environmental agreements to which independent nation states would voluntarily subscribe. The results from this literature show that non-cooperative equilibria will have higher current emissions and long-run stocks of greenhouse gases than cooperative equilibria, and that there are gains to cooperation. Two noncooperative equilibria are used - feedback Nash equilibria and open-loop equilibria, with the former having higher current emissions and stocks of greenhouse gas than the latter. The literature has also shown that it is unlikely that many countries will voluntarily agree to collaborate in reducing their emissions, in the sense that the number of countries that are likely to form a stable coalition is small. But this literature has ignored issues of uncertainty or learning.

There is also a substantial literature on uncertainty, learning and irreversibility in relation to climate change which has addressed questions such as whether the possibility of obtaining better information in the future should result in higher or lower current emissions of greenhouse gases (in the extreme case, should we do nothing to abate greenhouse gas emissions until we get better information about likely damages?) and what is the value of better scientific information? This literature shows that the possibility of getting better information in the future about the damages from global warming may raise or lower current period emissions depending on the functional forms for damage and abatement costs, and this is true whether greenhouse gas emissions are irreversible or reversible. There is always a positive value to better information. However, this literature has assumed a single decision maker, and so ignores the issue of many nation states taking decisions on greenhouse gas emissions independently.

In this I shall survey a small number of papers which have attempted to integrate these two literatures. There are two reasons for doing this. The first is to check whether the conclusions derived from models of dynamic games with no uncertainty still apply when uncertainty and learning are introduced, and similarly whether the conclusions from models of uncertainty and learning with a single decision maker apply when there are many non-cooperative decision makers. A second reason for integrating the two literatures is to allow issues to be addressed which simply cannot arise without such integration; for example, does the presence of uncertainty reduce the incentives for cooperation; and would countries agree on the benefits of better information?

On the first point, I shall show that the conclusions derived from the literature on dynamic games about the differences in emissions and stocks of pollution between cooperative and non-cooperative equilibrium largely carry over to a world of uncertainty and learning, as do the conclusions about the benefits from cooperation. Specifically, Ulph and Ulph (1996) showed that: (i) the ranking of current emissions and final stocks of emissions would be highest in a feedback Nash equilibrium, next highest in an open-loop Nash equilibrium and lowest in a cooperative equilibrium, and this was true both if there were no learning and if there were the possibility of learning in the future about true damage costs of global warming; (ii) there are always gains from cooperation with both learning and no learning. However, the conclusions from the literature on uncertainty, irreversibility and learning for a single decision maker do not generalize to a world of many countries acting non-cooperatively, for in a noncooperative equilibrium better information could make all countries worse off.

As I shall show, an important factor driving this result is the degree of correlation between the damage experienced by different countries. The result can only arise when there is less than perfect correlation between damages in different countries, that is, some countries may benefit from global warming while others lose substantially; this seems to be a likely description of the effects of global warming. Better information will then reveal that one country faces less damage than it had expected, while another country learns that it faces greater damage than it had expected. The non-cooperative response of these countries to this information is what gives information potentially negative value. This can also have important implications for policies for dealing with current emissions - suggesting that current emissions should be lower if there is the possibility of obtaining better information in the future than would be the case if there were no such possibility. These results also suggest that there is an important additional dimension to international environmental agreements - it is not just a need to secure a general reduction in emissions, but also a need to coordinate responses to new information.

In terms of the second reason for integrating the two literatures, it may be easier to secure cooperation between countries before uncertainties about global warming are resolved, and, as indicated above, that countries may differ in the value they attach to better information, with some countries attaching a positive value to information and others a negative value. In this I shall concentrate on explaining the theoretical arguments, and in most of this theoretical work I shall employ a very simple example, drawing on the more general analysis I have done in other papers.

This will allow me to illustrate the issues, and refer the reader to the source papers for the more general analysis. In the next section I shall introduce the simple model, and summarize the results from the two separate literatures — the analysis of learning for a single-country model, and the analysis of dynamic pollution games under certainty. In section 3, integrate the two problems and discuss the results that can be obtained. I shall also discuss briefly a related paper on the implications for reaching international agreements. I emphasize that I do not pretend that the very simple models used here capture the real complexity of global warming — what they are designed to do is to show why some of our standard intuitions may be wrong. In section 4 I shall say a bit about empirical work relevant to this; while this will bring the discussion somewhat closer to the reality of global warming, the models remain very simple.

Background Analysis

In this section I shall introduce a very simple model of global warming and use it to analyse first how the possibility of obtaining better information in the future about the damages from global warming would affect the emissions policy of a single decision maker (taken to represent the world) and then, second, to analyse how several countries would determine their emissions policies when there is certainty about the extent of damages from global warming. The analysis in this section draws heavily on Ulph and Ulph.

Uncertainty and Learning

There are two periods, t = 1, 2 which we can think of as the present and the future. In each period emissions of greenhouse gases are e_t and the utility or total benefits from emitting these gases is given by $U(e_{t)} = -0.5(e^*-e_{t)}2$. This simple utility function has the property that the marginal benefit of emitting greenhouse gases is a downward-sloping linear function, and in the absence of any concern about global warming, emissions in each period would be set equal to e, which I shall interpret as the business-as-usual (BAU) level of emissions. Any damages due to global warming are caused by the total stock of emissions of greenhouse gases at the end of period 2, denoted by X = e1 + e2, and the costs of any damages are given by the total damage cost functions D(X) = $0.5 \Theta X^2$. Again the simple quadratic total damage cost function implies that the marginal damage cost function is upward-sloping and linear. Note that it is implicitly assumed above that first-period emissions of greenhouse gases do not decay by the end of the second period. So the only way to reduce the stock of greenhouse gases and hence any damage from global warming is to reduce emissions of greenhouse gases.

There is uncertainty about the true extent of damages from global warming, which I capture by assuming that the true value of the parametre Θ in the total damage cost function is unknown. There are only two possible value states of the world, denoted by s = l, h, where in the low state, l, the parametre Θ takes the value 0 (that is, global warming is not a problem) while in the high state, h, it takes the value $2\Theta > 0$. The decision maker believes that each state is equally likely to occur, so that the expected value of the damage cost parametre is Θ. At the start of period 1 the true value of ˜ is unknown, but there are two possibilities for period 2. If there is no learning, then the decision maker is as uncertain about the value of Θ at the start of period 2 as at the start of period 1. If there is learning, then by the start of period 2 the decision maker has obtained perfect information, and so knows the true value of Θ. The importance of being able to obtain perfect information by the start of period 2 is that the decision maker can condition second-period emissions on what has been learned about Θ, and I denote this by saying that the decision maker sets emission level e_{2s}, S = l, h in period 2 if the decision maker has learned that the true state is s. If there is no learning, then the decision maker is constrained to set a single value for emissions in period 2, which can be written as $e_2 = e_{2l} = e_{2h}$.

To complete the description of the model, it is assumed that there is no discounting. Thus we have the simplest possible model of global warming, with only two periods, two states of the world, linear marginal benefit and marginal cost curves, no discounting or decay of the stock of emissions.

The key point to note is that when there is no learning, because second-period emissions are independent of the state of the world, Θ, and because of the simple multiplicative form of the damage cost function, expected damages with no learning are given by the total damage cost function with Θ replaced by its expected value, so with no learning there is certainty equivalence, that is, uncertainty can simply be handled by replacing the random variable by its expected value and then treating the problem as if it is one with certainty. On the other hand, with learning, because second-period emissions do depend on the true value of Θ, then even with the simple multiplicative form of the total damage cost function, expected damage costs do not display the certainty equivalence property.

A central question I wish to address is whether the possibility of learning more in the future about the true damages from global warming means that current emissions should be higher or lower than would be the case if there were no possibility of getting better information in the future. To understand how to determine first-period emissions, recall that if this is a one-period pollution problem under certainty, then the solution would require setting first-period emissions so that the marginal benefit of emissions equals the marginal damage cost of emissions. In a multi-period problem under uncertainty the solution has a fairly similar form, namely that first-period emissions should be set so that marginal benefit of first-period emissions equals the expected present value of marginal damage costs caused by first-period emissions. So we need to be able to calculate the appropriate present value expected marginal damage costs of first-period emissions under both learning and no learning.

In each case, the left-hand expression is just the marginal benefit of first-period emissions, the right-hand expression is the expected present value of marginal damage costs of first-period emissions.

It is easy to see from (1) and (2) that for any level of first-period emissions, the expected present value of marginal damage costs is lower with learning than with no learning. In turn this implies that the optimal choice of first-period emissions with learning, is higher than the level of first-period emissions with no learning. In other words, the possibility of getting better information in the future means that the decision maker need not cut current period emissions as much as would be the case with no learning. However, this does not support the extreme view that the decision maker should do nothing at all to cut emissions until better information is obtained.

It is important to understand what lies behind this result, and in particular that the result is not completely general. A general statement of the results that can be obtained is contained in the following set of sufficient conditions:

If $C'(e_1, \Theta)$ is concave in Θ then

If $C'(e_1, \Theta)$ is convex in Θ then

These conditions are shown by Ulph and Ulph to be equivalent to the sufficient conditions derived by Epstein for the particular model of global warming considered here. To see why these sufficient conditions apply, note that they are just a standard statistical result that the value of a concave (convex) function evaluated at the expected value of a random variable is no less (greater) than the expected value of the function. Recall that it is Jensen's inequality that explains why a strictly concave utility function implies risk aversion, since it means that the expected utility of a risky asset is less than the utility of the expected value of the asset.

In our context, Jensen's inequality means that if the marginal damage cost is strictly concave in Θ, the expected marginal damage cost of first-period emissions with learning (the analogue of a risky asset) is less than the marginal damage cost with no learning (a certain payoff); since the expected marginal damage cost of first-period emissions with learning is lower than with no learning, it is optimal to carry out more first-period emissions with learning than with no learning. As Ulph and Ulph note, it is difficult to provide general restrictions on the decision-making problem which guarantee that the marginal cost function $C'(e_1, \Theta)$ is either concave or convex in Θ, but a sufficient condition for the marginal cost function to be concave in Θ is that the total benefit and total damage cost functions are quadratic, which is what I have assumed.

International Environmental Agreements

The preceding analysis suggests two implications for the design of international environmental agreements. First, international agreements will need to consider more than just the usual question of how to get all countries to reduce their emissions – they will also need to consider what happens when better information becomes available, particularly if there is negative correlation among the damage costs to different countries. Second, and closely related to the previous point, while the analysis shows that there are always gains to cooperation, there may be much greater gains to cooperation when there is the possibility of learning better information than when there is not. This follows from a simple identity noted by Ulph and Maddison:

GfC (learning) – GfC (no learning) = Vol(coop) – Vol(non-coop).

GfC stands for gains from cooperation; Vol stands for value of information. Now we know that the value of information is always positive for cooperative equilibria. We also know that for sufficiently low values of the correlation coefficient the value of information will be negative for non-cooperative equilibria. Thus for these cases there are greater gains to be had from cooperation when learning is possible than when it is not.

However, the previous points are only suggestive of implications for international environmental agreements because the analysis to date does not explicitly analyse the question of how independent nations enter into such agreements, for it is one thing to show that there are gains from cooperation, quite another to show how they can be realized. A paper which explicitly examines the formation of international environmental agreements when there is uncertainty and the possibility of obtaining better information is Na and Shin, and this has some strong links with the analysis reported here. To understand their paper I need to summarize very briefly the kind of analysis used to study international environmental agreements. A widely used approach for studying what kinds of international environmental agreements might be formed is to look for stable coalitions of countries. A coalition of countries is simply a group of countries which act together to maximize the sum of the welfares of individual members, that is, to implement the cooperative solution among members, taking as given the emissions policies of non-members.

Countries have to decide whether or not to join a coalition by comparing their welfare in the coalition with their welfare outside the coalition. There are three factors that will influence whether to join a coalition: by joining a coalition a country will have to increase its own abatement of emissions, and hence increase its costs; on the other hand other members of the coalition will also increase their abatement of emissions, which will benefit the country; but non-members of the coalition will respond to the higher abatement by the coalition members by reducing their abatement. The balance of these considerations will determine whether or not a country will join a coalition. A coalition is stable if no member country wishes to leave the coalition and no non-member country wishes to join the coalition. The question studied in this literature is what is the largest stable coalition that can be formed?

However, almost all of the literature on coalition formation assumes perfect information about the payoff functions of countries, in particular the damage cost functions of countries. An exception is the recent very elegant paper by Na and Shin. They consider a three-country model, with a single period, where each country has a quadratic cost of abatement function and linear benefit of abatement function (in the terminology of this corresponds to a quadratic benefit of emissions function and a linear damage cost function).

However, there is uncertainty about the benefits from abatement, equivalent to my assumption of uncertainty about the damage cost function. Specifically, it is known that one country will have high benefits from abatement, one country will have intermediate benefits from abatement and one will have low benefits from abatement, but the identity of these countries is not known, and ex ante each country has an equal chance of being the high-, intermediate- or low-benefit country. Of course this is exactly analogous to the case of perfect negative correlation for my two-country example. Countries have to decide whether or not to join a coalition, and there are two timing possibilities.

In what I have called the no learning case, countries have to decide whether or not to join a coalition before the true state of the world is known, and of course they must then commit themselves to a level of abatement before the true state of the world is known. In the learning case, countries first of all learn the true state of the world and then have to decide whether or not to join a coalition. Na and Shin compare the expected benefits to countries in the no learning and learning case. What they show is that in the case of no learning, the only stable coalition is the 'grand coalition' of all three countries. In the case of learning it is much harder to form coalitions, in the sense that the grand coalition is unstable, and, depending on parametre values, either a coalition of the two countries with the highest benefits from abatement will be stable, or else there is no stable coalition – that is, the outcome is the non-cooperative outcome. What Na and Shin show is that whatever the parametre values, countries are always better off in the no learning case. The rationale is that it is easier to form coalitions the more similar countries are, and countries may be more similar before information is revealed, when they are faced with expected damage costs, than they are after information has been revealed.

It is clear that there are strong similarities between the Na and Shin analysis and that presented earlier in this section. The broad message is that if countries are likely to experience very different benefits and costs from global warming, then the strategic non-cooperative interactions between countries after information is revealed can offset the standard benefits decision makers have from being able to tailor their actions in the light of the better information provided to them, so that better information has negative value. The specific message from Na and Shin is that it may be better to try to reach international environmental agreements before too much information becomes available.

Migration and the Environment

Until the seventeenth century people believed that the Sun orbited the Earth. The long-lasting dominance of the Ptolemaean astronomy can no doubt be partly attributed to the intellectual authority of the Catholic Church and to the respect for the thinkers of antiquity. But perhaps a still more compelling reason is the fact that the geocentric world view seemed to be consistent with observations. Indeed, the Ptolemaean model with the Sun moving along its epicyclic orbit and the more modern Copernican universe where the Earth rotates around its own axis are two possible worlds where day follows night. For the alternation or light and dark the absolute velocity of the two celestial bodies is irrelevant. It is only the relative movement of the surface of the Earth with respect to the Sun that counts.

In this, the interaction of household mobility and environmental policy is analysed by using the story about Ptolemy and Copernicus and the principle of relative movement as guidelines. This develops a twoperiod game with accumulation of pollution and costly migration to suggest that the effects of household mobility on environmental policy are essentially equivalent to those of transboundary pollution.

By replacing the celestial objects figuring in the sketchy delineation of the two competing world views by concepts of environmental economics, the story can be retold. In a Ptolemaean economy people are immobile but pollution flows across national frontiers. In a Copernican world pollution is local but people can move from one country to another. In the astronomical context, both of these models give rise to the alternation of day and night. Now the claim is that the equivalence holds for international environmental economics as well: only relative mobility matters; just like mobile pollutants, mobile people create international externalities and distortions.

Demographic dynamics and environmental problems are known to be interlinked in a number of ways. A growing population increases the stress on the ecosystem. The state of the environment in turn influences death rates and people's incentives to have children. In recent years, more attention has also been paid to the interaction between migration and the environment. The term 'environmental refugee' was coined in 1985 by the United Nations Environmental Programme. Three years later a study by the Worldwatch Institute estimated that there were about 10 million people falling into this category in the late 1980s.Most of them had escaped soil erosion or desertification depleting arable land in developing countries, especially in sub-Saharan Africa. On the other hand pollution also played its role. The number of environmental refugees and migrants is expected to increase in the future.

The degradation of the environment influences people's decisions to migrate. On the other hand there is some evidence suggesting that mobile people can in turn be harmful to the environment. A bulk of studies has established that shifting cultivation and nomadism may be partly responsible for deforestation in the tropics and for desertification in sub-Saharan Africa. Shifting cultivators appropriate a piece of land by burning the forest. After a few harvests the field has to be abandoned and can be retaken into agricultural use, probably by others, only after a lengthy period of forest regeneration. Shifting cultivators move on and have no incentives to care for the ecological sustainability of the forest ecosystem.

Although population problems and the environment are acknowledged to be closely connected, economic research on international and interregional environmental issues has concentrated on studying transboundary pollution, trade and capital mobility. Furthermore, and perhaps somewhat surprisingly, the existing small literature on migration and the environment doesn't see household mobility as a source of international or interregional environmental problems, but rather as a mechanism inducing implicit cooperation between selfish national governments. Indeed, the literature shows that under costless migration, all international externalities caused by, for example, transboundary pollution are internalized by national environmental policies, and the resulting outcome is socially optimal.

Furthermore, the mechanism behind this result is found to be very strong: an attempt to increase one's own welfare at the expense of others, by cutting back emission abatements and letting neighbours affected by transboundary pollution carry a part of the environmental costs, triggers immigration.

As the population of the emitting country grows, the amount of fixed resources – for example, land or the carrying capacity of the environment – available per capita decreases, which in turn lowers welfare. Migration flows instantaneously cancel out all welfare differences: no country can be better off than any other country. As all countries can correctly anticipate the reactions of migrants and understand that a socially non-optimal policy is necessarily nonoptimal from the national point of view, each country ends up maximizing the aggregate welfare of the economy. In other words, perfect household mobility renders the objective functions of individual countries identical to each other and equal to that of the social planner. As there are no conflicts of interest, the decentralized outcome is fully efficient.

In this, our aim is to defend the opposite view, and to claim that the analogy between mobile pollutants and mobile people, and more generally models of the tragedy of the commons, constitutes a useful framework for the analysis of household mobility and the environment. When pollution flows across national boundaries, those who enjoy the fruits of production can avoid part of the environmental costs. National policies fail to recognize the damages occurring abroad: the inevitable consequence is over pollution. In the case of household mobility, the constellation is strikingly similar. People can produce, consume and pollute, and then escape the environmental consequences by moving away. Once again there's a discrepancy between costs and benefits.

A tragedy of the commons occurs when property rights over an asset are ill defined or cannot be enforced. Typically, the literature shows that common access leads to over consumption and underinvestment. When pollution flows across national boundaries, each country becomes a public dumping ground, and property rights over the environment are at best nominal. On the other hand, accumulation of pollution and household mobility together lead to the tragedy of the commons. A mobile household has incentives to consume now and to give a lower weight to future consumption and environmental amenities. If resources are saved, others will move in and appropriate them.

The nature of the migration-environment nexus may have several important policy implications. One of the objectives of the European Union is to reduce the obstacles to labour mobility between the member countries. Is an integrated European labour market a substitute for a common environmental policy or does it reinforce the need to delegate more power to Brussels? In the US environmental policy is conducted partly by states, partly by the federal government. The principle of subsidiarity adopted by the EU requires that all decisions be taken at the lowest possible level. What does the fact that Americans are more prone to move from state to state than Europeans from one country to another imply for the optimal division of power in the US and in the EU? How will the expected increase in the number of environmental refugees and migrants influence the relations between the North and the South?

In addition to the policy-oriented questions, there are more theoretical and methodological motivations for this study. Economic modelling always involves a trade-off between clarity and realism. In the literature on the local public sector it is standard to use static models and to assume that households are perfectly mobile. Studies on economic integration often start with a model with an immobile labour force, which is then compared to an economy with perfect labour mobility. For these ideal types to be relevant as stylized descriptions of the real world, the simplified settings should bear at least a qualitative resemblance to the more complex economic phenomena one wants to understand. One of the main results of this is that in a dynamic model setting imperfect household mobility is qualitatively different from costless migration. Comparing immobile households to free mobility would give a misleading picture of the effects of economic integration.

The rest is organized as follows section 2 presents two examples illustrating why household mobility can sometimes be harmful, sometimes beneficial for the environment section 3 develops a two-period game among selfish countries encompassing both the (partial) equalization of objective functions, resulting in implicit cooperation, and the tragedy of the commons as special cases. The model demonstrates that the effects of household mobility may depend crucially on governments' ability to make credible commitments. In addition we show that imperfect household mobility is qualitatively different from perfect mobility. Finally, section 4 concludes.

The case of perfect household mobility is particularly interesting. When people can move from one place to another without incurring any costs, the place where a person lives during a certain period doesn't affect his/her choice of location for the subsequent period: complete mixing of population is possible at each moment of time. If the tragedy of the commons is the right model for analysing the interaction between household mobility and environmental policy, the fact that people can escape the environmental consequences of their actions without incurring any costs should generate particularly strong distortions: indeed, perfect household mobility should be equivalent to global pollution. On the other hand the implicit cooperation argument, presented in the literature, tells us that costless migration implies social optimum.

In this section we develop two simple, and admittedly somewhat ad hoc, games to study environmental policy under perfect household mobility. We take seriously the claim that complete mixing of population is possible in each period, and assume that players are assigned to a country by a lottery. Although in a model, with the help of which one tries seriously to understand migration and the environment, the country where a person lives should depend on his/her own choice, not on pure chance, the simplistic approach we adopt in this section may give some useful insights. The following examples will illustrate that the effects of household mobility on environmental policy depend on at least two factors. (1) Does pollution accumulate to the environment? (ii) What is the exact sequence of events in the game? Does migration precede consumption and emissions or vice versa?

When people moving from one country to another have to incur sunk costs, migration decisions become forward-looking: the momentary stream of utility at the point of time migration takes place is not essential. The whole discounted sum of future well-being must be higher in the new home country. Furthermore, shifting costs make migration a process taking place in real time: the regional distribution of population doesn't instantaneously react to changes in policy.

Environmental policy, on the other hand, can influence both future and past migration. The link to the future operates through the accumulation of pollution. If environmental damages occur only after consumption has taken place, people can first consume and then escape pollution by moving away. On the other hand strategic over consumption, entailing a bigger pollution stock, is a way to preempt future immigration.

Environmental policy carried out at a certain point of time (t) influences migration taking place before that date, as well. If country 1 manages to increase its utility at the expense of its neighbours by over polluting from date t onwards, there will be a difference in the discounted sum of utility in favour of country 1 at each moment before t. This in turn triggers migration flows in the direction of country 1 before the date (t) the strategic over pollution begins. Finally, immigration lowers the welfare in the country trying to exploit its neighbours. Thus the effects of environmental policy on past migration create a feedback mechanism making countries' objective functions more equal to each other and inducing them to cooperate.

The incentives to strategic over pollution in order to cut back future immigration always exist if pollution accumulates to the environment. The strength of the mechanism forcing countries to cooperate depends, however, on the time horizon of environmental policy. If governments can make credible commitments, the decisions concerning the environmental policy carried out at date t can be made at a date t - h before t. It is evident that for the optimization happening at date t - h only the events taking place after that date are relevant. Thus, of all the labour movements happening before t, only the share of migration occurring between t - h and t is taken into account when designing the environmental policy. Now it is easy to see that the incentives to cooperation depend on the length of the period of commitment h. If the time horizon of environmental policy is long enough, incentives to cooperation outweigh incentives causing the tragedy of the commons. On the other hand, if commitment is impossible, only the incentives to overpollute remain: like mobile pollutants, mobile households create distortions.

The assumption that migration is costly is especially important. Indeed, perfect household mobility is qualitatively different from costly migration. When households are perfectly mobile the distribution of population reacts instantaneously to policy changes. The strength of the mechanism inducing countries to cooperate doesn't depend on commitment technologies. As all welfare differentials are instantaneously cancelled out, a socially non-optimal policy is always necessarily harmful from the national point of view, as well. In other words, in the case of perfect household mobility, the decentralized outcome is fully efficient.

One possible way to formalize the argument presented above is to develop a differential game taking place in continuous time: consumers can react constantly to welfare differences and can migrate at each moment of time; the role of commitment is captured by altering the time over which governments can make credible plans over the environmental policy. Such a strategy is adopted in Haavio. This study shows that the dynamic optimization problem faced by individual countries in the presence of migration boils down to the following basic structure: every time policy makers reoptimize, their decision entails a trade-off between present and future welfare.

The present essentially means the present period, of length h, over which the countries can make credible commitments. The future is in turn captured by a value function, having the stock of pollution and the regional distribution of people as its arguments. The present affects the future through the accumulation of pollution. The pollution stock, together with the distribution of population, in turn determines the pattern of future migration. In addition to the links between the present and the future, the other important thing is what happens inside the present period. Here the essential aspect is the length of the period. How much migration can take place during the period; how strong is the feedback mechanism inducing implicit cooperation?

It is this basic structure that we are trying to capture in the simplest possible way in this. To do so we shall develop a two-period model. The first period is the present, while the whole future is condensed into the second period. Through the accumulation of pollution, first-period emissions affect the second period: the quality of the environment and people's decisions to move from one country to another. The interaction between environmental policy and second-period migration leads to the tragedy of the commons.

On the other hand, the fact that first-period migration also depends on the level of emissions results in the feedback effect inducing cooperation. Governments' ability to make credible commitments also enters the model. Decisions concerning environmental policy are taken at the beginning of the game; when the second period comes, governments reoptimize. By letting the length of the first period h vary, we can study how the effects of household mobility on environmental policy depend on the time of commitment.

Chapter 3

The Nature of Environmental Management

APPROACHES TO ENVIRONMENTAL MANAGEMENT

Environmental management is an approach to environmental stewardship which integrates ecology, policy making, planning and social development. Its goals include:

- The prevention and resolution of environmental problems;
- Establishing limits;
- Establishing and nurturing institutions that effectively support environmental research, monitoring and management;
- Warning of threats and identifying opportunities;
- Sustaining and, if possible improving, existing resources;
- Where possible improving 'quality of life';
- Identifying new technology or policies that are useful.

It is clear that these goals conceal a wealth of issues. Clearly, short-term goals must be embedded within an overall vision. Without overall vision it is difficult to avoid fragmented decision making, or to adopt a long-term view, or to prioritize and identify urgent tasks. Environmental management thus demands 'scoping' (deciding goals and setting limits on efforts) before acting. However, this is often neglected. Since the early 1970s popular texts have often published variants of 'Laws of Ecology' (based on four 'laws' published by Commoner (1971) (environmental management implications are in parenthesis):

1. Any intrusion into nature has numerous effects, many of which are unpredictable (environmental management must cope with the unexpected).
2. Because 'everything is connected', humans and nature are inextricably bound together; what one person does affects others (environmental management must consider chains of causation, looking beyond the local and short term).
3. Care needs to be taken that substances produced by humans do not interfere with any of the Earth's biogeochemical processes (environmental management must monitor natural processes and human activities to ensure no crucial process is upset).

In recent years some environmental managers have begun to express their overall vision and goals by publishing an environmental policy statement—to show intent, identify priorities and principles, and give a sense of purpose. While this informs the public, it does not guarantee sound environmental management. Environmental managers must assume there is an optimum balance between environmental protection and allowing human activities. Establishing where that balance lies depends largely on ethics. Clark (1989) argued that at its core environmental management asks two questions: (1) What kind of planet do we want? (2) What kind of planet can we get? Even if agreement on an optimum balance can be reached, the approach to environmental management goals can take different paths.

Environmental management has not evolved in isolation: regional planners often adopt a human ecology approach, other planners a systems analysis or an ecosystem approach.

For example, McHarg used river basins, and Doxiadis (1977) tried to develop a science of planning settlement in balance with nature – ekistics. Rapoport recognized two main groupings: those who adopt a horticultural metaphor – Garden Earth – and those who prefer one that is more technological – Spaceship Earth.

The variety of challenges, and the fact that many different actors are involved (e.g. the public, commercial interests, professions, local and national government, special-interest groups, the voluntary sector), means that in practice environmental managers often focus on a region, ecosystem, sector of activity, or resource. Environmental managers may not achieve their objectives, might be criticized (or sued), fall into disrepute with those who employ them, and lose public trust. So, like most administrators, environmental managers are likely to follow risk-aversion strategies, including:

- Working to safe minimum standards;
- Adopting sustainability constraints;
- Following a 'win-win' or 'least regrets' approach (i.e. actions which seek benefits whatever the outcome; actions which seek to reduce unwanted impacts, respectively).

Effectively, these all conserve or protect the environment unless social costs are very high. Following the precautionary principle is not costless. In many situations it has high costs as some things have to be forgone to keep open escape options.

The Implications of Human Population Growth

In the late eighteenth century Thomas Malthus examined the factors limiting human population growth. His thesis was that human population growth puts pressure on the means of subsistence, throwing it out of balance with the environment so that there is population collapse. Interest in the limits to human population was rekindled in the 1970s by a group of ecologists, systems analysts, demographers and 'environmentalists' (There may be overlap between groupings, and within categories. Environmental managers may be more or less anthropocentric or ecocentric, more or less 'green', more or less supportive of technology. There is also a wide spectrum of political and philosophical stances, all of which colour the approach adopted) Ad hoc approach: approach developed in reaction to a specific situation Problem-solving approach: follows a series of logical steps to identify problems and needs and implement solutions Systems approach: for example

- Ecosystem (mountain; high latitude; savanna; desert; island; lake, etc.)
- Agro-ecosystem

Regional approach: mainly ecological zones or biogeophysical units, which can sometimes be international– i.e. involve different states, e.g. an internationally-shared river basin. For example:

- Watershed
- River basin
- Coastal zone
- Island
- Command area development authority (irrigation-related)
- Administrative region
- Sea (e.g. Mediterranean; North Sea; Baltic; Aral Sea, etc.)

Specialist discipline approach: often adopted by professionals. For example:

- Air quality management
- Water quality management
- Land management
- Environmental health
- Urban management
- Ocean management
- Human ecology approach

- Tourism management/ecotourism
- Conservation area management

Voluntary sector approach: environmental management by, or encouraged and supported by NGOs. For example

- Debt-for-nature swaps
- Private reserves
- 'Ginger groups' which try to prompt environmental management
- Private funding for research or environmental management

Commercial approach: environmental management for business/public bodies Political economy or political ecology approach: Human ecology approach: = biogeophysical systems who came to be known as neo-Malthusians. For a given species and situation, population tends to grow until it encounters a critical resource limit or controlling factor, whereupon there is a gradual or sudden, limited or catastrophic decline in numbers, or a shift to a cyclic boom-and-bust pattern. Neo-Malthusians saw population growth as the primary cause for concern, although a few also focused on the growing threat from 'careless technology'.

One of the neo-Malthusians, Hardin (1968), focused on collective damage as a consequence of inadequately controlled individual actions, something of concern to modern environmental management. Hardin's 'tragedy of the commons' essay (and related works) argued that commonly owned natural resources under conditions of population growth would be damaged because each user would seek to maximize their short-term interests.

This thesis is now largely dismissed as simplistic, together with much of the neo-Malthusian theory, for failing to examine the social and historical context of population growth. The link between population growth and environment is more complex than neo-Malthusians acknowledged. While 1970s neo-Malthusian and environmentalist publications were largely dogmatic warnings or pleas for change, weak on proof and workable strategies, they did trigger an awareness that in a finite world there were limits. In practice, there are complex environment–population linkages and feedbacks, for example, the speed of population growth related to the ability to upgrade technology may be crucial. Damage to the environment can be a function of:

1. Human population numbers;
2. High levels of consumption of that population (i.e. lifestyle);
3. Technology used to satisfy consumption and dispose of waste.

Contradicting neo-Malthusian theories, Boserup explored how population increase, provided it does not overwhelm the adaptive ability of people, may prompt social and technological changes leading to improved quality of life. Tiffen documents situations where not only has population growth led to innovation that improved quality of life, it has also reduced environmental degradation. This prompts the questions: How often can that pattern are achieved? What must be done to encourage such a pattern?

While there are Boserupian grounds for tempering Malthusian and neo-Malthusian pessimism, world-wide there has been breakdown of established livelihood strategies and environmental degradation. There are also situations where a very low human population, or trans boundary pollution of virtually undisturbed areas, are causing environmental damage. On a global scale there do seem to be too many humans, so environmental managers will have to establish what optimum sustainable population is, and how it can best be reached. Some demographers argue that only within the next decade or so will it be possible to achieve such a population with humane approaches.

Sustainable Development and Environmental Ethics

When neo-Malthusians were drawing attention to limits, the Club of Rome (an informal international group concerned about the predicament of humanity) reported on a systems dynamics computer world-model. This publication reported on studies to determine future scenarios, using global forecasts of accelerating industrialization; population growth; rates of malnutrition; depletion of non-renewable resources; and a deteriorating environment. The report was designed to promote public interest, and concluded that 'If present growth trends...continue unchanged, the limits to growth on this planet will be reached within the next hundred years'. Meadows and his colleagues concluded that by effective environmental management—a condition of adequate 'ecological and economic stability' could be sustained.

With The Limits to Growth in mind, some began calling for reduced or even 'zero growth'. However, any state embracing such ethics would face considerable disruption of its economy. From the early 1970s there was a much more palatable alternative—sustainable development. This seemed to offer a way for continued growth to avoid conflict with environmental limits. The goals of sustainable development and the Club of Rome are the same—adequate sustained quality of life for all without exceeding environmental limits. It is possible to stretch some limits, using technology, so sustainable development may be pursued not just by altering demands or finding resource substitutes.

In a sequel to The Limits to Growth the same principal authors refined their original systems dynamics model and fed in much-improved data. Beyond the Limits argued that the 1972 warnings were broadly correct, that some of the limits have already been exceeded, and that, if present trends continue, there is virtually certain to be global collapse within the lifetime of children alive today. However, they argue that it is still possible to have 'overshoot but not collapse', and to achieve the goal of sustainable development if excessive population growth and material consumption are cut and there is increase in efficiency of materials and energy use soon.

Beyond the Limits throws down an urgent challenge to environmental management and indicates a timescale for action. For effective environmental management there must be means of resolving controversies regarding proper conduct: to a large degree ethics enable this. Ethics can be defined as a system of cultural values motivating people's behaviour. They draw upon human reasoning, morals, knowledge of nature, and goals to act as a sort of plumb-line for development and shape a worldview. Ethics operate at the level of individuals, institutions, societies, and internationally.

Some environmentalists have blamed Judaeo-Christian ethics for the tendency over the last two thousand years for western peoples to see themselves in dominion over nature, and to pursue strategies of exploitation, rather than of stewardship. From the late sixteenth century the Protestant ethic spread in the west, and ideas of utopia were discussed—the individual was encouraged to be responsible for self-improvement through good acts and hard work.

However, few tried to shift laissez-faire attitudes towards environmental management before the 1960s. Activists in the 1960s and 1970s added little to environmental science; however, they did stimulate a quest for new development and environment ethics. From the 1980s interest in the environment has grown, stimulating books and journals (e.g. Environmental Ethics; Ethics & Behaviour; Ethics, Place and Environment; Environmental Values; Science, Technology & Human Values). Interestingly, some progressive environmental ethics literature has come from business. Unfortunately, there is plenty of environmental ethics theory, but little ethical pragmatism! Carley and Christie tried to summarize the range of environmental ethics, dividing them into:

a. Technocratic environmental ethics=resource-exploitative, growth-oriented;
b. Managerial environmental ethics=resource-conservationist, oriented to sustainable growth;
c. Communalist environmental ethics=resource-preservationist, oriented to limited or zero growth;
d. Bioethicist or deep ecology environmental ethics=extreme preservationist, anti-growth.

Grouping (a) is anthropocentric and places faith in the capacity of technology to overcome problems. Grouping (d) is unlikely to attract support from enough people to be a viable approach, and offers little guidance to environmental managers. Carley and Christie felt the ethics of groups (b) and (c) were more likely to support sustainable development and provide guidance for environmental management.

Problems andNneeds

Westerners have tended to see themselves as being at war with nature, rather than seeking to understand it and then trying to exist within its constraints. The environment was to be 'tamed', and unspoilt lands were 'wastelands'. Since the 1930s the last land frontiers have been closing, and unsettled areas capable of giving a good livelihood are increasingly difficult to find. By the mid-1960s the limitless world was seen to have shrunk to Spaceship Earth, a finite and delicate system which must be taken care of if it is to support humanity. The Gaian viewpoint goes further, regarding the Earth as a system which, if upset by careless development, might adjust in such a way as to make current lifestyles impossible or even eliminate humans.

Environmental management therefore faces complex environmental challenges which may reach crisis level within fifty years. It will have to cope with these in the face of growing human population, increasing poverty, likely social unrest, and perhaps natural disasters. Anticipatory action seems to hold most promise, and people will have to be involved more than has been the case with planning and management in the past. How will environmental management achieve its policy goals? Through a mix of moral pressure, the spread of appropriate ethics, and by ensuring economics, business and law are sufficiently sensitive to the needs of the environment. Environmental management will need to make use of education and the media to alter social attitudes so that there is an acceptance of a new ethics. It will also have to draw upon other fields to achieve its goals, and must have effective institutions. Manuals, guides, checklists, conventions and agreements can help guide the identification of goals and preparation of action plans and their implementation.

The reductionist approach of splitting problems into component parts for study and solution lies at the core of western rational, scientific study. Some feel a holistic 'overall view' approach should replace 'compartmentalized and inflexible science'; I feel that is a mistake—there is a need for both.

Environmental management involves a series of decisions. How these are made depends on whether a technocratic or a consultative model is adopted. The latter has become the usual pattern in the USA and Canada, and is increasingly being chosen in Japan and Europe, reflecting the trend towards freedom of information. Whatever the overall approach, environmental management is, as Matthews et al. noted, a 'myriad of individual and collective decisions by persons, groups, and organizations' and 'together these decisions and interactions constitute a process—a process that in effect results in management (or mismanagement) of the environmental resources of a society'.

Of the many problems that beset environmental management, inadequate data is a common hindrance: there are still huge gaps in knowledge of the structure and function of the environment, the workings of global, regional and local economics, and of how societies and individual humans behave. The ideal is adequate data that can be presented in real time, so that the scenario can be observed as it changes. With improved computers, software and the development of tools like geographical information systems (GIS) this may one day be possible, but often all that is available today is an occasional, incomplete snapshot view.

Decision making is often made difficult by politics; lobbying; media, public and NGOs' attention; lack of funding and expertise. Environmental managers are faced with two temporal challenges: (1) problems may suddenly demand attention and allow little time for solution; (2) the desirability that planning horizons stretch further into the future than has been usual practice. Decisions are easier to make and policies more easily adjusted if there is time available—for example, a 3°C climate change over 150 years may not be too much of a challenge, but if it happens over 20 years it certainly would be. Predictions are difficult enough with stable environments; once stability has been upset there may be unexpected and sudden feedbacks or shifts to different states, all of which are difficult to forecast. The behaviour of economic systems are even more difficult to predict, and human behaviour is especially fickle as tastes and attitudes alter. The unpredictability and rapidity of challenges prompted Holling to argue for adaptive assessment and management.

Sustainable development calls for trade-offs. For example, it may be necessary to forgo immediate benefits to secure long-term yields—which may far outweigh the former. Such trade-offs can be a cruel choice for individuals, groups or countries, and a minefield for the environmental manager (and it is a situation where foreign aid could be focused to cushion trade-offs).

Institutional problems probably present more difficulties for environmental management than technical or scientific challenges. Human institutions change and can be difficult to understand and control and building new ones may be hard. It is vital that the institutions involved in environmental management are effective. Even if there is technology and funding and a will to solve a problem, success will be unlikely without the right type of sustainable institution. A growing number of social scientists have been focusing on institution building: this gives us grounds for optimism.

The major international body charged with environmental management, the United Nations Environment Programme (UNEP), was designed in the 1960s (and founded in 1973), and needs remodelling to be more effective. The UNEP was located away from Paris, Geneva or New York, in Nairobi, which has had mixed results—some argue it is off the beaten track and this partly explains its poor funding and lack of power. To be fair to institutions like the UNEP, they must rely on the quality of their arguments to convince countries and multinational companies or transnational companies (TNCs) to accept a strategy, and have been given little in the way of sanctions to enforce policies.

ENVIRONMENTAL MANAGEMENT AND BUSINESS

By the late seventeenth century in the Caribbean, Mauritius, and many other places, trade in sugar, timber and other commodities by bodies like the Dutch East Indies Company and the (British) East India Company and clearances by numerous smaller plantation owners were causing deforestation and soil erosion. By the 1830s, English Romantic socialist-environmentalists like William Morris, and in Russia the proto-anarchist Pyotr Kropotkin began to criticize industrialization for its pollution, human degradation and shoddy products. But there was little popular protest until the 1960s, by which time people in developed countries had improved standards of living and enjoyed sufficient free time and access to a more or less democratic media, to become aware of and lobby for environmental issues. Accidents like the Torrey Canyon oil-tanker spillage and pollution disasters like Three Mile Island, Love Canal and Seveso had raised public awareness in USA and Europe by the mid-1970s. Also environmental NGOs, consumer protection groups and popular writers fanned public interest.

Accidents prompted environmental controls. Also by the 1970s American NGOs and groups of lawyers interested in environmental issues (notably the Environmental Defence Fund and the Natural Resources Defence Fund) began to fight group court actions against those damaging nature and lobbied for environmental legislation. In Europe and New Zealand green politics began to emerge. Research and contact between scientists increased after the 1957-8 International Geophysical Year, leading to improving awareness of environmental issues, better understanding of Earth's structure and function, the development of international standards, and sharing of data.

The USA passed the 1969 National Environmental Policy Act (NEPA) in 1970, and established an Environmental Protection Agency. The UN held the 1972 Conference on the Human Environment in Stockholm, and in 1973 established the UN Environmental Programme (UNEP). A deluge of publications fanned concern for the environment and realization there was a need to review practices and ethics, e.g. Schumacher's (1973) Small Is Beautiful voiced concern about material consumption, pollution and uncaring business. Overall, the mid-sixties to mid-seventies was a decade of increasing environmental concern. NEPA required developers to meet environmental standards, and effectively promoted the precautionary principle.

Business was also being prompted by legislation, public opinion and self-interest to pay attention to the environment. It was not enough to obey the law and reduce liability, there was a need to look concerned—what Brenton called 'defensive greenness'. Some companies saw opportunities for commercial gain through environmental management—building a green image and marketing environmentally friendly products or providing services for environmental management. There was a realization that 'end-of-pipe' solutions (i.e. cleaning up rather than prevention) were more costly, gave a bad public image, and that environmental management could be a way of cutting costs to get a 'competitive edge'. Other factors have prompted business interest in environmental management:

- Globalization (i.e. media, finance, etc., becoming global);
- 'Glasnost' (i.e. increasing public demand for access to information);
- Activity of green business groups, especially since the 1992 UN Conference on Environment and Development;
- Trade union and NGO concern for environmental issues;
- A wish by companies to reduce inspection by regulatory bodies;

- Insistence by funding, insurance and licensing bodies that impact assessment and eco-audit be conducted;
- Ethical (green) investment policies adopted by some companies (in the USA a group of powerful investors now apply a set of environmental policy principles—the 'Valdez Principles');
- Genuine sense of responsibility (some companies have been founded by people with a strong sense of moral duty);
- Avoidance of litigation;
- The establishment since the 1970s of increasingly powerful environmental ministries in most countries;
- Formation of bodies like the Institute of Environmental Management (UK);
- Promotion of the Integrated Systems for Environmental Management and the Business Charter for Sustainable Development (International Chamber of Commerce, 1991);
- Provision of courses on environmental management at university business schools;
- The UN Centre on Transnational Corporations has promoted sustainable development.

Corporate Environmental Management

Business interacts with a wide range of parties. Satisfying the investors and shareholders is at present the driving force; the adoption of environmental management implies concern for a wider range of stakeholders: the public, bystanders, employees, consumers, the regional and global environment. Environmental management must address its objectives within the context of company practices (e.g. if at all possible it should not slow completion schedules). As its value is proven, those practices may be modified to help environmental management. 'Company', 'firm' or 'business' is used in this, but environmental management, eco-audit and environmental management systems are also practised by government departments, city administrations, etc. The tasks of a business environmental manager include:

- Education of employees to be aware of environmental issues;
- Updating management on relevant environmental regulation, laws and issues;
- Selecting specialists and checking that environmental management tasks contracted out to consultants have been satisfactorily conducted and are properly acted upon;
- Ensuring waste management is satisfactory;
- Avoiding legal costs, reducing insurance premiums, risk and hazard assessment;
- If need be correcting mistakes of the past.

A typical definition of business environmental management would be: 'efforts to minimize the negative environmental impact of the firm's products throughout their life cycle'. The range of tasks is so wide, and involves working with so many people or bodies outside the company, that 'environmental co-ordinator' might be a better term. If business fails to adopt environmental management in a serious fashion there will be little progress, for, as Hawken (1993) noted, corporations are Earth's dominant institutions—many corporations have earnings in excess of those of most developing countries, and some command more riches than some developed nations. Governments are often lobbied and prevailed upon to do what national business, MNCs or TNCs want.

Big business often has better access to information, resources and skills than poor nations, and may have greater stability for year-to-year planning than some governments. For the last ten years there has been an increasing flow of books on environmental management and sustainable development for business. This literature may be subdivided into:

- Greening of business (often by sector, e.g. tourism management and environment);
- Environmental management for sustainable development of business;
- Green corporate environmental management;
- Total quality management/environmental management systems;
- Eco-audit;
- Impact assessment, hazard and risk assessment;
- Green business ethics;
- Green marketing, labelling, life-cycle assessment;
- Recycling and waste disposal;
- Health and safety;
- Environmentally sound investment and funding;
- Environmental law and business.

By 1992 the chemical industry in developed countries was spending an estimated 3 to 4 per cent of its sales income per annum on environment, health and safety in the USA alone: that constituted about US$10 billion a year. Spending is rapidly increasing. With accidents like the Exxon Valdez costing over US$2 billion it is easy to see why.

A Paradigm Shift to Environmental Management Ethics

'Fordism' of the 1920s to 1960s emphasized mass production, mass consumption, corporate control and resource exploitation. Since the 1960s various thinkers, 'barefoot economists' and environmentalists have questioned growing consumerism, i.e. excessive consumption, stimulated through marketing. The problem is, how will people (consumers) and business (supplying the consumers) shift to something more supportive of environmental goals? Hawken (1993) in The Ecology of Commerce argued that free market capitalism, the economic and social credo of most of the world, must rapidly shift to a 'restorative economy' based on 'industrial ecology'. Only business, he argued, and no other human institution, has the power to make adequate changes. Allenby and Richards (1994) also saw industrial ecology as a means of integrating environmental concern with economic activity.

Whether it is termed post-Fordian, postmodern or post-industrial, what Hawken and others argue is that the world's future economy should be organized with guiding principles coming from industrial ecology. These post-Fordians seem convinced that the profit motive will be replaced by a more environmentally sensitive approach. Some even suggest that environmental management values are supplanting shareholder interests and a paradigm shift is beginning. However, there is a risk that 'greening' of business is appearance rather than substance, simply the adoption of environmental management tools to improve profits and public relations.

While there might seem to be few incentives at present to encourage a shift to better environmental management, there have been efforts to promote it. One of the more significant moves has been the publication in 1991 of a Business Charter for Sustainable Development by the International Chamber of Commerce at the 1991 World Industry Conference on Environmental Management. One of the first questions asked by business of such proposals is 'can they improve financial performance as well as lead to sustainable development?' Klassen and McLaughlin put this to the test, and concluded from studies of firms' performances that the adoption of environmental management did increase profits.

Promote Environmental Management in Business

Klassen and McLaughlin noted: 'the long-term goal of environmental management is to move toward...considering environmental aspects in an integrated fashion in product design, the entire manufacturing process, marketing, product delivery and use, consumer service, and post-consumer product disposition.' Already, several fields are well developed, including: industrial ecology, green marketing, consumer protection bodies, ecolabelling, total quality management, covenants, and lifecycle analysis.

Industrial Ecology

This is an approach which examines industrial, economic and resource activities from a biological and environmental, rather than a monetary point of view. Allenby and Richards (1994) saw it as integrating environmental concern into economic activity. Industrial ecology regards waste and pollution as uneconomic and harmful, and seeks to 'dovetail' them with raw materials. This means that wherever possible industry should use by-products, and go beyond the reduction of wastes to make use of what remains by the producer or other bodies. The product does not cause damage, and leads to a system of commerce where each and every act is inherently sustainable and restorative. Effectively, the environmental price of a product is included in its retail price.

This application of the ecosystem concept to industry means linking the 'metabolism' of one company or body to that of others. This is not far-fetched: some groupings of companies and settlements do it already. For example, Kalundborg (Denmark) has a coal-fired power station, oil refinery, pharmaceutical companies, concrete producer, sulphuric acid producer, fish farms, horticultural greenhouses and district heating—which are well integrated. Kalundborg's industrial ecology has happened more or less spontaneously, as companies seek to minimize costs of energy and raw materials and cut the output of waste. There are a number of similar examples in Sweden and Denmark, where sewage, agricultural waste and household refuse disposal are often integrated with district heating and electricity generation.

Pigouvian Taxes

Some people advocate going beyond the sort of industrial ecology-based strategy adopted by Kalundborg to a fully cyclic economy, i.e. one which yields virtually no waste because recycling and by-product recovery are complete. Making manufacturers responsible for some or all of the costs of recycling or waste disposal is one way of encouraging waste reduction and industrial ecology. There are various ways of doing this: one is to levy Pigouvian taxes. Named after the 1920s UK economist Arthur Pigou, these aim to ensure a manufacturer pays all costs from raw material and energy provision to final collection and recycling.

Pigouvian taxes may present problems: large companies may make sufficient profits to afford fines, but small companies could be crippled. So, the 'polluter-pays' principle can be a virtual licence to pollute if the fines are not set high enough, and that can damage small businesses. One way of avoiding such problems is to use licences; for example, in Germany manufacturers pay a fee to the government to display a green dot on packaging which authorizes (compulsory) recycling. As the costs have to be passed on to the customer, this encourages companies to reduce expensive packaging and use cheap, recyclable materials.

Green Marketing

Some companies and public bodies had recognized by the early 1980s that a satisfactory green image could improve public relations, and perhaps provide a marketing niche. There are manufacturers that have gained from this, and offer genuinely improved products— e.g. refrigerators that use less electricity, do not leak CFCs, and which are easier to recycle, and firms which manufacture equipment for monitoring and managing environmental quality. Less enlightened companies may sell goods because of public fears about the environment—e.g. sunblock creams and sunglasses for those afraid of increased UV. AEG reputedly increased sales by ca. 30 per cent in a static market by running a marketing campaign on its green strengths. In America in the 1980s McDonald's commissioned an environmental audit and acted on it to shift from plastic packaging foamed with CFCs to environmentally friendly cardboard. This proved good for public relations and was much cheaper.

Consumer Protection Bodies

Alongside the growth in green marketing there has been a spread of green consumerism. Consumer protection bodies have been active since the 1960s, and have not been restricted to the developed countries, e.g. one Malaysian body has been active in its own country and works for consumers elsewhere – the Consumers Association Penang.

Ecolabelling

The marking of goods to indicate that they are environmentally friendly (ecolabelling) has been adopted in many countries, including Canada, the USA, Germany and Sweden. In most cases the product is judged against similar goods by an independent agency to establish whether it has less environmental impact (without formal eco-auditing). Germany was one of the first countries to introduce ecolabelling in 1978, with its Umweltzeichen or Blaue Engel system. This relies on a jury of experts supervised by the Federal Environment Ministry to award the right to display a mark on packaging or in adverts. This is a way of influencing the behaviour of consumers, helping them identify the environmental impacts of products, and encourages manufacturers to reduce the impacts of their products.

Ecolabelling assesses environmental impact and communicates this to the consumer or middle merchant. The focus is on the product and often nothing is said about the process of production or distribution. So, an 'environmentally friendly' product might come from a factory which causes pollution or present a disposal problem after use. There is also a need for standardization and policing of ecolabelling.

However, under current World Trade Organization (WTO) rules this may not be easy. West (1995) warned that without better legal enforcement, it tended to become a marketing gimmick.

Quality Management and Environmental Management

Total quality management (TQM) (also called company-wide quality management) aims to provide assurance of adherence to policy and specifications through a structured management system, and to enable demonstration of it to third parties through documentation and record-keeping. TQM was first formulated in the USA, and largely developed in Japan in the early post-war period to try to improve industrial competitiveness. Environmental management systems (EMSs) show adherence to a suitable environmental policy, the meeting of appropriate environmental objectives (equivalent to specifications in quality management) and the ability to demonstrate to a wide range of interested parties ('customers' in TQM) that the system requirements and objectives are met. EMSs, usually require that a company or body publishes and regularly updates an Environmental Policy Statement.

An EMS provides an organizational structure, procedures and resources for implementing environmental policy. It also provides a language of performance and quality that can be understood by management. So far, adoption of EMS has mainly been voluntary with rapid growth of interest and continuing modification and improvement. Hunt and Johnson suggested this indicates business has shifted from 'defensive environmental management' to accepting the need for probity.

There are critics of EMSs, who argue it is possible to rig them by setting easy-to-achieve targets; that it is more important (and difficult) to nurture satisfactory environmental ethics; and that EMS is still being developed and tested.

A government or other regulatory body can provide companies with a more stable regulatory environment and encourage development of better pollution control plans or adoption of an EMS through a covenant. This is a written, voluntary agreement signed by the company or other body and the government or agency seeking regulation. The Netherlands has made extensive use of covenants as part of an integrated approach to national environmental management policy. A Dutch company undertaking a covenant would be expected to produce a development plan every four years, to be reviewed by local authorizing bodies. The plan coverage includes pollution control and energy conservation and it is seen as a way of getting national policies implemented at local level. Measures were initiated by the National Environmental Policy Plans (adopted by the Dutch

Parliament in 1989), and by 1997 over 1,200 companies had signed covenants. The covenanting approach can be quite effective, particularly in cutting pollution. However, some NGOs are not keen on the approach, viewing it as closed or cosy and not sufficiently open to third parties to check. There are also some worries that it may lead to a softening of enforcement controls. Nevertheless, it is an approach which encourages company self-regulation.

Life-cycle Analysis

Many development activities are processes which have different stages—for example, manufacturing a car or running a power station involve raw materials and energy provision, plant construction, manufacturing, distribution, use and disposal or decommissioning. Equipment is usually subject to wear and tear, and so varies in performance and presents different risks as it ages and as management acquire experience (or become complacent). Industrial and power generation sites, for example, often accumulate contamination, and so the environmental threat is not constant. It is therefore undesirable to assess impacts or develop environmental management policies by simply taking a snapshot view. Life-cycle analysis (or assessment) has been developed to try to consider the whole of an activity, which may extend beyond the time horizon of a single owner. It is cradle-to-grave study of an activity or company.

The Current Situation

One may summarize the present situation as:

- The majority of businesses are aware that environmental issues are important;
- Some businesses are doing something—it may be from genuine concern, but often it is for public relations or profit motives;
- Too often businesses adopt a 'react and repair' approach, rather than following precautionary principles;

- Only a few businesses are acting at a strategic level;
- Business is in need of strategies like industrial ecology, but will need to be encouraged or forced to adopt them.

ENVIRONMENTAL MANAGEMENT AND LAW

Law should provide a framework for regulating use of the environment. Law is crucial for environmental management in a number of ways, aiding:

- Regulation of resource use;
- Protection of the environment and biodiversity;
- Mediation, conflict resolution and conciliation;
- Formulation of stable, unambiguous undertakings and agreements.

Environmental management may involve a number of resource situations, e.g. individually-owned (private) resources; national resources; shared resources; open-access resources; common property resources; global resources. Some of these are better covered by law than others. There are different legal systems—for example, based on Roman Law, on customary laws, Islamic Law, the Code Napoleon—to name but a few. Some countries have legal systems that combine more than one of these, say indigenous and colonial era legislation, plus Islamic Law. Areas may be subject to state and federal laws and to secular and religious laws. In most countries statutory law is written by politicians and passed by national legislature; and common law is compiled by judges (with reference to past cases and prior statutory law).

Most legislation evolves in response to problems, so there is often delay between need and the establishment of satisfactory law. Without effective legislation, resource use, pollution control, conservation, and most fields of human activity are likely to fall into chaos and conflict. Law can encourage satisfactory performance, enable authorities to punish those who infringe environmental management legislation, or confiscate equipment that is misused or faulty, or close a company; it may also be possible for employees, bystanders and product or service users to sue for damages if they are harmed.

Some countries have been active in developing environmental management law, notably Sweden, The Netherlands, the USA, Canada, Australia and New Zealand. Some environmental laws are ancient: Indian rulers promulgated controls on hunting and forest felling centuries ago; the UK had local pollution control laws as early as the twelfth century AD, and passed nationally enforced pollution control legislation like the Alkali Act (1863) over a century ago.

Environmental management increasingly involves transboundary problems that reach beyond traditional sovereignty limits, issues of negligence, and the need for nations to co-operate. International law is evolving to address such issues, although it is difficult to develop and enforce. Often powerful MNCs or TNCs are involved in issues and these may prompt and drive forward innovation, not necessarily to the benefit of the environment or the public. Walker likened them to seventeenth-century city states that had insufficient public accountability. The problem is to ensure that changes are for the good of the environment and the greater common good, rather than just suiting a large company or more countries.

Most laws, whether civil or criminal, are corrective—punishing wrong-doers and deterring others from infringing rules and agreements or from causing nuisance or injury. In the main, therefore, legislation has not been very pre-emptive. Environmental managers must also be aware that there is little point in passing laws or making international agreements if there cannot be adequate enforcement.

Three things are especially important for environmental legislation:

1. The precautionary principle, which has evolved to deal with risks and uncertainties faced by environmental management. The meaning is still not firmly established by law. The principle implies that an ounce of prevention is worth a pound of cure—it does not prevent problems but may reduce their occurrence and helps ensure contingency plans are made. The application of this principle requires either cautious progress until a development can be judged 'innocent', or avoiding development until research indicates exactly what the risks are, and then proceeding to minimize them. Once a threat is identified, action should be taken to prevent or control damage even if there is uncertainty about whether the threat is real. Some environmental problems become impossible or costly to solve if there is delay, so waiting for research and legal proof is not costless.

   Some hold that the principle should be applied in situations where both the probability and cost of impacts are unknown. The principle was stressed in many of the decisions reached at the Rio Earth Summit in 1992. For example, it was endorsed by Article 15 of the 1992 Rio Declaration on Environment and Development. Article 130r of the Maastricht Treaty (Treaty on European Union) of February 1992 states that EU policy on the environment shall be based on the precautionary principle.

2. The polluter-pays principle—in addition to the obvious—the polluter pays for damage caused by a development—this principle also implies that a polluter pays for monitoring and policing. A problem with this approach is that fines may bankrupt small businesses, yet be low enough for a large company to write them off as an occasional overhead, which does little for pollution control. There is debate as to whether the principle should be retrospective—e.g. today a purchaser who acquires contaminated land

in good faith is often forced to clean up the mess others left (if the polluter pays, how long back does liability stretch?). Developing countries are seeking to have developed countries pay more for carbon dioxide controls, arguing that they polluted the world during the Industrial Revolution, yet enjoy the fruits of invention from that era.

The polluter-pays principle is more a way of allocating costs to the polluter than a legal principle. OECD member countries adopted the principle in 1972, at least in theory.

3. Freedom of information—if the public, NGOs ('green watchdogs') or even official bodies are unable to get information, environmental planning and management is hindered. Democracies have begun to release more information—the USA has a Freedom of Information Act, the EU is moving in that direction, and in the UK the (1994) Environmental Protection Act has helped. Few countries have such well-developed disclosure as the USA, which requires public registers of development activities, publication of Environmental Impact Statements, hazard warning on products, etc. Some governments and multinational corporations fear industrial secrets will leak to competitors if there is too much disclosure, and there are situations where authorities declare 'strategic' needs and suspend disclosure.

   In many countries, court actions, even if they were fought in the public interest, had to be brought by an individual, who, if they lost, paid costs. This acted as a deterrent for anyone to tackle government or large company wrongdoings, because they lacked equivalent resources. It is desirable that NGOs and individuals be allowed to bring legal actions to protect the environment, if need be as group cases (class actions). In the USA the Environmental Defence Fund, the Sierra Club, and environmental lawyers like Joseph Sax managed to achieve the right to bring class actions (or group actions) in the 1970s. Subsequently Canada, the UK and several other countries saw similar legal changes.

US National Environmental Policy Act (NEPA)

Discussions leading to NEPA began in the early 1960s, when the need was perceived for the USA to have a basic declaration of national environmental policy and an action-forcing provision. The US Government was largely reacting to public opinion that conventional planning did not adequately take account of the environment; it already had responsibility to steward resources and protect the environment under the Public Trust Doctrine. However, before NEPA the USA had little effective federal control over the environment and lacked land use regulations which some other countries had. NEPA was signed into US Law on 1 January 1970, to reform federal policy-making, and influence the private sector to reorientate values.

Originally it was intended that NEPA would change the nature of federal decision-making. However, it has become more of a procedural requirement. Caldwell – one of the architects of NEPA – felt that, had it not happened in the USA, something similar would have appeared elsewhere. NEPA required environmental impact assessment (EIA) prior to federally funded projects that might 'significantly' affect the environment – a message to officials to 'look before you leap'. NEPA Section 101 set regulations to protect the environment, Section 102 (2) (c) ensured they were pursued, and Section 103 included provision for EIA statements to be challenged in court.

That happened a lot at first because NEPA was untested and used expressions like 'significant' and 'human environment' that were poorly defined. There was also some need to clarify which developments required EIA, and how and by whom it was to be conducted. Virtually the world's first use of the expression 'EIA' occurs in Section 102 (2) c of

NEPA, which requires US federal agencies to prepare an environmental impact statement (EIS) (bearing the costs against taxes, and sending copies to federal and state agencies and to the public) using EIA, prior to taking action. There were three main elements in NEPA:

1. NEPA announced a US national policy for the environment.
2. It outlined procedures for achieving the objectives of that policy.
3. Provision was made for the establishment of a US Council on Environmental Quality (CEQ) which was to advise the US President on the environment, review the EIA process, review draft EISs, and see NEPA was followed. Also in 1970 the US Government created the US Environmental Protection Agency (EPA), its brief to co-ordinate the attack on environmental pollution and to be responsible for the EIA process (the EPA is in effect 'overseer' of impact assessment in the USA).

NEPA was the first time US Law had really allowed for development to be delayed or abandoned for the long-term good of the environment, and for efforts to be made to co-ordinate public, state, federal and local activities. Effectively, NEPA put environmental quality on a level with economic growth, a revolution in values in a country where state intrusion was anathema—for this reason many see it as a sort of Magna Carta, although it stopped short of making a healthy environment a Constitutional Right.

Public participation is written into NEPA to the extent it might be described as a corner-stone. NEPA is statutory law: it was written after deliberation, and did not evolve from custom, practice or tradition. Consequently, like a charter, it was imperfect; there were problems, especially delay, as litigation took place over various issues.

Many felt NEPA had been abducted by lawyers and could become a bureaucratic delaying tactic. These teething problems have largely been resolved, although some feel NEPA should be strengthened, possibly leading to changes in the US Constitution to better manage the environment. NEPA has been a seminal concept and catalyst for EIA in other countries, although bodies like the Canadian Environmental Assessment Research Council and the International Association for Impact Analysis also deserve credit for spreading and developing mandatory development review processes. Effective implementation of EIA demands legislation and law enforcement to ensure that:

- There are no loopholes, so that no activity likely to cause impacts escapes EIA;
- The assessment is adequate;
- The assessment is heeded;
- The public are kept sufficiently informed or, ideally, involved in assessment.

European Law and Environmental Management

The European Community (EC) grew from the six original states which signed the Treaty of Rome in 1957 to form a closer European Union of 15 nations in 1995 which is set to expand further in the future. EU members like Sweden and The Netherlands have long-established traditions of environmental concern; others have given the environment far less attention. Growing EU integration should prompt and support better policies more widely. It will also ensure common rules and ways of monitoring, setting standards, etc. In 1992 the EU established a European Environmental Agency as a clearing-house for environmental information. Its role is also to evaluate and disseminate information and develop means for applying the precautionary principle, but not enforcement of environmental policy.

The Council of Europe had 35 EU and other member states in 1995 (many former colonies, trading partners, etc.), and is active in advocacy, cultural relations and raising awareness of issues including conservation and environmental protection. A UN agency that acts as a pan-European forum is the UN

Commission for Europe (UNECE), which supports sustainable development, environmental research, and has launched or serviced several agreements dealing with issues like pollution (e.g. the 1992 Convention on Transboundary Effects of Industrial Accidents). Environmental legislation is an important part of the emerging pan-European legal system (with the European Court of Justice as an overall arbitrator). The European Environmental Agency has not got as much enforcement power as the US Environmental Protection Agency, and serves mainly to gather information on the state of the European environment.

The EU has also established a European Environmental Information and Observation Network; a European Economic Community (EEC) Directive on Environmental Impact Assessment – which requires environmental assessment to be undertaken by developers; an EEC Directive on Freedom of Access to Information on the Environment – which requires authorities to ensure public access to relevant environmental information; and an EC Regulation on Eco-Management and Auditing (EMAS). One could make the broad generalization that EU environmental law has focused on co-ordination, codification and integration.

Since about 1973 there has been more interest in integrating wider environmental issues into politics alongside concern for achieving economic growth. In 1985 the European Commission decided environmental protection should be an integral part of economic and social policies at macroeconomic level and by sector. This was incorporated into the Treaty of Rome in 1987 and was strengthened by the Maastrict Treaty (1993), which included a statement of concern for sustainable growth. EU legislation seems to be increasingly aligning itself with global conventions such as those relating to global warming or waste management. Since 1993 EU law has been enacted to support more freedom of environmental information, better standard setting, the precautionary principle, and the polluter-pays principle; Winter has listed the core objectives:

- Preserve, protect and improve the quality of the environment.
- Protect human health.
- Prudent and rational use of natural resources.
- Promote measures at international level to deal with regional or world-wide environmental problems.

Hughes has noted that environmental management law should be 'vertically integrated' between regional, national and international systems. The EEC system allows this to some extent. Efforts to develop an overall EEC environmental policy resulted in the publication in 1973 of the First Programme of Action on the Environment; the Second, Third, Fourth and Fifth Action Programmes appeared in 1977, 1983, 1987, 1992 (reviewed in 1995), and lay down principles that EEC environmental legislation should adhere to. The Fifth Programme of Action on the European Environment seeks to incorporate good environmental policy into all Community policies. In the UK the 1995 Environment Act created a powerful, wide-ranging Environmental Agency for England and Wales, which brought together the functions previously spread among many agencies (pollution control, fisheries management, flood defence, etc.).

International Law and Environmental Management

International law governs relations between states, and has no direct effect on domestic law or individuals. It is often difficult to force a sovereign state to sign, and then honour, a treaty or similar agreement. International law must thus depend a great deal on voluntary agreements by governments and international bodies (the Brussels and Lugano Conventions on Environmental Law cover this issue of ensuring compliance). When negotiation fails a possibility is to refer the case to the International Court of Justice (not a very friendly process), or set up an International Joint Commission. International law has tended to be laissez-faire and ad hoc.

From the mid-nineteenth century until the 1950s co-operation, exchange of information, agreement and international guidelines or rules were often initiated by international public unions, e.g. the International Postal Union, or the International Telegraphic Union. Nowadays, the UN and its 15 specialist agencies (the FAO, WHO, UNESCO, UNEP, etc.) often initiate the development of international environmental law. For example, the UNEP has published guidelines on principles of conduct over shared natural resources (1978) and, more recently, on exchange of information on chemicals in international trade. NGOs like Greenpeace, Friends of the Earth and the World-Wide Fund for Nature also lobby for environmental legislation.

Various observers note the UN-supported system of environmental treaty making is valuable, although it needs strengthening—e.g. the UN General Assembly can only recommend, not insist that law be made. Developing countries have complained that international law is too US- or Eurocentric and there is a wish in some countries to see more application of Islamic Law. Since the 1972 UN Conference on the Human Environment (Stockholm), most of the UN-prompted multilateral treaties have been developed by a two-step process: a relatively vague framework convention which acknowledges a problem is presented (most countries are happy to sign such a non-binding agreement); that step prompts action, especially data collection, discussion and propaganda, which reduces opposition and raises interest so that a protocol can be introduced and agreed to.

International law faces a number of challenges. One of the greatest is the management of 'global commons': oceans and their resources; world weather and climate; atmosphere; stratospheric ozone; space, etc. Many resources, and also pests, migrate or move, so that effective management of ocean fisheries, migratory fish in rivers, whaling, disease or locust control, etc., needs to be through multilateral agreement.

In the late 1970s a class action by an NGO forced the US Agency for International Development (USAID) to insist on pre-development environmental assessments before granting funds. In effect the precautionary principle embodied in NEPA was extended to the Third World with respect to aid. Within a few years most aid agencies had adopted environmental guidelines and rules. The end of the Cold War may mean more opportunities and resources for international environmental law to develop.

Indigenous Peoples and Environmental Law

IUCN estimates suggest there are over 250 million indigenous peoples who interact with environmental law with respect to:

1. Protection of natural environment together with indigenous people;
2. Rights of indigenous people over natural resources;
3. Rights over traditional knowledge—e.g. to prevent ethnobotany becoming 'biopiracy' (gathering indigenous knowledge which is patented and sold);
4. Damages to indigenous people for past environmental wrongs by 'outsiders';
5. Views of indigenous people which could be fed into environmental law making.

Indigenous people often retain knowledge, skills and beliefs that relate closely to the natural environment. The protection of the environment is often vital to their physical and cultural survival, and they have insight which may aid environmental management and law making.

The rights of indigenous peoples are recognized by the UN Commission on Economic Development 1992 Convention on Biological Diversity and by the 1994 Draft UN Declaration of the Rights of Indigenous Peoples. Nevertheless, indigenous people often still have no written land tenure, making them vulnerable to abuse or resettlement if there are natural resources to be exploited.

In recent decades several countries have made changes to improve indigenous peoples' control of their environment and natural resources. Whether this will lead to better environmental management is debated. In Australia, New

Zealand, the USA, Canada and Amazonian Brazil aboriginal people have fought for their sovereign rights to control and manage, or at least share in, resources.

In Australia debate about aboriginal territorial rights has become heated recently. The Australian High Court has ruled that Australia's indigenous people enjoy native title and access rights to land leased by Euro-Australian farmers, which means two land-users should legally coexist. An Aboriginal claim to coastal waters and the Great Barrier Reef, if awarded, would have considerable impact on fishing and coastal resorts.

A question increasingly asked is: who should bear the cost of rehabilitation after resources exploitation? For example, the Pacific island of Nauru, now independent, provided phosphates for some 90 years. Does it have any claim on past colonial powers to remedy damage? Nauru claimed through the International Court of Justice for damage done before its independence in 1967. Similar retrospective actions have arisen in Australia and in other Pacific islands, over nuclear weapons test sites, and in Papua New Guinea concerning mining.

UN Conference on Environment and Development

Sometimes referred to as the 'Earth Summit' or abbreviated to UNCED, held in 1992 the Rio Conference was a test of the ability of the international political and legal order to reach a consensus for the good of the whole world. Originally there were hopes that UNCED would agree an Earth Charter, but this was not achieved, although several new declarations were made and conventions were established. Freestone reviewed the implications of UNCED, stressing that it did crystallize principles which contribute to the development of international environmental law. However, some feel the Earth Summit tended to weaken international environmental law by focusing on development issues. A follow-up meeting to UNCED, the Rio II Conference was held in New York in 1997.

Agreements made at the Earth Summit, 1992

- Rio Declaration on Environment and Development updated version of the Stockholm Declaration (of 1972); published general principles for future international action on environment and development.
- Framework Convention on Climate Change framework for negotiation of detailed protocols to deal with control of greenhouse gas emissions, deforestation, sea-level change, etc.
- Convention on Biological Diversity intended to arrest alarming rate of species loss (criticized for having been poorly and hurriedly drafted).
- Declaration on Forests a principle, not legally binding, this was substituted for original idea of a Forest Convention.
- Agenda 21 an action plan for the rest of the century and framework for dealing with environment and development issues. Consists of 40 chapters (not a legally binding instrument).
- Global Environmental Facility a fund established for global problem-solving. Under the auspices of the World Bank, UNEP and UNDP. Designed to be 'democratic and transparent' and helpful to poor nations. Amongst other things, intended to support Biodiversity and Climate Change Conventions.

International Law and Sovereignty Issues

Sovereignty affects access to data and monitoring, and can be a major constraint on environmental management. Countries are usually reluctant to sign any agreement which affects their sovereign powers. Yet growing transboundary and global environmental problems make it important to get co-operation. There are transnational and multinational corporations sufficiently powerful to threaten and bribe their way around sovereignty and other controls. Terrorism can have transnational or global impact, so there should be better international controls and co-operation to counter it. Unfortunately for many environmental management issues, getting multi-state agreements is a slow process.

In 1977 the Stockholm Declaration on the Human Environment affirmed the sovereign right of states to exploit their own resources and their responsibility to ensure that activities within their jurisdiction or control do not cause damage to the environment beyond the limits of their national jurisdiction. This affirmation has had considerable influence on subsequent international environmental law making.

International trade agreements, notably the GATT/WTO provisions, mean that if a country has environmental protection laws, say controlling the import of pesticide-contaminated produce, timber cut in an environmentally unsound fashion, or fish caught using nets that kill dolphins, these measures may be unenforceable because they impair 'free trade'. The level playing field demanded by trade agreements may make it difficult to control importation of food and commodities produced by means of genetic engineering and growth- or lactation-enhancing hormones.

Conversely, there may be situations where globalization helps countries adopt and enforce better standards (care must be taken to ensure that the motive is to improve environmental quality and not an attempt to make production costs uniform or create a global market for standardized products that enjoy economies of scale). Globalization of patent rights has generated concern; MNCs and TNCs seek to recoup research costs and control markets; poor countries fear bio-piracy with corporations patenting and claiming intellectual rights on genetic resources and ideas derived from such resources. The patenting and control of sales of crop seeds (modern varieties) and pharmaceutical products has also caused much friction.

Protection and extension of sovereignty can lead to wars; testing and storage of weapons; and territorial claims. These affect the environment and need to be more firmly addressed by international agreements and law. The pollution associated with the Gulf War underlines the importance of negotiation. Hostile environmental modification is covered by the 1977 Environmental Modification Convention (invoked to hold Iran to reparations for damage to Kuwait), and there are controls on nuclear, chemical and biological weapons.

A number of trends are apparent here. There has been a move towards the precautionary principle—since about 1972 countries have been guided to try to prevent pollution accidents and misdemeanours. Obtaining damages for, or penalizing, transnational pollution has been patchy, e.g. there were no adjudications over Chernobyl, Amoco Cadiz and many similar disasters. There has been little progress in establishing 'environmental rights' (i.e. rights of natural objects or organisms), although in some western countries there is a vociferous animal rights lobby.

Various agreements and conventions have reaffirmed and there are many areas agreed by scientists, social scientists and other specialists to be in need of formal protection. Protection may be supported by a state; privately funded by a group or individual; or by an international body or bodies. For example, there is a worldwide scatter of Biosphere Reserves; the UK has state-protected Sites of Special Scientific Interest (SSSIs); many countries have reserves and national parks. Some conservation areas are established and watched over by international treaty—the 1971 Ramsar Convention (Convention on Wetlands of International Importance) provides a framework for protection of wetland habitats, especially those used by migrating birds. The UN Educational, Scientific and Cultural Organization (UNESCO) supports and oversees many sites of special cultural value.

The Antarctic

In Antarctica territorial claims have been put aside (but not eliminated) under the Antarctic Treaty which came into force in 1960 (signed 1959). Basically this is an international treaty by which signatories have agreed to keep Antarctica and its surrounding seas open for scientific research by all nations deemed to be pursuing scientific exploration south of 60°S. The treaty requires demilitarization, no nuclear weapons and a commitment to conservation.

While it has been quite a flexible treaty, modified as need arose, it has been put under some pressure as interest in resource development (notably oil, minerals, krill, squid and fish) comes into conflict with its conservation requirements. There are also demands from non-treaty nations (basically those which have not maintained a significant research presence there) and some NGOs for there to be changes to give the whole world (probably through the UN), not just signatory nations, control of Antarctica (a coalition of over 200 NGOs and non-treaty nations—the Atlantic and Southern Ocean Coalition—has been seeking such a goal). There have been some moves which in theory could allow mineral resources to be used—the 1988 Convention on the Regulation of Antarctic Mineral Resource Activities allows exploitation only if very stringent environmental assessments are made and accepted by treaty nations. The Falklands conflict is a warning that if potentially attractive mineral resources are identified territorial claims may reappear in Antarctica.

Transboundary Pollution

In 1965 Canada and the USA became involved in the Trail Smelter pollution case. The outcome was acceptance that no state has the right to permit use of its territory in such a way as to injure another territory. The 1972 UN Conference on the Human Environment in Stockholm was in part called for by Sweden, because of concern about acid deposition generated by other countries. In 1979 the Geneva Convention on Long-Range Transboundary Air Pollution addressed the problem of transboundary sulphur dioxide atmospheric emissions, but did not lay down firm rules. By the late 1980s the resolution of transboundary impacts had become an increasingly active field of diplomacy. The 1991 UN Economic Commission for Europe Convention on Environmental Impact Assessment in a Transboundary Context obliged signatory states to act to control transboundary environmental impacts from proposed activities.

Controls on Global Warming

The UN Framework Convention on Climate Change obliged signatories to stabilize CO2 emissions at 1990 levels by AD 2000. The 1997 Kyoto Conference was intended to settle details of CO2 reduction and to see that targets were enforced by international law. However, a coalition of USA industries was opposed to any limit on greenhouse gas emissions, and lobbied to hinder agreements. Finally agreements were made by the EU to make an 8 per cent cut in emissions by AD 2010 and arrangements for Tradeable Emissions Quotas (TEQs) were approved (with Russia able to sell its unused quotas to the USA).

Ozone Damage Controls

Efforts to phase out and if possible ban the use of CFCs were made at the 1985 Vienna Convention for the Protection of the Ozone Layer. The 1987 Montreal Protocol on Substances that Deplete the Ozone Layer—revised 1990—derives from the Vienna Convention. The protocol aimed for a 50 per cent cut in CFCs over a short period (24, mainly developed nations signed—by 1994 this had increased to 74, including some developing countries) and was signed in the face of considerable uncertainty about ozone damage. The protocol is a landmark, in that for the first time nations agreed to impose significant costs on their economies in order to protect the global environment. India and China held out, seeking agreement for funding to assist with ozone controls.

The Law of the Sea

In 1954 the International Convention for the Prevention of Pollution from Ships was undertaken to try to reduce the discharge of waste oil from oil-tankers and other ship-related discharges (with limited success). For ocean pollution control to be effective, agreements that cover rivers, effluent outfalls, air pollution, etc. are required, because pollutants arrive in the sea from such sources. In 1958 the First Conference on Law of the Sea took place (the second was in 1960), and in 1959 the

UN established the International Maritime Organization to deal with marine safety, law, pollution control, etc.

From the early 1970s some of the nations with coastlines began to declare extensions of their territorial waters from the accepted 3 to 12, or even 200 nautical miles. The 1950 Continental Shelf Convention was largely behind this trend towards extension of exclusive sovereign rights to continental shelf or seabed resources. To try to formalize these trends the Third Conference on Law of the Sea was held in 1974.

The UNEP's Regional Seas Programme has brought together coastal states of a number of marine regions, resulting in several Regional Seas Treaties, covering: the Mediterranean; the Gulf; West Africa; Southeast Pacific; Red Sea; Caribbean; East Africa; and the South Pacific. These treaties led to the development of Environmental Action Plans and then co-ordination to fight pollution, etc. In 1977 the North Sea ceased to be 'high seas' as far as fish and mineral exploitation were concerned, when the EC established zones laying claim to the continental shelf. A number of the regional seas, e.g. the North Sea, Japan's Inland Sea, the Baltic and the Mediterranean have been the subject of convention or treaty agreements in addition to the efforts of the UNEP to try to control pollution more effectively.

Meeting in Jamaica in 1982, the UN launched the Convention on the Law of the Sea (with agreements effective to 2500 m depth from the shore). Some developing countries are keen to see the oceans, like Antarctica, declared common heritage, rather than becoming de facto possessions of those countries with the wealth and technology to exploit the resources. There has been some progress, e.g.: the EU is developing a form of supranational legislation, and the UNEP argues that international law should deal with protecting the world's life support systems.

Alternative Dispute Resolution

Disputes about resource exploitation and environmental management can be addressed in a number of ways:

1. Through legal measures (judicial);
2. Through political measures;
3. Through administrative measures;
4. Through alternative dispute resolution measures (which may not use law).

Legal measures rely upon courts, litigation, protocols and procedures, etc. Political measures rely upon elected or established representatives to decide. Administrative measures can be used to improve resources and environmental management. Alternative dispute resolution can be through a range of measures, including:

- Negotiation;
- Mediation;
- Arbitration;
- Public consultation.

Environmental management legislation may specify the use of some of these measures, or they may be adopted voluntarily. Negotiation is a process whereby two or more groups agree to meet to explore solutions, in the hope of reaching consensus. Mediation is similar to negotiation, but involves a mutually accepted neutral third party who finds facts and tries to facilitate discussion. The mediator may act with groups that are unwilling to meet face to face, if need be 'filtering' the exchanges to help reach agreement. Arbitration involves a third party like mediation, but at the outset the parties involved agree to give the arbitrator power to make decisions (which may or may not be binding).

Chapter 4

Environmentalism and Social Science

ENVIRONMENTAL ECONOMICS

The products and by-products of environmentalist thought are all around us. The campaign literature of environmental groups is delivered to thousands of homes. Green slogans compete for our attention from the packages on supermarket shelves. Television programmes inform us about the threats of global warming, the intimate details of the lives of plants and animals, the deficiencies of government policies on energy and transport. The advertisements that interrupt those programmes try to entice us with green images. Bookshelves and catalogues display a bewildering array of environmental literature, from official reports to fictional adventures. Development projects are subjected to environmental assessments, companies and government departments to environmental audits, and the curricula of schools and colleges have been invaded by courses on environmental science, law, politics and management.

As the products of environmentalism have multiplied, so have the attempts to describe and understand it. My task in this is less daunting; it is to present an analysis of the analyses, or rather of some of them, in order to argue that an approach from the viewpoint of cultural theory is both possible and useful. This task is complex enough, however. In the 1970s, when public interest in environmental issues was beginning to have significant political impacts, the relevant body of social scientific literature was small and relatively easy to digest because it focused on a few key areas: changes in public values, the social bases of environmental concern and pressure group politics. In the mid-1990s it is enormous, diverse and extremely complex. The task of analysing it is made more difficult (but also more interesting) by the fact that the boundary between advocacy and analysis is often difficult to detect. In other words, social scientific studies of environmentalism cannot always be distinguished from literature advocating environmentalist points of view. This is to be expected, for several reasons.

First, ideas are refined and advanced through critical analysis, so anyone wishing to further environmentalist thought is likely to do so through an analysis of existing ideas. In this sense, authors who see themselves primarily as advocates have also to be analysts in order to substantiate their views and give them credibility. Second, social scientists who become interested in environmentalism are often motivated by their own concerns for the environment and a personal desire to contribute to environmental discourse. Thus some authors who regard themselves, or may be seen by others, primarily as analysts use their research to advance or defend particular environmentalist perspectives, or to suggest how environmentalist ideas might be made more practicable. Finally, in environmentalism we are dealing with a part of culture and, culture is both the object of our analyses and a phenomenon in whose creation we inevitably participate, even as we analyse it. In this sense it is impossible for analysts of culture, even if their motives are purely academic, not to contribute in some way to the development of the object being analysed.

In order to argue that cultural theory offers a distinctive way of analysing environmentalism, I need to compare it with other social scientific projects of the same kind; in other words, those analyses which have treated environmentalism itself as an object of study, and which have addressed questions about its nature. Sociology and political science have been the leading disciplines in this enterprise, and studies which fall within these fields form a central focus of discussion in this. But, the boundaries among the social sciences are, to say the least, blurred, and some of them become indistinguishable when the veneer of specialist terminologies is chipped away. In what follows, academic niches are not important. Having said this, there is one major field of analysis which should at least be mentioned if I am to avoid the accusation of having ignored much of what seems relevant: environmental economics, whose contribution to environmental discourse has received more public attention than those of the other social sciences.

Environmental economics is a rapidly growing field which encompasses several schools of thought, though it tends to be identified (as does economics in general) with the most influential of these, the neoclassical tradition. This approach is primarily concerned with ways of enabling environmental values to be taken into account in economic activity. This has meant exploring techniques for assigning measurable values to environmental benefits, such as clean air, unpolluted rivers, pleasant landscapes and wildlife, and incorporating them into costing and pricing procedures, such as cost-benefit analyses and fiscal practices. Some of these techniques were already being developed by the early 1970s, but they have come to public attention only during the past ten years or so, as ways of making industrial economies sustainable have become central to environmental discourse.

They have met with considerable criticism, not only from conservationists who have argued that environmental benefits are often seen as priceless, and that assigning monetary values to things such as pleasant landscapes and wildlife can only serve to undervalue them, but also from economists who have explored the limitations of the neoclassical model and argued that its valuation techniques are fundamentally unsound. In response to these criticisms, neoclassical environmental economists have pointed out that environmental goods are assigned implicit values in much of what we do, and that it is the failure to make these values explicit that has effectively undervalued the environment; things that are implicitly regarded as priceless are often treated as worthless in economic decision making.

Economists have been the most conspicuous social scientists to participate in environmental discourse because, on the whole, they have been the only ones to whom policy makers in industrial societies have been prepared to listen. Indeed, politicians throughout the industrial world have actively sought the advice of economists, while specialists in other disciplines have struggled to demonstrate the value of their skills. It is the quality that makes economics attractive to politicians which effectively makes it marginal to the discussion in this. Economics, as Simmons has pointed out, is about means rather than ends. Economists are technicians, who explain how goals might be achieved, while supposedly remaining indifferent to the goals themselves.

This indifference to goals makes economics a favoured political tool. Economists can be called upon to examine how pre-defined political goals might be achieved, in the knowledge that they will not question the goals themselves. Sociology and political science are unpopular with politicians for precisely the converse reason: their practitioners see it as their role to question, not only political goals, but also the values and assumptions from which those goals are derived. While sociology and political science (and, for similar reasons, cultural anthropology) are inherently subversive, economics, at least in its neoclassical form, cannot be.

Environmentalism is about goals as well as means; it is about protecting the environment through human activity. As the brief summary above indicates, economics can be (and has been) enlisted to examine how this goal might be achieved, to consider what its achievement might mean in practical terms, but it cannot provide an analysis of environmentalism itself, since this means examining the goals of environmentalism, the interpretations of reality from which those goals are derived, and, quite possibly, the perceptions which accompany environmentalist interpretations of the world. So while the contribution of economists to environmental discourse has been conspicuous, it has not enabled them to become theorists of environmentalism, since this is not the nature of their enquiry.

In fact the role of economics in environmental discourse is similar to that identified in the previous for anthropology, as the study of human ecology. This is not surprising, given that economy and ecology both embody the material relations between human beings and their environments, and that the two concepts have been virtually inseparable in the work of some anthropologists. It was suggested in the previous that, by studying the relationship between people's understanding of the world and the ecological impacts of their activities, it might be possible to assess whether or not particular cultural perspectives are ecologically sustainable.

Such knowledge could then be applied in a search for more sustainable ways of living. This kind of role for anthropology would be a technical one, which would help to establish whether the means for achieving a sustainable way of living were available, without examining the goal itself. It would thus parallel the role of environmental economics, which considers ways of achieving environmentalist goals through economic activity, but does not analyse those goals.

Environmentalism and Political Theory

When scientists encounter a new object, they try to establish its place in the order of things by assessing its characteristics in terms of what is known and familiar. Is it genuinely new or merely masquerading in new attire? Does it represent a new class of objects and, if so, is there perhaps more than one kind of it? How is it related to objects in the known universe? When environmentalism first gripped the public imagination in the 1960s and early 1970s, and when, contrary to the expectations of some analysts, it became clear that it was not going to go away, social scientists were faced with the problem of how to characterize it. Did it fit a known pattern of social events, or did it represent a genuinely new way of thinking and acting? Did it break the mould of traditional political allegiances or merely reproduce them in a new idiom? Was it an internally homogenous category, or was there more than one kind of environmentalism? The answers to these questions have formed the nexus of a debate within social science about the nature of environmentalism; they also set the agenda for the following discussion. The most pervasive points of argument in the debate have been the identification of two kinds of environmentalism, the status of environmentalism as a (new) social movement and as a political ideology, and the relationship of environmentalism to established cleavages in politics.

It appears that there have always been two environmentalisms, or at least since the beginning of this century when the battle of words between Muir and Pinchot, over the damming of a river in Yosemite National Park, laid the foundations of a split between the 'conservationists' and the 'preservationists'. While conservationists wished to protect nature as a resource for human use, preservationists recognized a moral obligation towards nature itself and wished to protect it from human use. This distinction was easy to recognize because it was played out in action-people took sides-but the current environmental debate, throughout its development during the past thirty years or so, appears to have been characterized by less distinct and more variable cleavages. The result is that, while analysts have continued to recognize two environmentalisms, they have not always been the same two.

The most pervasive distinction in the literature is between an environmentalism which can be accommodated within the structures of contemporary industrial society and one which demands fundamental change to those structures. In this sense it is useful to speak of the two environmentalisms as 'conservative' and 'radical'; it is the nature of the conservatism and radicalism that appears to shift, often in quite subtle ways, from one analytical perspective to another, or even within a single analysis. Cotgrove made a distinction between those environmentalists (including conservationists and preservationists) whose policies offer no challenge to the dominant economic value system, and those who would wish to replace economic goals with 'welfare values which are incompatible with or in conflict with purely economic ends'.

In this formulation, the distinction is between different evaluations of the economic vis-à-vis other kinds of value. But he also followed Kruse (1974) in describing the division between two environmentalisms in terms of evaluations of technology; a faith in human ability to overcome environmental problems as opposed to a conviction that human ingenuity is subject to limits imposed by nature.

He offered yet another variation, a distinction between environmentalists who preach an holistic message based on ecological principles, and those who advocate a 'piece-meal tinkering' with industrial processes to bring about environmental improvements. The former is revolutionary and millenarian, the latter is reformist. A later version of the distinction identifies 'catastrophists' as those who consider industrialization per se to be the cause of environmental breakdown, and 'cornucopians', who blame 'the exploitative and predatory nature of capitalism'. In each case, the distinction is between a more radical and a more conservative environmentalism, but the idiom in which the conservatism and radicalism are expressed changes from one formulation to the next.

Cotgrove's second formulation is similar to O'Riordan's distinction between the 'technocentric' and 'ecocentric' forms of environmentalism. Technocentrists have faith in technology and assume that humankind is in control. They may wish to make industrial society more environmentally benign, through changes in policy and practice, but they do not question the goals of industrial development, nor the values which drive it; they thus represent a conservative form of environmentalism. Ecocentrists see humankind as subject to, rather than in control of, nature. They preach humility towards the natural world and respect for its processes and products. The practical implications of this view include low-impact technology and self-reliance, which could not be achieved to any significant degree without a radical overhaul of the foundations of industrial society.

An important component of both Cotgrove's and O'Riordan's conceptualization of the division was the observation that people hold different understandings and evaluations of science. Sandbach brought this into focus by distinguishing between an environmentalism which seeks to influence economic and technological change by presenting scientific arguments based on the analysis of ecological systems, and one which questions whether science itself is compatible with humanistic values. But in this formulation, ecology seems to have changed sides. Both Cotgrove and O'Riordan observed that an holistic understanding of ecology was the inspiration for the more radical mode, whereas for Sandbach it formed the rational basis of conservative environmentalism.

This apparent contradiction shows how ecology, as a body of scientific knowledge, is amenable to different interpretations, and therefore plays a part in the pursuit of diverse, often contradictory, objectives. It is seen both as a route through which human management of the environment can be improved, and as the basis for an alternative vision of our relationship with the rest of the natural world. Just as the complex structure of the eye, for one analyst, proves the existence of a divine creator, and for another denies it, so a knowledge of ecology leads some to a greater faith in our ability to control natural processes, while for others, like Douglas Adams' 'Total Perspective Vortex', it creates a sense of our relative insignificance in the natural order.

The distinctions considered so far refer to environmentalism as it was understood by analysts before 1980. In more recent analyses the division into two environmentalisms has persisted, but the terminology used does not sit easily upon the earlier interpretations. Cotgrove, O'Riordan and Sandbach all referred explicitly to types of environmentalism. Dobson, rather confusingly in the context of this discussion, used the term 'environmentalism' to refer to just one side of the distinction; the more conservative mode, green with a small 'g', which assumes that the environment is a resource for human use, manageable through human ingenuity, and that environmental problems can therefore be solved 'without fundamental changes in present values or patterns of production and consumption'.

'Ecologism', the contrasting radical mode (Green with a capital 'G'), is based on the understanding that the environment has a value of its own, independent of its use to human beings. Our proper treatment of it therefore requires a fundamental change in the way we understand our relationship with nature; it requires us to see ourselves as one element in a complex ecological system, rather than as the centre of the universe. The logic of Dobson's terminology is clear. An environment is that which surrounds, 'and can exist... only in relation to what is surrounded'.

'Environmentalism' therefore only makes sense if we assume the existence of a centre. An ecosystem is viewed as if from without, as a complex of interacting organisms and other factors. An ecological perspective has no central focus, and it therefore makes little sense to refer to such a perspective as 'environmentalism'. However, despite its undeniable logic, Dobson's terminology has not been widely adopted, and most analysts continue to refer to kinds of environmentalism. The substance of his distinction, on the other hand, has been recognized by other analysts as the most important cleavage in current environmentalist thought. Eckersley characterized the two perspectives as 'anthropocentric' and 'ecocentric', respectively (1992).

There are both shifts and continuities in the way the two environmentalisms have been characterized by analysts over the past twenty years. The main continuity is in the distinction between a conservative and a radical environmentalism; this cleavage can be detected in each of the formulations discussed above. The main shift is in the definition of the radical perspective. In the earlier analyses, it is difficult to identify a unity underlying the various expressions of radical environmentalism, other than the fundamental nature of its challenge to industrial culture (in other words, its radicalism). In the later analyses, a more developed 'ecologism' (to use Dobson's term) or 'ecocentrism' (to use Eckersley's) has emerged. The significant cleavage is clearly identified as an opposition between a perspective which values the natural world in terms of its use to human beings, and one which sees it as having value independently of human use or, indeed, of human existence.

The most obvious explanation for this emergence is that it reflects a real trend in environmentalist thought, that the 'New Ecological Paradigm', which was undeveloped and unarticulated in the 1970s has, during the 1980s and early 1990s, become a coherent and well-defined ideology, partly through the work of environmentalist writers and ecophilosophers, and also through the work of analysts such as those discussed here, whose thoughts, as I have suggested, feed into and help to shape the object of their analyses.

It is possible to detect, in the recent analytical literature, suggestions of an alternative interpretation. Atkinson pointed out that the debate over the desire to adjust the relative importance of human beings and nature 'suffered from a lack of rootedness in social conditions and practice'. Norton suggested that the dichotomy between the two environmentalisms has been exaggerated by theorists and ecophilosophers. While acknowledging the long-standing presence of two distinct world views, he argued that those who openly and conspicuously espouse one or the other should be seen as 'idealized arguers', whose polarized perspectives are not reproduced in environmentalist policy and practice.

Instead, a consideration of what environmentalists want and do reveals a remarkable unity. Norton did not underestimate the importance of a common environmentalists' dilemma, that of how to sustain and advance a moralist perspective on nature in the face of economic and utilitarian arguments, but he pointed out that only some environmentalists opt for one or other horn of the dilemma; it does not, therefore, divide environmentalists into two exclusive camps. Many, perhaps most, experience it as an internal, personal quandary which influences, sometimes in one direction, sometimes the other, their everyday decisions.

Norton's analysis raises the question of whether the identification of a fundamental split between two environmentalisms, with a coherent ecocentric position emerging over the past ten years or so, represents a rather narrow characterization of environmentalism. The literature on the divisions in environmentalist thought clearly says something about environmentalism, but it does not say everything, and it may say very little, about the everyday experiences of environmental activists and policy makers. In fact, there is a huge number of empirically grounded analyses of environmental movements, groups, protests and debates, and, especially during the 1970s, studies of the social bases of environmental concern. But these have failed to influence the theoretical characterization of environmentalism and have, in turn, been little influenced by it. The gap noted by Lowe and Rudig, between empiricism and theorizing, still remains.

One reason for this gap may be that those writers who have emphasized the dichotomy between two environmentalisms have focused on environmentalist thought rather than environmentalist policy and practice. They have drawn their material from environmentalists' own accounts of the way they understand the world. Much of this literature is, itself, strongly analytical and therefore tends to interpret through categories and boundaries. Environmentalists, like other ideologists, have been keen to draw attention to the differences between their views and those of others, in order to establish the nature of the 'true' faith. Unless they pay attention to the empirical studies, analysts of environmentalism have no reason to suppose that the practice is significantly different from the theory.

Environmentalism as a Social Movement

The term 'social movement' designates the principal category into which social scientists have slotted the new phenomenon of environmentalism. As a prelude to examining how they have done this, it is helpful to consider briefly the relationship between objects and categories. When scientists of any variety allocate a new object to a familiar category, they do so as part of the process of investigating its place in the wider scheme of things, however that might be conceptualized.

The initial allocation is usually pro-visional; a close examination of the object may indicate that it would be better placed elsewhere. A set of broad categories thus forms an analytical framework within which the specific characteristics of objects can be examined and compared. But the categories themselves are not immutable; science leaves their boundaries open to question, and, to recall Bohannan's comment, one person's black box is another's field of investigation. It is the continuous examination of their contents that results in analytical categories being redefined. Categories and their contents are thus held perpetually (though not continually) in suspense.

This has been the pattern of social scientific studies of environmentalism as a social movement. Some analyses, probably the vast majority, have taken for granted the status of environmentalism as a social movement. They have used the category as a broad framework within which to examine the special features of environmentalism, such as its relationship with science and its global character, without questioning the boundaries of the category. Rudig et al. noted this tendency in British writing on social movements:

A notable feature of much of British writing is the frequent but perfunctory use of the term social movement without exploration of its potential connotations or efforts to set it into relevant theoretical or conceptual contexts. Typically it is undefined and is often used quite promiscuously.

This comment is presented as a criticism, and is valid as such in the context of their discussion of social movement theory. But in broader terms, every analysis needs to leave some concepts unquestioned. If everything were open to investigation, there would be no solid ground in which to anchor an interpretation, no way of tying it to a broader field of study. Thus, in two of the early empirical studies of environmentalism, Harry et al. (1969) and Devall (1970) used 'social movement' as nothing more than a convenient label. It served to locate the object of analysis within a broad typology of social phenomena, in order to relieve the reader of any concern about what kind of a thing was being discussed, and direct their attention to what most interested the analysts, in these instances, the social characteristics of conservationists.

In a similar way, McCormick referred to the phenomenon whose history he was describing as 'the global environmental movement', but paid no attention to the sense in which it might be called a movement. Numerous studies have used the label in a similar way to provide a context for analyses of environmentalism in different countries. The label signals that, in all these cases, something similar is being discussed, and that comparisons are therefore valid and possibly interesting, but suspends interest in how that broad something might itself be understood.

According to Yearley's (1994) analysis, this use of the category is more in line with the American interpretative tradition than that established in Europe. In the American tradition, 'social movement' is typically treated as an 'empirical generalization', recognized by its broad organizational features: 'more organized than protesting crowds or mobs, less formalized than political parties and more concerted than simple social trends'. European theorists have tended to identify social movements in terms of 'their perceived capacity for major social transformation', perceived, that is, by the analyst, who is drawn to search for signs of transformative capacity.

For Touraine, it is present when one class struggles against another for control of historical processes. For Melucci it is present when norms are contested and sources of power are challenged. For Eyerman and Jamison it resides in what they call 'cognitive praxis', an attempt to generate new knowledge through communicative action. A considerable amount of interpretation of observed reality is required in order to recognize any of these criteria, leaving no clear, non-arbitrary way of identifying social movements for analysis.

In addition, although it is the capacity to transform that defines a social movement, there is a tendency to regard as 'true' social movements only those which actually transform (there being no other proof of transformative capacity than actual transformation). In other words, true social movements can only be identified retrospectively, not only after a movement has been analysed, but also after its social consequences have become clear.

This effectively rules out the possibility of identifying a phenomenon as a social movement as it develops and as a framework in which to examine its special features. The European tradition, while it may have advanced our understanding of the role of social movements in a wider context, has therefore not produced the kinds of definitions which can form a useful framework for analysis. In a similar vein, Eyerman and Jamison made the observation that movements, by definition, are transitory, they live and die, and whatever innovations they introduce are either rejected or adopted by wider society. However reasonable this might appear, it could not be used as a criterion for identifying social movements empirically, unless we were to confine our studies to movements that had already died, and whose transitory nature was therefore confirmed.

Jamison et al. forged their own definition of social movements by combining transformational and organizational criteria, and in doing so claimed to bridge the divide between theorists in the European tradition, for whom social movements are sources of new collective identities, and those in the American tradition who see social movements as mechanisms for 'resource mobilization', and identify them empirically by their organizational features. However, their comparative analysis of environmentalism in Sweden, Denmark and Holland shows that their new composite definition is found wanting as an empirical tool. Environmentalism takes on different shapes in different countries, because environmentalists have to organize their activities according to the political context in which they operate.

The analysis showed that in Sweden environmentalism did not develop a distinctive oppositional character, for two main reasons. First, there are financial incentives for new organizations to formalize their structure along the lines of established political groups, with the result that 'the borders between the established and the oppositional are blurred'. Second, it is difficult for new political actors to loosen the grip on Swedish political culture, of the long-established cleavage between the socialist and bourgeois blocs. Instead, new interests tend to be incorporated into those of the existing blocs and promoted through their activities. As a result, in Sweden, 'environmentalism can hardly be called a social movement'. Thus, despite their declared intention to combine transformational and organizational criteria, the analysts fall back on the organizational when identifying social movements empirically. Although environmentalists in all three countries share the same collective identity, environmentalism in Sweden is less of a social movement because it does not possess the appropriate organizational features.

The distinction between organizational and transformational criteria is significant in relation to the perceived existence of two environmentalisms. Both the conservative and the radical forms (or indeed, in some cases, a single undifferentiated environmentalism) have been seen as displaying the organizational features of a social movement. But almost by definition, only the more radical form has the capacity to transform society, and so analysts who have understood social movements in this way have tended to restrict their use of the term to the more radical form. Thus Cotgrove who, quoting Banks, saw social movements as self-conscious attempts 'to introduce innovations into a social system', suggested that 'something more like a coherent movement emerges' if we focus only on the groups that fundamentally challenge dominant economic values. However, it would probably be more accurate to say that the transformative capacity of radical environmentalism has more often been seen as identifying it as a 'new' social movement. More will be said about this when discussing the relationship of environmentalism to established political allegiances.

Environmentalism as a Political Ideology

Social scientists have treated 'political ideology', like 'social movement', as a category within which to examine the distinctive features of environmentalism. Again, the term is left undefined and 'used quite promiscuously' by some analysts and subjected to quite close scrutiny by others, though this does not always yield a clear definition. Cotgrove, following Mannheim (1966), defined ideology as 'beliefs and values which are justifications for the status quo, the preservation of existing institutions and the interests which they serve'. As such, they contrast with environmentalist perspectives which he regarded as 'utopias', visions of a better society. And yet he also referred to environmentalist ideologies, and identified the function of an ideology as 'legitimating or justifying courses of action', regardless of whether the actions concerned support or oppose the status quo.

Dobson, following Donald and Hall, also defined ideology in terms of its function: political ideologies provide 'the concepts, categories, images and ideas by means of which people make sense of their social and political world, form projects, come to a certain consciousness of their place in that world and act in it'. In this sense, ideology fulfils both cognitive and practical functions; it enables people to understand the world and their place within it, and forms a basis for action. Paehlke provided a more purely substantive definition: an ideology is 'a worldview both value laden and comprehensive', but he also saw the practical component of ideology as definitive. His aim was to develop 'a political theory with ideological potential', a potential which he identified as lying in the ability of environmentalism to present an effective challenge to the dominant political order.

From these and other studies it is possible to identify three features of environmentalism which analysts have seen as signifying its status as a political ideology: its comprehensiveness, its coherence and its practical potential. The comprehensiveness of environmentalism lies in its ability to present a vision of a complete alternative society, a 'post-industrial' and 'sustainable' society. Not surprisingly, some analysts identify this feature only in the more radical form of environmentalism.

By definition, radical environmentalism rejects a managerial and piecemeal approach to environmental change and seeks a comprehensive overhaul of society's values and institutions. Thus for Dobson, 'ecologism' is an ideology, whereas the more conservative perspective (which he calls 'environmentalism') is not. Paehlke, however, made little of the radical/conservative distinction, and identified environmentalism in terms of a single though wide-ranging set of values. He observed that 'the opponents of environmentalism apparently saw its ideological potential before its advocates did', in that they recognized that the values espoused by environmental campaigners (respect for nature, a need to reduce waste) held far-reaching implications for social change.

The internal coherence of environmentalism has been examined at some length by Goodin (1992) who, though he did not identify environmentalism explicitly as a political ideology, analysed it in ways consistent with the concepts of ideology discussed above. For Goodin the distinction between conservative and radical environmentalism (expressed as 'shallow' and 'deep' ecology;) is less significant than the relationship between what environmentalists value and the kinds of actions they advocate. A theory of value implies a theory of agency, in the sense that what is seen as valuable should be protected through action. Goodin identified nature or 'naturalness' as the core environmentalist value. People value nature, he suggested, because it provides them with a context in which to set their own projects and activities and, in so doing, enables them to see some sense and pattern in their lives.

He argued that, although this theory of value has clear implications for the kinds of public policies that environmentalists might advocate, it does not necessarily hold implications for individual lifestyles. The need to see personal lives set in a larger context demands that the context itself (nature) be protected, but it also demands that personal lives be somehow distinguishable both from the larger context and from each other. It is therefore 'logically coherent', according to Goodin, for environmentalists to advocate policies which protect the natural world, while refusing to adopt a green personal lifestyle.

Goodin's analysis would seem to hold out some promise for the practical potential of environmentalism as a political ideology. Individuals are more likely to support environmentalist goals if they are not expected to give up their cherished patterns of activity. Not so Dobson's analysis which, in exploring the implications of radical ecologism, emphasizes the practical difficulties of pursuing 'Green' objectives in a society which appears receptive only to a more conservative 'green' message. He pointed out that in Britain, Green activists tend to speak with a green voice in order to make their message more palatable, with the result that the true voice of ecologism is not heard in public.

What Paehlke would call the 'ideological potential' of radical environmentalism is thus destroyed by the perceived need to compromise. In contrast, Paehlke's own analysis seems to suggest that some degree of accommodation between environmentalism and other political perspectives is necessary in order for the ideological potential of environmentalism to be fulfilled. Paehlke saw this potential in the ability of environmentalism to present a realistic alternative to 'neoconservatism', which he saw as the dominant ideology in Anglo-American democracies during the 1980s. The ability of environmentalism to achieve this, he suggested, depends to some degree on its relationship with other established perspectives in the political spectrum.

Environmentalism and the Political Spectrum

Social scientists have been interested in the relation of environmentalism to the established political ideologies for two main reasons. First, as part of a broader interpretation of social processes, they have considered its status as a 'new' social movement. 'Old' social movements are those derived from class politics, which reproduce the struggle between labour and capital. New social movements are those which take politics out of a class framework. Thus the women's movement and the peace movement are typically seen as 'new' social movements. Second, radical environmentalists have claimed that they offer a genuinely new political perspective, that breaks away from or transcends the old division between right and left. They claim that the similarities between the established ideologies of communism and capitalism are more significant than their differences and that the old order of right and left needs to be replaced by a new opposition of green against the old, grey politics of industrialism. Social scientists have considered the place of environmentalism on the political spectrum specifically in order to test this claim.

Analysts have presented at least four responses to the question of how environmentalism is related to the left-right spectrum in politics: that the division between left and right is not a useful analytical framework, that environmentalism's perceived place on the spectrum will vary according to the perspective of the perceiver, that environmentalism really does offer a genuinely new departure from the left-right spectrum, and that the division between left and right is actually reproduced within environmental politics.

Eckersley saw the main thrust of radical environmentalism as emancipatory, and suggested that ecocentrism can be seen as seeking 'emancipation writ large', in the sense that it allows all human and non-human entities to develop 'in their own way unhindered by the various forms of human domination'. Her analysis explores the place of ecocentrism within the broader field of emancipatory thought and, since contributors to this field 'cluster to the left' of the traditional political spectrum, she did not consider this spectrum to be a useful framework.

The value of the left-right spectrum as an analytical framework has also been questioned by others, on the grounds that there is no universal agreement on what is meant by left and right. Paehlke argued that a line between left and right, though it captures the popular perception of ideology, is not a particularly appropriate shape for depicting established political perspectives, in that it fails to acknowledge both the view that the extreme poles have much in common, and the deep rifts that divide apparently adjacent ideologies, such as communism and democratic socialism. Dobson pointed out that left and right may be taken to mean different things.

If the left is seen as favouring equality and the right as favouring hierarchy, then ecologism, which seeks a kind of equality among all beings, human and non-human, leans to the left. If, on the other hand, the right is seen as favouring minimal intervention, and the left as favouring the management of nature for the maximal benefit of all human beings, then ecologism, 'which is in principle averse to anything but the most timid engineering of the social and natural world' appears firmly on the right. It all depends how right and left are defined, and what criteria are used to identify environmentalism itself.

In view of these ambiguities, Dobson found it useful to distinguish between the left-right dichotomy and that between communism and capitalism. Environmentalist critics of established politics tend to treat these as more or less synonymous, arguing that environmentalism transcends the left-right spectrum though its attack on industrialism, as the basis of both capitalism and communism. By distinguishing the two pairs, Dobson showed how the 'Green' claim that capitalism and communism are similar in their environmental consequences is, from the perspective of the left, a right-wing view. By attacking industrialism, environmental politics is failing to confront capitalism, therefore helping to sustain it. From this left (socialist, rather than communist) viewpoint, ecologism belongs to the right. Paradoxically, from this perspective, the more conservative environmentalism identified by Cotgrove appears more left-wing. While the radical 'catastrophists' saw industrialism as the cause of the environmental crisis, the 'cornucopians' saw the greed of capitalism as the main problem.

The clearest indication of how environmentalism can be seen as a genuinely new departure from the established political spectrum is offered by Paehlke. Again, the way in which this spectrum is defined is crucial. Paehlke observed that traditional politics is about distribution-who receives what-and that interests are generally interpreted in these terms. The left-right spectrum, insofar as it is useful, represents a range of views about distribution. Environmentalists do not ignore distributive issues, but they give a higher priority to matters of technology-how resources are used and how our relationship with the rest of the natural world is organized. Thus, once environmentalism is included within the political spectrum, the distributive axis between left and right is no longer an adequate representation of that spectrum.

But Paehlke also made the point that, in order to fulfill its potential as a political ideology, and offer a realistic alternative to neoconservatism, environmentalism should break away from its 'neither left nor right' image, and be prepared to engage in distributive politics. In other words, environmentalism can only become an effective player in the political arena if it is seen to be concerned with the kinds of issues that have traditionally fuelled political debate in the industrial world. Such is the 'central tactical dilemma' that haunts environmentalists and undermines their aspirations to become an effective political force while remaining truly 'Green'.

Paehlke's analysis can be seen as having rather contradictory implications for the status of environmentalism as a new social movement. 'Old' social movements, which were concerned with the distribution of economic resources among classes, helped to establish the distributive character of political discourse. If environmentalism defines interests in terms other than distribution, and therefore appeals to social groups which are not differentiated along distributive lines, its status as a 'new' social movement, which takes politics out of a class framework, appears to be substantiated.

And yet it makes some sense to argue that it is not distribution itself that distinguishes old and new politics, but the question of what is being distributed. It could be argued that the new social movements-the women's movement, the peace movement, the environmental movement-are also about distribution, but not of material wealth. Instead, they seek to distribute access to power, rights and freedoms more equitably throughout the human and (in the case of environmentalism) non-human world. Seen in these terms, it is the economic basis of old politics that distinguishes it from the new, not its concern with distribution.

The observation that old and new social movements might be seen as sharing a concern with distributive issues would seem to lend weight to Scott's argument that, instead of transcending the left-right cleavage as some activists and analysts claim, environmental politics reproduces this division. Scott observed, for instance, that the German Green Party developed out of a number of citizens' initiatives with diverse ideologies and that left and right political perspectives had already crystallized within this movement by the time the

Party was launched in 1979. He went on to argue that this diversity is represented in environmentalism generally, because its supporters have drawn on existing ideologies in formulating their message. In consequence, environmentalism as a whole has been difficult to locate on the left-right spectrum precisely because the different points on that spectrum are reproduced within environmental politics.

Thus it is difficult to generalize about where analysts have placed environmentalism in relation to the established political spectrum. Perhaps all that can usefully be said is that it depends on a number of factors. For instance, it depends on what criteria are used to characterize both environmentalism and the established spectrum: whether they are seen in terms of a concern with distribution, with emancipation, or with intervention in natural processes. It also depends on whether the analyst is examining environmentalist ideas, assessing the practical potential of such ideas or analysing actual (if limited) political achievement. Once again, we seem to be faced with the reality that, the closer one comes to practical involvement in politics, the harder it is to sustain the claim that environmentalism offers something different.

Environmentalism in Anthropology

So far, this has concentrated on some of the frameworks employed by sociologists and political scientists to understand environmentalism. It is now appropriate to consider what anthropology has to offer. Several anthropologists have turned their attention to environmental issues in recent years, but the best-established and most consistent application of cultural theory in this field is presented in the work of Douglas and those who have used her ideas. Since this approach is widely known both within and outside the discipline, it provides an appropriate starting point from which to explore an anthropological approach to environmentalism.

Douglas' Theory of Culture

Expressed simply, Douglas' theory states that culture is determined by social organization. She used 'culture' to refer to people's understanding of the world-what they think, feel and know-in a manner comparable with that outlined as being typical of post-structuralist anthropology. 'Social organization' refers to the way people run their social relationships: the degree of freedom they accord each other and the level of constraint they impose, the patterns of authority they establish, the extent to which they act in groups or as individuals. Her approach thus conforms to the broad pattern established in post-structuralist anthropology. Culture, assumed to exist in people's minds, is distinguished from actions and patterns of behaviour (society, social structure, social organization) in order to focus on the relationship between them.

However, she differs from most other post-structuralist anthropologists in the way she conceptualized this relationship. Others saw the relationship between culture and social organization as dialectical, and set themselves the task of exploring the workings of the dialectic through human choice. Douglas saw it as deterministic, and thus appeared to deny the possibility of choice playing a role, though on this point, her work is ambiguous, as we shall see. For Douglas, a particular form of social organization gives rise directly to a particular way of understanding the world. The influence of Durkheim, which Douglas fully acknowledged, is clearly visible here, though she felt that 'Durkheim did not push his thoughts on the social determination of knowledge to their full and radical conclusion'. Douglas' approach to culture has been to explore the paths down which such thoughts lead. Environmentalism is just one of the many fields she has visited on the way.

One of the central pillars of Douglas' approach to culture is a model which defines forms of social organization in terms of two variables, which she called 'grid' and 'group'. 'Grid' represents the regulation of activity, 'group' represents the degree of social cohesiveness. Grid is high when people's actions are strictly controlled by authorities, and low when they are free to act as they please. Group is high when people show allegiance to collectivities, and low when they act primarily in their own interests. These two variables combine to produce diverse forms of social organization. High grid and high group produce a hierarchical form; freedom of action is tightly constrained from the centre, and activities are directed towards collective interests.

Low grid and low group produce a 'market' form of organization; people are free to act in their own interests and pursue personal gain. Low grid and high group produce an egalitarian or 'sectarian' form of organization; people pursue collective interests but do not tightly regulate each other's activities. High grid and low group produce a society in which people do not pursue collective interests, but also have no freedom of action to pursue their own interests. Although Douglas originally used this model to develop a loose typology of whole societies, she also recognized, as did others who have used her model, that the different forms of social organization might exist in combination in any one society.

The essence of Douglas' theory is that the different forms of social organization give rise to different ways of understanding the world, different cosmologies or, to use the term suggested, different 'cultural perspectives'. If a society is homogeneous in its organization it can be expected to hold a single cultural perspective; its whole culture will consist of one perspective. A society that embodies several forms of organization will be culturally heterogeneous; it will support and maintain a number of cultural perspectives. Douglas' theory makes connections between specific forms of organization and specific perspectives, through the following line of reasoning. The moral order-what people take to be right or wrong, appropriate or inappropriate-protects the social order-the existing form of social organization. The moral order is sanctioned through fears of dangers and threats-things that people assume will befall them if the moral order is violated. A simple illustration of this is the belief, held in many societies, that sexual misdemeanours, such as incest or adultery, cause the transgressors or members of their families to become ill and die; fear of the sanction protects the structure of the family.

There are many dangers about which societies and social groups could be concerned: illness, war, witchcraft, divine retribution, crime, environmental damage. But societies and groups tend not to be equally concerned about all these things; they tend to fear some more than others, and some not at all. Douglas' theory asserts that societies and groups select those fears which most closely reflect their social order, enabling people's fears and concerns to be explained in terms of their forms of social organization. In an entrepreneurial context, in which individuals compete for personal gain, the most feared dangers are likely to be the mechanisms through which individuals harm each other: witchcraft and sorcery, gossip, crime and litigation. Among the Cewa of Zambia, for instance, contests for political office were often accompanied by sorcery accusations, usually between close maternal kinsmen, among whom competition was most intense. In western liberal democracies, attempts to discredit opponents by revealing (or perhaps fabricating) financial or sexual misdemeanours have become a normal part of political life. Not surprisingly, some of the most successful entrepreneurs occupy roles which offer individuals protection against these threats, or retribution should their fears be realized: insurance and security companies, the legal profession, diviners and witch-doctors.

Hierarchists might be expected to worry most about losing their power and are therefore likely to promote fears which help to sustain that power. A hierarchical priesthood may invoke divine retribution as a threat to enforce continued submission to their authority. In traditional Australian Aboriginal societies, the continuation of life was seen as depending on the expertise of ritual elders, for only they knew how to perform the sacred ceremonies which guaranteed the supplies of essential resources. For other members of the population, an ever-present fear was that of incurring the anger of these elders, who could order the execution of those they considered guilty of sacrilege (violating sacred norms or objects), and who could withhold ritual knowledge from anyone whom, because of some misdemeanour, they considered unworthy to hold it, thereby blocking their access to power.

Douglas' theory establishes a category of phenomena in which environmental concern can be placed. Fear of pollution, resource depletion, species extinction and so on become, like other fears, mechanisms through which society protects its institutions. In this sense, concern about environmental pollution in industrial society is the functional equivalent of the fears of ritual pollution expressed in many other societies. They do the same job: they protect the moral order on whose fulfilment the continuation of social order depends.

Surprise Theory and the Myths of Nature

Douglas' grid-group model has been adopted by several analysts investigating the diversity of people's responses to environmental change. Ecologists have been found to conceptualize 'nature' in different ways: as robust, fragile, capricious or robust within limits. These four 'myths' of nature have been associated by the 'surprise theorists' with the forms of social organization described in Douglas' grid-group model and the cultural perspectives that Douglas has suggested are associated with those forms. Hierarchists (high grid-high group) believe nature to be robust within limits; egalitarians (also referred to as 'communards'), with a sectarian form of organization (low grid-high group), believe it to be fragile; entrepreneurs, who favour market organization (low grid-low group), see nature as robust; and fatalists (high grid-low group) see it as capricious.

Thus fatalists see little point in planning, since it is impossible to predict how the environment will respond. Entrepreneurs act on the understanding that, whatever they do, the environment will recover. They are thus free to pursue personal profit, unconstrained by worries about environmental consequences. Hierarchists, on the understanding that the environment will tolerate a certain amount of abuse but no more, urge caution and central control. Egalitarians worry that even the slightest additional burden placed on the environment might push it over the edge into inevitable decline.

These associations of forms of social organization with cultural perspectives and myths of nature are useful to the surprise theorists in enabling them to identify possible responses to environmental change. Douglas' summary of these responses is as clear as any:

> Supposing in the event nature turns out to be really ephemeral and the biosphere splits and slides away; then the communards will not be surprised. Saying 'We told you so' will be small comfort to themselves and to the surprise holders, in this case the entrepreneurs and the hierarchists. But supposing in the event nature turns out to be robust enough to take all the punishment we mete out to her. Then the surprise-holders will be the communards. They will find that they didn't need to reduce their style of life, that they have gained little while their opponents have made large fortunes. And so it goes on. The only people who will get no surprise are the fatalists because they made no bets.

In the surprise theorists' models, environmental dangers thus appear as those most likely to be feared by egalitarians (communards), which makes environmentalism a cultural perspective most likely to be associated with sectarian forms of social organization (low grid-high group), but also present (with a lesser sense of urgency) among hierarchically organized groups (high grid-high group). These accords closely with the observations made by Douglas and Wildavsky in their study of environmentalism in America.

Cultural Theory and American Environmentalism

Douglas and Wildavsky set out to explain why environmentalism became an important part of American culture during the 1960s and 1970s. They identified, in American society, three of the forms of social organization defined by the grid-group model; hierarchy, market and sect. Hierarchical and market forms of organization (characterized, respectively, as high grid-high group, and low gridlow group) are established central components of American society, while sectarian organization (characterized by low grid and high group) is more typical of the 'border' or, to use a more common term, the 'periphery'. Sectarian groups tend to develop in opposition to central institutions.

The chief characteristic of sects is that their membership is voluntary (low grid); they are held together by commitment to communal interests (high group). Douglas and Wildavsky suggested that the rise in environmental concern in America in the 1960s and 1970s was related to a growth in sectarian organization.

Sects sustain themselves by opposing the centre. Environmental concerns are an appropriate mechanism for doing this because they question the values and assumptions on which the continuation of hierarchical and market forms of organization depend, such as the supremacy of science and technology and confidence in established laws and procedures. By sustaining fear of pollution and other forms of ecological damage, environmental groups kept their members with them, so ensuring their own continuation: 'these ideas and these dangers respond to the problems of voluntary organization: they are the daily coinage of debate in groups that are trying to hold their members without coercion or overt leadership'. Environmentalism thus developed as a means whereby sects, groups held together by voluntary association, sustained themselves; an environmentalist perspective was produced or determined by this form of social organization.

Douglas and Wildavsky recognized that, rather than explaining the rise of environmentalism in America, this argument merely shifted the focus of the enquiry. If environmentalism developed in order to sustain sectarian groups, the central question becomes, why did this form of social organization become important in America in the 1960s and 1970s? The analysts answer this question by pointing to historical and technological factors that helped to shape post-war American society. For instance, the broadening of access to higher education, together with the development of labour-saving technology, produced a large number of educated people for whom industry had no room. This surplus fed the development of the service sector, which, they suggested, is less tolerant than industry, both of hierarchical control and of the pursuit of individual gain. Faith in individualism as a guiding principle was undermined by the exposure of social injustice, particularly racism, and faith in the bases of central authority was shaken by events such as the Vietnam War and Watergate.

As well as relating environmentalism in general terms to the spread of sectarian organization, Douglas and Wildavsky drew attention to the fact that some environmental groups are more sectarian than others. They pointed out that the older, well-established conservation organizations, such as the Sierra Club and the National Audubon Society, tend towards hierarchy. David Brower, as Director of the Sierra Club during the 1950s and 1960s, involved the organization in several large-scale campaigns against environmentally damaging developments, with two significant consequences: the membership of the Club grew from 7,000 to 77,000, and its tax-exempt charitable status was withdrawn by the Internal Revenue Service. The resulting split in the Club's leadership led to Brower's resignation as Director. Shortly afterwards he became a founder member of Friends of the Earth, which was organized along less hierarchical lines and adopted more sectarian principles.

Although my purpose here is to argue that cultural theory can provide a complementary understanding of environmentalism to those offered by social and political theory, it would be misleading to suggest that there is no overlap among these fields. Some of the studies conducted by sociologists and political scientists have much in common with an anthropological approach. There is a striking similarity between some of the analytical concepts used by social and political theorists and those used by anthropologists.

Take another look at Donald and Hall's description, quoted by Dobson, of the functional character of ideology: 'the concepts, categories, images and ideas by means of which people make sense of their social and political world, form projects, come to a certain consciousness of their place in that world and act in it'. If the phrase 'social and political' were removed, it would become an acceptable description of what many anthropologists in recent decades have understood by culture. Paehlke's understanding of ideology as a comprehensive, value laden world view is also close to what anthropologists would call a cultural perspective. Eyerman and Jamison's concept of 'cognitive praxis', the generation of knowledge through communicative action, which they see as the essential feature of social movements, is similar to the way in which anthropologists view the process of cultural change, which they assume to be going on all the time in all social contexts.

It is not surprising, then, that the insights provided by social and political analyses of environmentalism appear similar in some ways to those provided by Douglas' cultural approach. For instance, in describing the rise of sectarian organization in America, and relating it to the emergence of environmental concern, Douglas and Wildavsky, it could be said, effectively presented an account of environmentalism as a social movement. Their interpretation appears similar to that of Jamison et al. who, by examining how environmentalists organize their activities in different political circumstances, also pointed to the conditions under which environmentalism might become a social movement.

But the similarities are only superficial, for an important element in Douglas and Wildavsky's framework, that cultural perspectives (or ideologies, or world views) are caused by forms of social organization, is not shared by the social and political analyses. Thus for Jamison et al., specific conditions lead people, who are already concerned about the environment, to organize their activities in certain ways, but for Douglas and Wildavsky it is the organizational form that generates environmental concern, that turns people into environmentalists. As indicated above, it is this causal or deterministic element that sets Douglas apart from most post-structuralist anthropologists and which is seen by many as the main difficulty with her approach to culture. I shall return to this point in the next section.

There is also some similarity between Douglas and Wildavsky's framework and the social problems approach which Yearley used to analyse the development of environmentalism in Britain. Both share the assumption that public concern for an issue is generated and sustained, not by 'objectively' existing conditions, but as a result of claims made by groups and individuals. Yearley showed, for instance, how the Royal Society for the Protection of Birds (RSPB), throughout the hundred years of its existence, has generated and sustained public sympathy for birds by drawing attention to the problems they face. The problems have changed over the years. Concern for the impact of the plumage trade was replaced by concern for the impact of egg collecting, of pesticides, of the live-bird trade, of afforestation in Scotland and deforestation in the tropics. What has remained constant is the fact that it has been the efforts of the group that have kept public concern alive. However, while Douglas' theory of culture would lead us to assume that the RSPB did this for the purpose of sustaining itself, Yearley made no such assumption. This difference highlights a second major difficulty with Douglas' approach to culture, as the discussion in the next section will show.

Used Douglas' model as an illustration of how cultural theory has been used in the analysis of environmentalism, but I would not wish to argue that her approach to culture is the most appropriate. In fact, there are contradictions in it which make it impossible to swallow whole, and it is important to identify these in order to be able to select from it what is valuable. The most controversial feature of Douglas' theory is the assertion that forms of social organization cause or determine cultural perspectives. Determinism was seen as one of the major evils of the various structuralist approaches in anthropology and which post-structuralist anthropologists sought to leave behind. The main problem with determinism is that it appears to deny the possibility of choice and therefore of change, since change is assumed, in post-structuralist approaches, to result from people choosing to act or think differently.

Like the structural-functionalists before her, Douglas denied that her model precluded change, and indeed used it to interpret changing situations, such as the rise in American environmentalism. But in doing so, she contravened the logic of her theory. The theory states that cultural perspectives change as a result of changes in social organization. In other words, the social change is prior to, and causes, the change in culture. Social change, in turn, is the result of new conditions. For instance, the emergence of a highly educated sector of American society with no role in industry provided the conditions in which a sectarian form of social organization could flourish. But how did the increase in sectarian organization actually take place? According to Douglas and Wildavsky's analysis, it happened when people lost faith in existing institutions. In other words, the social change, the rise in sectarian organization, depended on a prior cultural change, a loss of faith in existing social forms.

It is also clear from their analysis that Douglas and Wildavsky did not intend to deny the possibility of choice. In fact, choice is presented as playing a pivotal role in the generation of both cultural perspectives and forms of social organization: 'people select their awareness of certain dangers to conform with a specific way of life'; 'the selection of dangers and the choice of social organization run hand in hand'. Sectarian organization is founded on choice-the voluntary association of people in groups which persuade (not compel) their membership to remain with them.

Thus, the hard determinism of Douglas' theory of culture appears to give way, in the analysis of American environmentalism, to a softer, more flexible representation of the relationship between social organization and culture, in which choice is central to the generation of cultural perspectives and social forms. Once choice is admitted into the interpretation, several specific questions arise which are not directly addressed by Douglas and Wildavsky's analysis. Why, for instance, do people choose one form of social organization in favour of another? Why sectarian organization was considered an appropriate alternative to the established institutions in which faith had been lost? And once sects had been 'selected', why were environmental threats considered more appropriate than other kinds of danger as a mechanism for holding them together?

In stating that social organization determines culture, Douglas' theory implies that culture determines (or defines) reality. Indeed, her views are often taken to be typical of what I have described as the more moderate form of cultural constructivism: the view that culture imposes meaning on an otherwise meaningless world. For Douglas, the source of meaning is society itself. The content of cultural perspectives is determined, not by what exists in the 'real' world, but by the form of social organization they are required to sustain. People's knowledge of what constitutes dirt, for instance, or of what is or is not edible, or of animal categories, is generated by their social structure. There is no room here for knowledge to arise from any source other than society, for people to discover things about the world that are not derived from their social conditioning; no room for direct perception.

This is the logical entailment of the view that knowledge is socially determined, and yet Douglas' own analyses, again, seem to deny this logic. The 'real' world, unconstructed by society, is assumed to enter human consciousness: 'The perils of nuclear wastes and carcinogenic chemicals are not figments of the imagination'. It would not be possible to say this without assuming that we have access to a world independent of cultural construction, that not all knowledge is socially determined. The same point can be illustrated using Douglas' analysis of the dietary laws listed in the Old Testament. Pigs, among other species, were not allowed to be eaten because they were seen as unclean. The reason for this, according to Douglas, was that they only possess one of the features which identified animals as edible-they have cloven feet, but they do not chew the cud. Thus, pigs straddle the boundary between cloven-footed, cud-chewing (and therefore edible) animals and the rest. The prohibition against eating pork served to protect these cultural categories. But whatever the social function of these categories and the rules that protect them, the categories themselves, as Douglas has acknowledged in her more recent work are defined on the basis of empirical observation. People first had to observe the ways in which pigs differ from other animals before they could select these criteria as socially significant. People cannot select from a meaningless reality; knowledge of the world as meaningful is a precondition for whatever influence social organization might exert on our cultural understanding.

Notwithstanding the inconsistencies and contradictions discussed above, Douglas' theory states that social organization will always be the prime mover in cultural change. The implication of this for environmentalism as a cultural perspective is that it exists to serve the purpose of generating or sustaining some organizational form. Like most functionalist explanations, this model appears to make some sense in some situations, but is clearly denied by others, which leads us to be highly sceptical about its general explanatory value. It is possible to envisage an environmental organization whose participants, in order to perpetuate the group, select and promote those concerns that appear most likely to keep their members with them. But there are also many environmental groups that are created in response to specific problems and then disperse once opposition becomes either futile or unnecessary.

Given Douglas and Wildavsky's argument that environmental concerns are appropriate for sustaining sectarian forms of organization, it is ironic that the groups which seem the most likely to perpetuate themselves are those that tend towards hierarchy. A large organization with central facilities, established political connections and many paid employees is much less easily dismantled than an informal group with little established political or economic commitment. Indeed, some form of hierarchical organization seems to be implied in the idea that fears are selected and promoted for social purposes, for such an enterprise, in order to work, surely needs both activists and an attentive following.

The only alternative interpretation consistent with Douglas' theory is that each environmentally concerned individual is 'really' worried about something else; that environmentalism is an expression of some more fundamental and more significant fear about society and is not, as environmentalists themselves believe, about the physical threats posed by polluted air and water, or the loss of valued landscapes and species. Anthropologists used to explain witchcraft and sorcery and other apparently 'irrational' beliefs in much the same way, by arguing that they were really expressions of something else, inevitably something that made more sense in terms of the anthropologists' own cultural perspective. One of the most important advances of post-structuralist anthropology has been that we no longer consider it our role to legislate on what counts as reality for the people whose cultures we study.

What is the purpose of all this theorizing? Why have social scientists been concerned to classify environmentalism as a social movement, an ideology or a cultural perspective? These categories constitute part of the social scientist's known and familiar world into which the new and unfamiliar needs to be slotted if it is to be understood. Establishing the status of environmentalism as a social movement is seen as increasing our understanding of it because we know, more or less, what a social movement is; we have certain expectations of it. If environmentalism can be shown to fit into this category, then we can reasonably expect the same things of environmentalism. This approach is one of the principal ways in which scientific knowledge of the world is assumed to advance. But it carries an inherent and inescapable limitation: the understanding of what is new and unfamiliar is restricted by what is already known. Most scientists, social or otherwise, will have experienced the frustration of this limitation at an individual level; the feeling that their own knowledge is not adequate to make sense of their data, the frantic search through the literature, the mining of other scholars' knowledge, in order to extend the boundaries of their own familiar world, in the hope of turning up a more satisfactory approach or explanation.

The reason why social scientists call for interdisciplinary approaches to the environment or any other issue is because they recognize that this limitation also exists at the level of whole disciplines. Although the boundaries between disciplines are hazy, each is nevertheless a product of its own tradition. Anthropology developed as the study of 'other' cultures with non-industrial, mostly land-based economies whose members live in small communities. Anthropologists consequently have an elaborate array of concepts for discussing economic exchange, kinship relations, ritual and so on, but they are ill equipped to discuss large-scale economic and social processes. Sociology and political science, on the other hand, have tended to focus on social and political processes that operate within and between contemporary industrial states. This bias is revealed in the call for 'internationally comparative and interdisciplinary approaches' to the environment. To an anthropologist, the assumption that nations will be the appropriate units of comparison seems restrictive, and an interdisciplinary approach based on this assumption would threaten to exclude anthropology, in which nations have never been as significant as cultures, societies or communities.

The question of whether or not an interdisciplinary approach to environmental issues is a realistic option will be considered in the final. For the moment, my purpose is to indicate what understand by an anthropological approach to environmentalism, in order to define the parametres for the analysis presented in the following. Although Douglas' model is seen by some outside the discipline as providing the anthropological slant on environmentalism, it does not represent a consensus among anthropologists and, as we have seen, there are serious problems with it, but it also demonstrates what I regard as one of the main strengths of a cultural approach.

Explanation and Interpretation

The Durkheimian influence in Douglas' theory of culture makes it, in part, a survival from a previous era of anthropological thought. The battle against causal theories in anthropology was fought during the 1960s and 1970s. The assumption that social and cultural phenomena are somehow causally linked to each other belonged to the old structuralist and functionalist models which the 'revolution' in anthropology sought to overthrow. As explained, the purpose of narrowing down the concept of culture and confining it to what people hold in their minds was to open up the possibility of examining how it is related to people's activities and forms of social organization.

It was precisely because many anthropologists considered a causal model inadequate for understanding this relationship that the shift in thinking occurred. Social and cultural systems, once treated as machine-like entities composed of functioning parts, came to be seen as the emergent products of human activity, 'the statistical outcome of multiple individual choices'. The central importance of choice in this new paradigm made causality an inappropriate analytical concept. Choices are made, it was assumed, in order that goals might be achieved and not because certain conditions prevail.

The abandonment of causality had a significant effect on the way anthropology is viewed by its practitioners. In the early part of this century it had struggled, alongside other social sciences, to establish its status as an explanatory and predictive discipline. The assumption that cultural phenomena have causes-be they environmental, as in some of the models discussed, or social, as in Douglas' model-enabled anthropologists to claim that, by identifying those causes, they were explaining culture in some final and definitive sense. Once the concept of choice became central to analyses of culture, anthropologists felt less able to claim that those analyses produced definitive explanations.

This was not because a concept of choice is incompatible with explanation, but because the task of explaining how a cultural feature is generated and sustained becomes so much more complex once choice is involved. Countless individual decisions contribute to the processes that sustain any one cultural feature, and many analysts feel uncomfortable generalizing about something as variable as human choice. Anthropologists have not given up the effort to explain cultural features, and some regard this as their ultimate goal, but since the 1970s many have seen their task as interpretative rather than explanatory.

Their role has been to reveal how cultural perspectives make sense, by showing how they are related to the activities of those who hold them, and how their various components-assumptions, values, norms, goals-relate to one another.

As indicated, many anthropologists would also dissent from Douglas' model in another way. For Douglas, social organization was primary and cultural perspectives the secondary products of social forces. Many anthropologists would see the relationship between the cultural and the social as dialectic.

What people know, think and feel forms a basis for their social activities, and these activities generate experiences which both sustain and modify their cultural perspectives. I have taken this formula as the starting point for developing a model of culture appropriate for exploring anthropology's contribution to environmental discourse.

But, a departure from it. I argued that culture does not relate only to people's social activities and does not, therefore, consist only of what they learn through their interaction with others. Instead, it consists of all the meanings through which we understand the world, whether they are communicated to us by others or discovered through our active engagement with our surroundings (in the process referred to as 'direct perception'). It is partly because we acquire some of our culture outside social contexts that it makes little sense, in my view, to regard our understanding of reality as being 'socially constructed'.

This model makes culture the mechanism through which we interact with our environment. It also allows for the possibility (which the constructivist model logically does not) that individuals from very different social backgrounds might come to understand their environments in quite similar ways. This is important for examining environmentalism as a perspective that can be shared and communicated beyond the confines of what anthropologists have called cultures. It acknowledges that, in a world in which communication transcends the boundaries of communities, societies and nations, perspectives can effectively become 'transcultural'.

A great deal of social scientific analysis proceeds through comparison: the characteristics of social and cultural phenomena are identified by comparing them, and the factors that generate and affect them are isolated by comparing the contexts in which they occur.

In such analyses, categories such as 'social movement' and 'political ideology' have the role of defining the limits of comparison. By defining environmentalism as a social movement, we are stating that it is valid to compare it with other social movements.

Through this comparison, our understanding of environmentalism itself and social movements in general is assumed to advance. One of the most striking features of anthropological analyses, which sets them apart from those of other social scientists, is the breadth of material on which they draw for comparison. Instead of comparing, say, political processes in (more or less) similar nation states, an anthropologist is more likely to draw on ethnographies of distant communities in Africa or New Guinea to elucidate what is happening in contemporary Europe or America. These points to what I see as one of the most significant insights provided by Douglas' model and cultural approaches in general. For Douglas, ritual pollution and environmental pollution are phenomena of the same kind. It makes sense, therefore, to ask whether they are generated by similar forces or play similar roles in human society. While not sharing her deterministic assumptions, I applaud the breadth of vision that makes such comparisons possible.

If environmentalism is identified, for the purpose of studying it, as a social movement or a political ideology, we are precluded from considering what else it might be, how else a concern to protect the environment might be expressed. Our analysis is constrained by what we know about social movements and ideologies.

If environmentalism is identified as a cultural perspective, we can ask under what conditions it might be expressed as a social movement or an ideology. These phenomena are seen as types of environmentalism, or forms it might take. Of course, the analysis is still constrained-it is the purpose of a theoretical perspective to constrain analysis-but it is constrained by different parametres. It is shaped by our understanding of culture, which is universal in human experience, rather than our understanding of social movements or political ideologies, which are less widely distributed.

If culture in its general sense is the mechanism through which we interact with our environment, then specific cultures and cultural perspectives can be treated as distinct forms of this relationship, and environmentalism as one such form. In other words, environmentalism is one of many ecological alternatives employed by people-it is a basis for interacting with the environment-and we can advance our understanding of it as such by isolating its essential cultural features. The established anthropological technique for doing this is cross-cultural comparison.

Just as treating environmentalism as a social movement provides a basis for its comparison with other social movements, so treating it as a cultural perspective enables us to compare it with other cultural perspectives, in order to identify more closely its distinguishing features. I suggest that, in the broad spectrum of cultural perspectives, there will be some that are overtly environmentalist in character, others that are capable of accommodating environmental concerns, and yet others that effectively exclude or are hostile to such concerns.

If we can determine which is which, and why, then we might go some way towards understanding what constitutes environmentalism; which particular assumptions and values make it a legitimate and practicable way of understanding the world. This is the task for the next, in which the environmentalist credentials of a range of cultural perspectives are examined and compared.

Chapter 5

Environment in the Third World

The environment in developing countries is said to be under threat, and this is certainly true: nature and humans are equally endangered creatures in those countries. Lack of sanitation has polluted water and soil and jeopardized people's lives in all poor areas of the globe. It is estimated that 75 per cent of the world's population lacks basic sanitation, and that 57 per cent has no access to clean water. This unhealthy situation has serious consequences for both the physical environment and population health, since WHO believes that 80 per cent of disease cases—cholera, typhoid, hepatitis, leprosy, typhus, trachoma, schistosomiasis—in the Third World is caused by impure water and poor sanitation. As part of the same environmental problem connected with human settlements, housing conditions of seventeen Third World countries have been surveyed by researchers from the International Institute for Environment. They found that both housing and land tenure conditions of poor people are getting worse since Habitat. An expressive example of this is seen in India and Nigeria, where over half of urban families live in one-room shelters.

In Asia, Africa and Latin America, landless peasants use the soil up to the point of its exhaustion and erosion. Another way people cause soil erosion and fertility loss is through clearance of forests, which happens mainly due to shifting cultivation or removal of wood for either energy purposes or grazing. GEMS monitoring data show that, from 1976 to 1980, closed forest removal yearly reached the amount of 1.3 million hectares in Africa, 4.1 million hectares in the Americas and 1.8 million hectares in Asia, with even worse projections for Latin America alone in the period 1981-85. Equally gloomy are the data concerning open forests in those continents.

Erosion, loss of fertility and desertification are replacing forests in developing countries at the rate of 20 million hectares yearly; in South America, Africa and Asia, 82 per cent of the soils already presents serious limitations for agriculture. This situation resulted in 450 million people—of whom 200 million are children—being chronically underfed in those places during the seventies, and life expectancy at birth in developing countries is still 55.1 years.

Poor education and lack of both economic and technological means for survival could explain the main causes of the Third World's environment degradation. However, this actually constitutes only one third of the picture.

Second causes for environmental damage are local government policies. Developing countries are given incentives to emulate patterns of development from industrialized countries, to look for a higher GNP and to spend more on technology than on satisfying human and social needs. An example of this bias is seen in the enormous investments made by poor countries like Brazil, Ecuador, Colombia, Nepal, Philippines, Pakistan, India and Egypt in building up gigantic hydrodams and manmade lakes. Receiving approval and loans from both developed countries and development aid agencies to fulfill their projects, those countries have cleared forests, destroyed genetic species, created conditions for the development of disease vectors and may have triggered unforeseeable conditions for global climate change. Besides these consequences, a financial commitment is contracted by those governments against society's will; nevertheless, society will have to pay for the debts, even though it was not given the chance to choose the kind of investment it would prefer.

Another aspect of the perverse economic policy of local governments (pressed by international development aid agencies and foreign banks) is the emphasis on the export of goods, even if, as a result, this action inflates internal prices and generates hunger. An example of such a policy can be observed first of all in Brazil, which exported all its 1982 production of maize and beans, which are the basic food of the low-income population. Another example is cow raising in Central America and Colombia to feed North Americans. Another facet of the same environmental problem caused by overemphasizing export of local products are the cases of unfair exploitation of wood and mineral resources by multinational companies from Europe, the United States and Japan, which now replace the old colonizing metropolises. The third factor of environmental degradation in the Third World is external, represented by policies of specific rich countries and international organizations.

Developed countries usually impose severe restrictions concerning industrial pollution in order to clean up their environment and protect their people's health; thus, polluting factories are relocated in developing countries. For instance, the European Economic Community (EEC) suggests that European polluting industries be transferred to developing countries, the Japanese aluminum industry has been relocated abroad, the petroleum refinery industry found a haven in Indonesia, and asbestos factories have been installed by the United States in Mexico and Brazil.

Accepting this transfer of polluting industries would imply agreement with a new form of unfair international division of labour, where developed countries host "clean" research and industry, while the Third World hosts all the industrial pollution. Brazil, as a typical developing country, has been producing and importing pollution, in spite of aspiring to a better environment. In this contradiction lies the core of its main environmental disruptions, which have been identified in interviews with environmental managers throughout the country:

- The problems concerned with the social environment are the most acute, mainly in relation to sanitary and housing conditions, public health, distribution of wealth and basic education.
- Fresh water pollution is a widespread problem, caused by domestic, industrial and agricultural waste, while atmospheric pollution affects only big industrial centres.
- All regions to a greater or lesser extent have been affected by land misuse problems associated with either agriculture or urbanization.
- There is a conflict between the central government's ambition for Brazil's short-term development and the ecological concern of both environmental agencies and the population.

Those problems still persist and have accrued by the magnified dimension of socioeconomic problems of the population, resulting from the economic policy long since adopted by the authoritarian government that has ruled Brazil from 1964 through a sequence of five military presidents.Except for political control, which is not a feature of the Indian government anymore, the above environmental problems of Brazil may be compared to those of India, if one takes as reference the gloomy but humane view presented by the Centre for Science and Environment in The State of India's Environment, 1982.

The main difference is that Brazil leans toward the industrialized world, leaving unsolved the problems of the hungry masses, while India is becoming viable through its own cultural model of development. Although those problems have a local colour and so demand a local approach, it is important to realize that many of those malaises seem to be common to most Third World countries. This can be inferred from the regional seminars organized by UNEP, in cooperation with UN regional economic commissions in 1979 and 1980, to analyze development patterns. Some of those common environmental problems to be tackled are:

- Economic limitations, such as poverty, inequalities in the distribution of wealth, unemployment and underemployment;
- Health and sanitation insufficiency, such as endemic diseases, malnutrition and lack of both safe water supply and waste disposal facilities;
- Problems associated with urban and industrial development, such as rapid urbanization, poor housing conditions, various forms of pollution (industrial and agricultural), insufficient energy and transport inefficiency;
- Land-use malpractice, such as wildlife destruction, deforestation and related problems like erosion and desert encroachment;
- Consequences of adopting Western capitalist life and development style, such as overexploitation of resources by transnational companies, external dependence and loss of cultural identity.

Although innumerable projects of environmental interest are being implemented in most of the Third World countries individually—on their own initiative or that of UNEP or of any other international organization—the interchange of knowledge and experience among Third World countries to solve common problems is not yet the usual pattern. However, as their common problems have been identified, developing countries should now combine efforts in research, exchange of relevant information, organization of educational programmes and various forms of technical cooperation in order to find their own model for sustainable development leading to appropriate solutions for their problems. The Third World nations are not insensitive to the environment, and their concern is manifested both through governmental actions to prevent and to control pollution and through public awareness of ecological matters. In the following pages these manifestations will be analyzed with respect to environmental information, in aspects such as:

- Legislation as the basis of national environmental policy;
- The media's role in raising public consciousness;
- Educational programmes leading both to the formation of ecologically minded citizens and to the advancement and communication of specialized knowledge.

Formal systems of environmental information will be dealt with separately. Governments of different countries, starting from the most technologically advanced, have responded to public manifestations against environmental nuisances by setting up a central environmental agency, by creating and enforcing legislation, and also by establishing quality standards, all equally important measures in the control of pollution. The first two of these measures have already been adopted by most of the developing countries. However, up to now only a minority has established its own standards, because this measure would require technological knowledge and a basic amount of equipment not possessed by the bulk of the Third World countries. Some others among them have just utilized alien models, but by adopting foreign standards they are frequently misled into imposing a too severe control upon emission, which is likely to discourage industrial expansion, so much welcomed by most of the developing countries. This contradiction suggests that some conflicts between developmental strategies and environmental policies still remain.

Usually, the first wave of legislation passed to prevent or to abate pollution in any country comes as part of a sanitary legislation package. This is why legislation about water pollution—the earliest to be developed as part of sanitation measures—is more voluminous and advanced. Nevertheless, the first comprehensive legislation on water pollution is North American, enforced in 1948. In the same line, Mexico adopted, in 1973, its Regulation to Prevent and Control Water Contamination, which was amended in 1975. India, in 1974, passed the Water Act, which is still in force.

The control of atmospheric pollution comes after that of clean water. England was the pioneer in air pollution control as a result of its earlier industrial development. In 1863, as part of the Alkali Act, the country got its first legislation about air pollution and industrial effluents. At the beginning of the fifties more strict control became necessary to abate London fog, and the Clean Air Act of 1956 was passed and later amended. Among developing countries it seems that India awoke earliest to the problem of air pollution, establishing its control through the Indian Motor Vehicle Act of 1939, via the adoption of a series of measures related to industrial pollution control (such as the Indian Boiler's Act of 1923) and finally through the Air (Prevention and Control of Pollution) Act of 1981.

The problems of solid waste disposal and noise abatement are quite recent in legislation. The United Kingdom Litter Act was the first legal control of solid waste in England, followed later by new legislation on the disposal of generic solid waste and specific waste, such as industrial and poisonous wastes. In the Third World, the central control of solid waste disposal is not yet frequently legislated under specific acts, but is integrated with either sanitary or industrial legislation. Nevertheless, the Brazilian government, through the Ministry of the Interior, passed the Solid Waste Edict no. 053 in 1979. In Egypt, as in other countries, solid waste is controlled at the municipal level.

English legislation about noise started with the Noise Abatement Act of 1960, one of the earliest in developed countries. In most developing countries, noise is either not yet considered a problem or its control is left to municipal authorities, as it is in the case of Egypt. Brazil, which adopted Edict MINTER 092/ 1980; India, with its Noise and Nuisance Act; and Mexico, that passed in 1976 the Federal Regulation for the Prevention and Control of Environmental Contamination by Noise, are the few exceptions having a national regulation, even though the control is loosely performed by local authorities.

Although very late in industrial development, many Third World countries have already adopted specific legislation to prevent and to control industrial pollution. Among developing countries the concern of the Indian government for the effects of some chemical products upon human health should be highlighted. This concern can be observed from India's adoption of the following regulations: the Poison Act of 1919, the Prevention of Food Adulteration Act of 1954, the Drugs (Amendment) Rules of 1964 and the Insecticides Act of 1914 (updated in 1968 and 1969). Egyptian Act no. 509/ 1954 also falls within the same orientation.

Another interesting facet of developing countries is the incorporation of environmental ethics in their political Constitutions. Examples of this incorporation are found in the Mexican Constitution (art. 27) and the Indian Constitution (arts. 48 and 51a), where the main framework for natural resources management is outlined.

Although developed and developing countries had started some kind of pollution control many years ago, a comprehensive view of environmental pollution is really an issue of the seventies, when those countries passed inclusive legislation and established their national environmental agencies, following recommendations of the Stockholm conference.

Among developed countries, the beginning of the seventies showed West Germany (1970), France (1971), Japan (1971), England (1974) and the United States (1974) establishing their institutional structure for national environmental control.

As far as the Third World is concerned, W. Bassow, referring to a survey performed by the World Environment Centre of New York, unveils that, by 1980, 102 developing countries already had some kind of environmental agency, in contrast with only 11 in 1972. Some of those countries have created fully fledged ministries to deal with environment, as in Indonesia, Gabon, Ivory Coast, Upper Volta, Malaysia and Jordan. In other developing countries, environmental agencies have been embodied by either a secretariat, department, committee, bureau, board or council. Among the countries that have adopted this latter approach are Brazil, Mexico, Egypt, Ghana, Zaire, Uruguay, Oman, Iran, Thailand and Korea. India has a Department of Environment with the status of a ministry. Malaysia (1974), Iran (1974), Thailand (1975), Korea (1977), Indonesia (1981), Brazil (1981), Mexico (1982) and Oman (1982) constitute quite good examples of developing countries that have already approved comprehensive legislation on environment.

In a superficial analysis of the bulk of environmental legislation in the Third World—focusing mainly on Brazil, India, Mexico and Egypt-some facts show up: there are many gaps in the subject range covered; developmental policies conflict with environmental enactments; legislation toward natural resources conservation is quite voluminous; institutional control is sometimes duplicated because it is scattered under different authorities; and legislation neither keeps pace with national evolution nor reflects local culture. On the other hand, environmental authorities in developing countries recognize that legislation does not suffice, since they find it difficult to implement it because of lack of funds, technology and trained personnel.

Those drawbacks met by developing countries in the implementation of legislation result from characteristic underdevelopment scarcity which could easily be resolved if cooperation and interchange among nations were real and founded on a more just basis. In order to get all nations into the spirit of such a mutual assistance, the concept of "only one Earth" should also be reconsidered through an inward view: in spite of being artificially divided into countries, the Earth is a unity, essentially indivisible, if one considers vigilant concern for life as the guiding principle of international ethics.

It is not possible to approach Third World advances toward environmental consciousness outside the international context since the ecological movement tends to be universal. Besides, in this concern, as in many other aspects, the Third

World started later and has just followed the track of industrialized countries, sometimes being directly advised by foreign organizations or consultants.

The environmental movement presents two distinct phases according to the predominant interest in each period: first, the conservation of natural resources and, later, the struggle against pollution. From the end of the nineteenth century up to the early sixties, it was not really a popular movement, even in rich countries. There was concern by individuals and small groups, but the concern was directed only to the conservation of natural resources, including their protection and restoration. G. H. Siehl reminds us that most of the major conservation organizations active today were founded in the late 1800s and early 1900s, such as the Sierra Club, the Audubon Society, the U.S.

National Parks Association, the Society of American Foresters and the International Association of Game, Fish and Conservation Commissioners. Some other organizations, such as the Civilian Conservation Corps, Friends of the Earth and Resources for the Future were founded later. Besides their efforts in defending the environment, conservation organizations have played a major part in educating the public to the importance of protecting the environment, and quite certainly they may be acknowledged for preparing the actual environmental movement, which started in the 1960s.

The passage from a purely conservationist attitude to an antipollution cry is said to have been provoked by R. Carson's Silent Spring in 1962. The emotional style she used to denounce the pollution of rivers and land by chemical pesticides alarmed the public, which increased its participation, both directly and through pressure on the government, to maintain vigilance on environmental issues. The danger of pollution and other environmental threats then became a popular subject among scientists, too.

The conservation organizations, which previously concentrated on the only objective of natural resources, broadened their interest to include the quality of the environment. Pressure groups have been created to fight specific problems. Different segments of the adult population have been sensitized. Youth expressed its concern about nature through the philosophy of the "hippie" movement. So, by the end of the sixties and early seventies the control of environmental pollution was already a sensitive subject with a very political content.

This has happened in both developed and developing nations. Examples of NGOs undertaking the responsibility for public information and education in the developing world can be observed in India, where over 100 of such organizations are active in the field of the environment. In Indonesia there are 400 such organizations. The most traditional environmental NGO in Brazil is Fundacao Brasileira para a Conservacao da Natureza (FBCN). The Environment Liaison Centre (ELC) in Nairobi has played a catalytic role in relation to the Third World NGOs, besides having taken some initiatives on its own in the fields of environmental education and information.

A particular case in Brazil is the strong presence of the Catholic Church in defending both the natural and the social environment. On the whole, the part played by the Church in the ecological movement consists of educating and alerting the population about threats to human rights, which includes the right to a better quality of life.

In some countries, like West Germany, England and France, the people have established an ecological party, which has been influential in government decisions. In Brazil, during the campaign for 1982 elections, some politicians characterized themselves as the "green candidates" and the most representative parties—PDS, the government party and PMDB, the main opposition party—included ecological concern in their platforms. The same movement was observed in the 1980 elections in India, when politicians incorporated environmental concerns in their programmes as an answer to the efforts of the Indian Department of Environment, which promoted the sensitization of politicians by publishing a book – Environment: The Choice Before Us.

In the United States, the Environmental Protection Act of 1970 provides for public participation in the protection of the environment. Many actions have since been taken by the EPA and similar agencies, as for instance, the Citizen Awareness/ Information Exchange Programme under the Federal Water Pollution Control Act Amendments (FWPCAA), the Inform and Involve Programme (Forest Service), the creation of EPA's Office of Public Awareness and the different task forces incapsulated in many environmental programmes."

In the same way, most governorates of Egypt have combined to create an advisory Environmental Committee, which includes members from both government and the public, the latter being represented by NGOS. This Committee advises local government in the identification and solution of problems that affect people.In countries such as Indonesia and India, the national environmental agency, working with environmental study centres or different kinds of NGOS, stresses community awareness in their programmes. In Egypt as well, the Ministry of Public Information is supposed to be preparing a programme to heighten environmental consciousness in the population.

Although public awareness on environmental matters is a reality in every country, social scientists are still investigating the kind of participation people have in ecological movements, and they are also surveying people willing to participate. Thus, J. F. Wohlwill reviews previous research on the sociopolitical content of environmental attitudes. The results of these previous research studies, plus J. F. Wohlwill's own findings and the observations made by W. W. Hines and G. E. Willeke, indicate that environmental concern cuts across different segments of our society, although it has been found more strongly correlated with the following socioeconomic characteristics:

1. Income: the upper-middle class people, who tend to have higher income, are more likely to join the

environmental movement, as long as it does not threaten their right to land and home ownership.

2. Education: a characteristic of the defenders of the environment is a good education, at either an average or a high level. They are also well informed through literature and the media.
3. Political preference: the environmental attitude has been associated with sociopolitical liberalism, for instance, the Democratic Party in the United States (as opposed to the Republican Party).
4. Social group: Ecological sympathy, as a manifestation of social group, is possibly more closely related to the dominant group than to racial minorities.

It seems that the above findings can be applied to developing countries as well. So, both C. E. Lins da Silva observing Brazil and R. Claxton observing South America as a whole come equally to the conclusion that ecological concern in those places is restricted to elites in the affluent middle class.

These comments could be extended to explain by analogy why the concern about the environment is an attitude more frequent in developed countries. In backward countries, natural resources are considered a commodity to be used in order to survive and possibly to reach development, their main goal. Where the protection of nature has to compete with alleviating hunger and oppression, it is understandable that the environmental movement is not so popular or it evolves slowly.

Considering the important role media can play in raising the population's ecological consciousness, some environmental agencies of developing countries—like Pakistan in 1979—have prepared special seminars and workshops on environmental awareness for journalists and other media personnel. Media have actually played an important part in educating and alerting the population against pollution risk and in voicing people's opinions and complaints about the quality of life they experience. It happens in both developed and developing countries, as concluded by C. E. Lins da Silva when analyzing North American and Brazilian contexts. He understands that newspapers have had an important political role in alerting the population to environmental issues, but he suggests that they should also catalyze society's efforts toward the attainment of solutions for environmental problems. More specifically, W. W. Hines and G. E. Willeke show television as the most active medium in the environmental mission, followed by newspapers, the latter being important for people of higher education and social class.

Television has proved to be an important medium to reach mass population through ecological messages in the Third World as well. In Brazil, from the late seventies on, news and documentaries on environmental topics have been shown on TV; even soap operas have assimilated the ecological motif. Mexican television (both governmental and commercial channels) presented in 1982 sixty programmes on sanitary education prepared by the Secretaria de Salubridad y Asistencia, besides many others on the TV stations' own initiative. A daily ecological news bulletin is now programmed for TELEVISA (the private Mexican channel) in cooperation with the Subsecretaria de Mejoramiento del Ambiente.

Preparation and distribution of short films on environmental topics for TV is also an important activity performed by the film divisions of the governments of India, Bangladesh, Philippines and Pakistan. Similar to TV is the power of radio among poor people. Thus, the Voice of Kenya, in collaboration with the Kenyan National Secretariat for the Environment, presented a series of radio programmes on various aspects of the environment. In Mexico, a daily radio programme advises the population about community development. In Brazil even novels have discussed the environmental debate, as is the case of Tieta do Agreste, by the popular writer Jorge Amado, which approaches the pollution problem in Bahia.

J. W. Parlour and S. Schatzow investigated the role of the Canadian mass media (newspapers, magazines, TV and radio programmes) in communicating news and in changing people's attitudes in relation to the physical environment from 1960 to 1972. These authors concluded that media played a very important part in that concern, mainly in the period between 1968 and 1971. Besides alerting the population, the Canadian media had the merit of getting the political recognition and the institutionalization of environmental concerns at all levels of the political system.

Similarly, J. S. Bowman analyzed eight leading American mass circulation magazines from 1960 to 1979 and found that six out of eight devoted an increasing attention to ecological subjects. The author suggests that magazines could be the ideal media – in periodicity and style-to give a sustainable coverage to environmental issues.

The power of media in changing governmental policies was apparent in India, when public pressure through the media caused authorities to reconsider projects like the Silent Valley hydroelectric plant in Kerala and the industrial complex of Mathura, which was likely to damage the Taj Mahal.

The argument against generation and use of nuclear energy, a constant theme of the media, was the subject of two important movies: in the cinema, through The China Syndrome, and on TV, through The Day After. On the musical scene, the suite Minamata, by Toshiko Akioshi, echoes complaints made by Japanese fishermen against the mercury poisoning of water in that town. In Brazilian popular music, a few good examples of ecological themes may be mentioned: Aguas de Marco, by Tom Jobim, Baleias, by Roberto Carlos, Asa Branca, by Luiz Gonzaga, and O Reino Encantado da Natureza Contra O Rei do Mal, the official tune of the Salgueiro samba school, written by Ivan Jorge for the 1979 carnival in Rio de Janeiro.

So varied are the problems and manifestations that, if one looks through newspapers or any publication that advertises public events in any metropolis of the world, one is certain to find either a demonstration or a meeting to protest against the armaments race, the installation of a nuclear power plant, the transport or burial of nuclear waste, the poisoning of water, land or air or some other kind of environmental threat.

All these observations show that, as the lay people become better informed about the causes and consequences of pollution, they begin to participate in the debate and are prepared to take action in defence of a better quality of human life compatible with respect for nature. That is why both environmental education and environmental information systems have such an important role in developing countries.

As far as environmental education is concerned, since 1976 and even more intensively after Tbilisi Conference, UNEP has been working with UNESCO to implement pilot projects in developing areas—Egypt, Kenya, Indonesia, India, Thailand and Latin America among others-aimed at either formal students or staff training. UNEP also helps governments in the preparation of regional seminars to orient teachers and school supervisors, as it did for Latin America in 1979. The same help is granted by UNESCO in the training of specialists, as it happened in Brazil, India, Argentina, Cuba, Philippines and Senegal.

Third World governments also have organized their own programmes for both formal and informal education. So, some Asian countries-for example, Sri Lanka and Pakistan—have included environmental topics in the curriculum of primary schools. In central African countries, primary education, as well as secondary education, includes environmental matters, following the orientation of the African Curriculum Organization. Many Asian universities and research centres have introduced environmental education programmes in their activities, for instance, in Thailand, Philippines and Indonesia. Also in the Philippines the important policy of teaching nonconventional energy technologies at secondary schools prevails. In Indonesia, priority is given to the specialization of university lecturers and government officials.

In Brazil, attempts have been made to introduce environmental education at primary and secondary levels, mainly by changing the focus of approach of conventional subjects. At Brazilian universities, environment is taught through either Master's courses (ecology, environmental engineering, and so on) or as a specific discipline. The Universidade de Brasflia (UnB) has been the first one to introduce a Master's course in ecology.

Environmental engineering is also part of all sanitary engineering courses. Workshops and seminars for the public are often prepared by universities. The Brazilian Secretariat of the Environment (SEMA) endeavours to assist all levels of environmental education and to prepare some special audio-visual materials as teaching help, mainly at primary and secondary levels. Most of SEMA's actions in this area—research, teachers' training, courses and so on—are performed in conjunction with state governments or other organizations.

The Mexican government considers education as fundamental for the success of environmental programmes. That is why the Secretaria de Educación Publica decided to integrate ecological concepts in the existing programmes and disciplines at all levels of formal education, always taking into account the real economic, social and cultural needs of the country. According to this approach at both primary and secondary levels, environmental education is emphasized in disciplines connected with natural and social sciences, technological and health education, discussed from the viewpoint of the community interest.

In higher education, the broad objective of Mexican policy is still related to forming positive ecological attitudes in future professionals in both social and technological careers. However, at this level, specific courses of environmental interest exist at the Universidad Nacional Autónoma de México (UNAM) (environmental engineering, hydrological engineering, biochemical engineering, chemical engineering and marine sciences), at the Universidad Autónoma Metropolitana (ecology, environmental engineering, biology and chemistry) and at the Instituto Politécnico Nacional.

At the Master's level, the environment constitutes a specialization in four Mexican universities, while at the Universidad Nacional Autónoma de México environment is the object of a Ph.D. programme.

Regarding informal education, the Subsecretaria de Mejoramiento del Ambiente established and is implementing a programme of ecological training divided into three phases: emotional appeal, enhancement of concern and information for self-reliance of the whole population.

In India, emphasis is first of all given to primary education, where students analyze their own living environment and the importance of nature conservation to human beings. In order to select topics, to guide teachers in the use of appropriate teaching methods and to prepare educational material (books, audio-visual materials, special kits and so on), the Department of Environment works closely with the National Council of Educational Research and Training. At a higher level, many universities have already created courses on environmental sciences. Jawaharlal Nehru University (JNU), entirely funded by Indian government, maintains courses at the postgraduate level at the School of Environmental Sciences, taught by an interdisciplinary group of highstandard professors and researchers, who have behind them the support of a good library, macro- and microcomputers for bibliographic and scientific research and well-equipped laboratories.

In Egypt, policy and orientation for environmental education are provided for by the National Board of Environmental Education, part of the National Academy of Scientific Research and Technology. The general system of education, at the basic level, offers students short lessons about their living environment, and at the university level, students are encouraged to take disciplines of environmental content. There are ten universities in Egypt and all of them have at least one course on sanitary engineering and another on public health medicine. At the High Institute of Public Health in Alexandria, both the Environmental Health Department and the Occupational Health Department offer diploma, Master's and Ph.D. courses. Research at Egyptian universities is mainly funded by sources from the United States, where most of the scientists are also trained. Germany has also cooperated by offering equipment.

From the above described panorama of environmental education in the Third World—especially from what happens in Brazil, Mexico, India and Egypt—one realizes that most of the burden of formal education lies on governmental structure and funds; some foreign cooperation exists for research support and high level qualification of manpower only; NGOs are deeply involved in the work concerning informal education of the population; and industries are not willing to cooperate with either government or universities for the promotion of environmental education and research.

Information and education together have the potential to lead the population to care for nature, since they are the basis for public awareness and for changes in attitudes. This is the reason to believe that all the above actions concerning environmental education and information indicate that developing nations—governments and society—are progressively becoming conscious of their environmental problems. On the other hand, thanks to the media, NGOs and even to official environmental agencies, the populations in those countries have slowly realized they have duties and rights in regard to a clean environment. In spite of the remaining economic and sociopolitical hindrances, environmentalism within Third World societies evolves into an enduring concern, and this move cannot be reversed.

In addition to this process of the environmental awakening of the Third World, it has been evidenced that information is a strategic element for nations to reach environmentally sound development. But, like a vicious circle, the existence of an environmental information system in developing countries is determined by factors inherent in the characteristics of underdevelopment.

Environmental Information Systems in Developing Countries

Economy and sociology of development are still evolving and there is neither a conclusive definition nor a universally accepted interpretation of underdevelopment, as one can deduce from R. H. Chilcote's review. Having this argument in mind and avoiding playing the expert, this attempts to identify—from living experience rather than from theory—some key variables to understand the connections between underdevelopment and environmental information.

Taking this personal approach to underdevelopment, two groups of political and socioeconomic factors, can strongly influence the design, implementation and management of government environmental information systems in developing nations. These determinants derive partially from the very nature of society of backward countries, that is, from their underdevelopment. There are some basic features of underdevelopment—focused on in the next section—which are common to all developing countries and likely to interfere with the quality and sometimes with the very existence of an official environmental information system. Some of those features (for example, bureaucratization) are not peculiar to underdeveloped countries. However, in combination with the other factors of underdevelopment they are more likely to be a drawback to the existence of information systems than when they occur in advanced countries.

The other group of intervening factors that will be discussed in this results from the environmental policy adopted by a government in the management of its natural resources and in the control of pollution. Three basic kinds of policies of environmental ideologies can be adopted: conservationist, ecodevelopmental or technocratic. Each of these lines considers the environment from a different perspective. The focus and concern officially given to the management of the environment will determine the level of priority given to an environmental information system. Since the users of such a system would be principally authorities in environmental agencies, governmental policy would be a strong indicator of the type of demands for data and services placed upon the information system.

The identification of some of these two groups of factors has been tried, and the result is exhibited concisely. In this respect, the factors discussed hereafter should be seen not as overriding influences but as tendencies that in any case will confirm the sensitive character of an environmental information system and its political role in a developing country.

The status and characteristics of underdevelopment affect every single area of planning, including that of information systems.

H. Bernstein sees development as resulting from a desire to overcome malnutrition, poverty and disease and embracing such features of social justice as equality of opportunity, full employment, generally available social services, equitable distribution of income and basic political freedoms. H. Bernstein comments that this scenario embodies a value judgment concerning society's needs, which suggests the principle of self-determination as a right of developing countries.

His statement is an indirect description of the syndrome of underdevelopment, which the poor nations strive to overcome. Some indication of these problems can be gained by examining the features of underdevelopment, which are relevant factors in the life cycle of an environmental information system.

The first factor—poverty—can be expressed both through shortage of capital as far as government finance is concerned and paucity of per capita output. According to P. Baran, these are the two main characteristics of backward countries and account for their designation as underdeveloped.

As far as information systems are concerned, the main implication of poverty, in both its facets, is that information is not a priority at all. Poor countries have to struggle for survival, and their scarce resources are allocated to basic areas, such as health, agriculture, education, transportation and the implementation of industries. As a consequence, the entire information process, from its generation to the internal dissemination and exchange among the agencies, is seen as a luxury and either kept at an inadequate level—quantitatively or qualitatively—or not embarked upon at all. Collecting and processing local data are problematical and unsatisfactory as the result of deficiencies in equipment and personnel.

Attempts to access foreign information meet technological barriers (like obsolete computers or inadequate communication systems) and financial restrictions (such as devaluation of local currency at the international financial market, balance of payments, reimbursement of royalties and strict financial legislation concerning importation). Last, salaries are low and do not attract professionals from the environmental sciences to work as information scientists.

The second characteristic of underdevelopment is what the structuralists call a "dualistic economy," resulting from the penetration of modern capitalistic enterprises into archaic structures. According to C. Furtado, it is likely to produce a hybrid structure, part tending to behave as a capitalist system, part perpetuating the features of the previously existing system.

It is worth mentioning that the concept of dualism is rejected by authors like L. Pereira and A. G. Frank, who prefer to explain underdevelopment through either a historic or a more dynamic approach. Disregarding theoretical discrepancies among specialists, dualism has been included in the present with the intention of emphasizing the contrasting faces of the socioeconomic reality of developing countries. These faces correspond to different stages of the history (either evolution or involution) of different regions or cultural groups, which coexist with unequal shares of benefits and opportunities within the same country. Regardless of terminology, this idea expresses the level of development characterized by L. C. Bresser Pereira as "industrialised underdevelopment." The exogen and endogen causes of such inequalities, as well as strategies for their elimination, are important matters still waiting for practical solutions.

Duality is reflected on the information scene by the fact that there are often just two kinds of services: either the "grass roots" information of a practical character for some specific groups of workers or the scientific and technological information for the elites. An example of the first is the dissemination of agricultural information for rural workers, usually conducted at the instigation of, and with help from, FAO. The second—scientific and technological information for research workers—is more prestigious and receives a better share of scarce resources. This happens partially because of its elitist characteristics and links with the international scientific community.

A further reason is that, in the eyes of government, information for research workers indirectly supports technological advancement, a goal usually set in development programmes. Unfortunately, most of the scientific and technological research follows the lines of developed countries in order to satisfy demands of the higher layers of society in developing nations. These higher layers of society have a pattern of consumption that resembles that of developed countries, which is a feature of dependency, as discussed by C. Furtado. Thus, society as a whole does not benefit from scientific and technological research and local science and technology do not reach their autonomy.

Information support from government is often given to the scientific community by supplying them with either foreign "models" (patents, processes and so on) or theoretical information to tackle specific problems on a short-term basis. This narrow focus may be explained by the existing tendency in developing countries not to invest in long-term research programmes, usually because they are pressured by immediate needs.

This leads to the consideration of the third factor, which is the existence in developing countries of a technological inadequacy or inviability (called technological "gap" by the analysts from developed countries). Lack of resources, information and freedom cause developing countries to select and to use a technology that is not often the most convenient to their own needs or to their local environment. This impasse leads developing countries to a kind of technological inviability, followed by perplexity upon realizing that local problems need local solutions. To make this situation even more complex, poverty and inefficacy of communication interfere in the exchange with other countries within the Third World. This inadequacy sometimes affects the process of information transfer, noticeably in electronics (data processing and communication), transport and micrographics.

Sharing information resources among organizations within the same country is a big problem where long distances cannot be overcome by good communication and transportation systems. This same barrier is found when trying to access international networks or database systems if the appropriate communication technology is not available. Poor countries face with concern the prospect of a paperless society, like that foreseen by F. Lancaster, as they are not technologically prepared to participate in this progress. Far behind in being self-sufficient, they have no money to import the necessary technology from abroad, and yet they could not survive without information generated in the advanced countries. New technology invented by developed countries for their own practical purposes and economic reasons creates enormous problems for developing countries.

One of the options presented to the Third World is the adoption of alternative technologies more suitable to their present conditions. However, as seen by D. S. Price, the adoption of intermediate technologies would probably mean a return to the traditional printing stage as the West goes paperless, a return to mechanical processes while the developed countries take advantage of electronics and holography. Obviously, these options very often do not satisfy developing countries either. It is sometimes believed that intermediate technologies are merely methods promoted by developed countries to divert the more backward countries from full development. The adoption of alternative information technology would not solve the problem, however, if foreign information was presented in a higher technological form because developing countries would not be able to integrate with an international network to "decode" the information they could get.

The question of scientific information and the technology necessary to its processing in developing countries has therefore the same socioeconomic and political components as the whole subject of development itself. P. Baran points out the existence of a vast unproductive bureaucracy and a military establishment as typical handicaps of backward countries, and that they are among the principal obstacles to their economic growth. When developing countries are ruled by a military government, a frequent situation, the result is military red tape in official organizations and services. Just as this factor obstructs general development, so it also negatively influences the promotion of information systems:

A huge amount of resources is wasted in these redundant institutions to the detriment of the productive sectors of the country.

An excessive hierarchization slows the administration and the decision-making process hinders communication between different levels within the same organization and among different ones. A further problem for information systems is that, in such governments, they are usually placed at a low hie archical level. Military beliefs and attitudes promoted by the central government make very rigid and illiberal. Because defence is overemphasized by a military government, excess secrecy obstructs the free flow of information.

An internal struggle for power among civil organizations and between civil and military organizations results in gaps and overlaps in the areas to be covered, in loss of authority and in discontinuance of the system or service question. As far as information is concerned, there is a tendency for son "fashionable" subareas to be covered by a number of institutions while others receive no attention at all.

Linked to the above is the fact that development programmes are, in practice, contingent upon a number of other factors. As a result of these contingencies, some government programmes never come to be reality; others are interrupted, with a waste of effort and resources. Both internal and foreign pressures are responsible for these contingencies along with incompetence of authorities, absence of long-range planning and lack of resources. In such conditions, the stability of an environment information system will depend on:

- The convictions of the ruling group in the central government about the value of formal information;
- The position given to information in general and to the specific subject-environment—in the main plan of government and government's short-range goals toward development;
- How highly assessed is this specific sector supported by the information system, both by the internal and international market; and

Approval granted by foreign creditors and political controllers. The sixth factor control of information media-is a part of the political scenario within which the movement to development occurs. All means to bring information and education to the population are under certain kinds of control by both national government and foreign bodies, the latter being represented by foreign government agencies (including intelligence services), transnational companies, political groups and supranational organizations. Nation government itself operates through a system of either direct or indirect censorship, since it is usually very sensitive to criticism, does not believe in the public's capacity for participation and values excessive secrecy about official plans and data.

Government secrecy affects the transfer of information to the local population and to foreign governments. Not only are newspapers, radio and television affected, but the printing industry also is affected, mainly as concerns publishing in the area of the social sciences (books and periodicals). In addition to censorship, government may control the media by imposing severe economic constraints, like limitation of credit and obstacles to importing equipment and material. Both forms of control upon the media are highlighted by P. Marconi, who uncovers the history of the Brazilian press in the period 1968-78, and by W. A. Rugh, who discusses the Arab press.

Foreign influence in the control of information channels is part of a broader politico-economic domination of the poor by wealthy countries. So, it is manifested through both politico-ideological control and economic measures. Control may be exercised over the government, a specific national group or economic area or directly over the population. Thus, funding may be offered to a project or withdrawn from it according to the circumstance, depending on the interest of the specific foreign group or country at the time. Political ideology is disseminated in reading material and conferences on the grounds of foreign cooperation in the national programme of education. Public opinion is frequently misled by campaigns carried through the media by foreign economic groups interested in starting a business in the country, which would despoil the environment as a result.

Another facet of the international control of information channels is represented by the international news agencies. Rare and powerless are these agencies in developing countries; only from 1978 on have some of them joined the Yugoslavian Tanjub in a pool of nonaligned countries. So, news is transmitted to the world via international agencies, which tend to select maliciously the news to be published or distort the message received from local correspondents. This unfair situation has been the object of attention from UNESCO, which produced the MacBride Report, defending a new international order of communication and information. A more direct analysis of the transnational news agencies is presented by F. Reyes Matta.

Government control over environmental information may become even tighter because, overall, the subject area deals with the knowledge of existing natural resources, the performance of industries and the health condition of the population. National governments try to hide this kind of information from the local public to avoid pressures and from other governments in order to preserve national sovereignty. Foreign governments, however, do their best to obtain this key information so that they may achieve domination of the political scene and have a hold on the economic potential of the observed country. Despite the vigilance of developing countries, data on their natural environment can be collected and processed with more accuracy by developed countries, thanks to the higher technology owned by the latter; for instance, images obtained by satellites, which are easily available in the United States, but sometimes considered a "national security matter" in the country from which the image is taken.

Dependency on developed countries is another characteristic of underdevelopment and is apparent, in a broader context, in the slavish imitation of foreign models by developing countries. This attitude is contradictory, since they also reject intellectual colonization and overvalue their own national characteristics. This is the result both of media control by foreign agencies and of a whole politico-economic manipulation of backward countries by the developed nations, which has prevailed for centuries. Foreign products and ideas are promoted so massively in developing countries that they inhibit the generation of a national model or an appropriate technology.

R. Prebish blames transnational companies for this situation, as they promote the intnernationalization of consumption in the Third World, causing new forms of dependency and deeper inequalities within those societies. T. dos Santos identifies this syndrome with underdevelopment itself and calls it "dependent capitalism,", while A. G. Frank explains it through his theory of "metropolis-satellite polarization.", Both theories imply a condition of stagnation, within which the dominated country is tamed to consume products and information that the dominant country wants to disseminate and to sell. In such a context, an information system in an underdeveloped country must attempt to deal with (and may break) the monopoly of information by some foreign groups and with the difficulty in selecting what is really needed from what is an artificial need created by the external producer or controller.

It is a further complication that, within this setting, an environmental information system has the role of encouraging and supporting research groups to develop indigenous knowledge and consequent technology appropriate to the local environment. Reaction to foreign domination can range from "idolatry" of foreign models to an overestimation of national values. Nationalism is a common feature of developing countries, which is revealed at the international forum by overstressing each country's right to self-determination and control over its own natural resources. Extreme nationalism tends to have a negative effect on information systems, as it makes the country impermeable to external ideas and developments, besides creating obstacles to the exchange of information.

Here again, the question of secrecy is relevant, since oversecrecy might impede the supply of information about specific aspects of the environment, such as natural resources and health, to both foreign countries and supranational organizations. A last factor—a deficient educational system—is one of the basic handicaps of developing countries. As far as environmental information systems are concerned, it affects all levels: information professionals need better training in both information techniques and subject content; the specific users, that is, the environmental managers and scientists, are not aware of the information resources available and how to obtain and use them; and the whole population needs to have free access to all levels of education and information in order to be able to achieve a better quality of life and then value a clean, balanced environment.

Implications of Environmental Policy

The sensitive nature of a national environmental information system makes it entirely dependent on the policy adopted by the central government in relation to the human and the natural environment, since it is intended to support government programmes, and it is, moreover, maintained by government. Six points have been identified as the main components of environmental policy which could determine the basic characteristics of an environmental information system. These components are:

- Strategy on natural resources
- Industrial development objectives
- Pollution criteria and parametres
- International exchange platform
- Attitudes toward public participation
- Subject areas of R & D encouraged

Conservationist Policy

When the central government adopts a conservationist policy in the management of environment the results may be as follows:

Strategy on natural resources. Emphasis will be on natural resources, in a search for their protection for ecological reasons and their preservation for future generations. As a whole, in this situation there will be a smaller volume and less variety of data to be managed by the information system than under either of the other two policies. However, the area of natural resources will probably be the strongest feature in the system.

Industrial development objectives. The government will probably not encourage the implementation of industries because it values a clean environment more than the economic growth of the country. Environmentally sound technology will be welcome, even though government is not deeply involved in supporting its development. Thus, the information system will have a weak monitoring activity and lack of data on pollution and the socioeconomic environment but a good deal of information on alternative technologies.

Pollution criteria and parametres. Regulations to control pollution are very restrictive as part of the scheme to discourage industrial development. There will be emphasis on the promotion and collection of studies like environmental impact statements.

International exchange platform. Conservationists are usually prone to considering the environment as a common inheritance of all living beings. If held in governmental circles, this attitude is likely to lead authorities to adopt, in diplomatic and international discussions, an open position about environmental subjects. It may also lead to a disposition toward the free international exchange of information and willing participation in any international information networks.

Attitude toward public participation. Government will welcome public participation in environmental affairs. However, the fact that government is already meeting environmental needs may mean that less public pressure is exerted on the subject and, accordingly, that less information support is demanded. If it really occurs, the information system will not be a priority for government unless channelled for public education on ecological matters.

Subject areas of R&D encouraged. Government will tend to sponsor educational and research programmes in subject areas related to natural sciences and landscape planning, and so the supporting information systems will be sponsored as well. There will be a tendency for users of the information system to be scientists and researchers, followed by environmental managers.

Ecodevelopmental Policy - When government has taken an eco-developmental line, the whole planning system is directed to environmentally sound socioeconomic development, presenting the following specific tendencies:

Strategy on natural resources. Nature is seen as a benefit to be shared by the whole world and a resource to be thoughtfully used and individually managed by each country. Information will be needed about: (a) the basic components of the environment (air, water, soil), both from the theoretical approach to nature and from a practical view of local environment; (b) products of soil and water, the so-called renewable natural resources, from both naturalistic and economic points of view and under both global and local approaches; (c) mineral resources, their nature, reserves, careful means of exploitation and research data on potential renewable substitutes; and (d) recycling of resources.

Industrial development objectives. Industrial expansion is an important issue, and government emphasizes the development of technology appropriate to the physical and the socioeconomic environment of the country. Transfer of technology is considered in accordance with priorities of the recipient country, and exchange of information—especially on AT—among developing countries is highly considered.

The information system will develop a collection of data and documents on technological and socioeconomic facets of industrial development. Hard data will be demanded as much as qualitative information. All possible information on resources—conserving, raw material saving, low-energy, low-waste and nonencroaching technologies should be collected and made available. Information should also be supplied on methods of assessing environmental impact and undesirable deterioration by natural disasters and human misuse. The social subset of the information system dealing with the human environment is going to be highly considered and demanded by the government.

Pollution criteria and parametres. Pollution control regulation is quite comprehensive and more flexible, as the parametres vary regionally according to the carrying capacity of the local environment. This flexibility is part of the strategy to attract industries and keep them under the control of the local environmental agency. Monitoring systems, in this case, must be quite complex, and the resulting data are going to be a subset of the information system. The environmental impact statements are equally valuable. Information on the social aspects of pollution associated with poverty and bad sanitary conditions might receive high consideration.

International exchange platform. Ecodevelopment pays particular attention to developing countries sharing the same problems and similar environmental conditions. However, most of the studies and research are carried out in developed countries. Backward nations adopting an ecodevelopmental policy are usually open to an international exchange of information, even though they are also very zealous in the pursuit of their national sovereignty.

Developing countries will always expect to receive information from the developed world, but they tend to be reluctant to supply information about their own resources and policies if the requesting country is not an ally or does not belong to the same politico-economic group. In this context, the developing country may participate officially in international information networks, but the ambivalent nature of its participation is likely to create some practical difficulties with the other members and ethical problems for information workers.

Attitudes toward public participation. Government will encourage public participation, which is expected to occur in all representative groups of society, which will be manifesting different positions. It will result in high pressure on the government and, consequently, on the information system. Data and document collection must range from conservation of natural resources and the social aspects of the human environment to high technology for industrial development, not disregarding information to the general public about means of solving routine environmental problems. All forms of community information will come under the umbrella of an ecodevelopment policy of government.

Subject areas of R&D encouraged. Government will give incentives to educational and research programmes in a variety of environment-related subjects, such as natural sciences, agriculture, environmental and sanitary engineering, AT, environmental education, environmental medicine and urban and landscape planning. Therefore, environmental information systems must be prepared to satisfy demands related to these programmes. Users will also represent the following variety of interests: environmental managers, governmental planners, scientists and technologists, social scientists, researchers, lecturers and, by extension, the population as a whole.

Technocratic Policy

A technocratic government tends to mean development at any cost, with environmental disruption accepted as a by-product of progress. In these circumstances the tendencies are as follows:

Strategy on natural resources. Nature is regarded solely as an economic resource to be used in the most profitable way. The information required about natural resources will always show the economic bias of government and will stress the demand of quantitative aspects and the available technology to exploit existing resources. Data on natural resources, mainly mineral reserves, are a fundamental requirement of government and usually considered a sensitive subject.

Industrial development objectives. A technocratic government tends to understand development as being synonymous with economic growth and to consider industrial expansion as the way to reach it. It will have little concern for protecting the environment and preventing pollution. Information will be demanded on cheap, profitable technologies, whether or not they are harmful to the environment or to people.

Pollution criteria and parametres. Pollution control regulation is quite limited and parametres very lax, so that industries are not deterred from coming to the country in question. Some monitoring is performed in order to alleviate the consquences of heavy pollution. Social information related to pollution of poverty may eventually receive some consideration, with marginal interest, to back up development programmes.

International exchange platform. Backward countries with great ambitions to develop try to get the maximum in resources and knowledge from outside in order to reach their goals more quickly. At the same time they attach some secrecy to information about their own natural reserves, which they plan to exploit on their own behalf in the future. These countries have a very conflicting international relationship, as they need and want help, but they are not willing to renounce some rights to their national sovereignty in exchange. It rebounds on the information scene by creating an ambiguous position: central government controls main decisions about international exchange and is eager to receive information but is very secretive in giving it to foreign countries. This position makes it more difficult for them to participate in international networks or to collaborate with information systems of supranational organizations.

Attitude toward public participation. Government will not give incentives to public movements in favour of protecting the environment, but these will certainly occur as a result of the official neglect of the natural and the social environment. Nor will programmes of environmental education be given much incentive. However, information systems will be asked to follow the development of the ecological movement, at both national and international levels, in order to provide government with necessary information to support its policies and promote its good environmental public image. The information system will probably be a high priority for a technocratic government, as it associates scientific and technological information with economic development.

Subject areas of R&D encouraged. Government will give incentives to development of applied knowledge. R&D information will be accordingly promoted, mainly in areas of industrial technology, agriculture and all different branches of engineering, where the abatement of pollution will also be included. Users will be mainly government planners and technologists.

Since the political process is very dynamic, the overall policy adopted by government in the management of a country's environment will determine the specific policy of environmental information. Reciprocally, that policy is also likely to be influenced by the information available to policymakers. In the potential of information professionals to persuade environmental policymakers lies a great deal of their power to cooperate for the betterment of life quality on Earth and especially in the Third World. This improvement cannot be achieved without environmentally sound development and the assurance of justice for all.

Chapter 6

Heritage in Environmental Management

BROADENING ENVIRONMENTAL MANAGEMENT

Environmental management should be considered as a means for attaining sustainable development. However, the direction of this development should not be solely determined by a purely ecological environment, but must include the human aspect, as expressed by cultural diversity. Although present-day indigenous populations may still display original characteristics that illustrate their unique ways of adapting to the natural as well as to the human environment, often the most authentic expressions of knowledge and know-how are hardly remembered and lie hidden in the archaeological heritage. These remains of the past may hold a huge potential for understanding how we became what we are and what lessons past successes and failures may teach us, but they are, at the same time, prone to destruction for multiple reasons.

Current protection measures don't work well, partly because of a lack of efficient enforcement, and partly because of the great complexity of the problem. All development projects in archaeologically interesting areas should therefore include an archaeological impact assessment (AIA), and foresee appropriate measures for protecting ancient remains. This means that political will, at all levels, must exist to include

AIA in the project cycle and to execute it properly, after which monitoring of the archaeological heritage must be organised. Hence the need for awareness-raising and capacity-building at all levels. A possible way of reaching this objective could be to include the cultural dimension in existing legally binding environmental agreements on the international level, or to negotiate a convention *sui generis* that combines both aspects.

If sustainable development means that we can continue to use all kinds of resources for our own development, while guaranteeing that future generations can also establish and enjoy a good quality of life, and if, furthermore, we accept that sustainability comprises aspects of natural environment, social welfare and economic well-being, then the very concept of sustainable development must be broad enough to encompass the multiple facets of human society.

The omnipresent, though mostly unconsidered, cultural characteristics of human society in general make up a very important aspect of the driving forces that ultimately determine the direction of development. However, human society varies widely according to historical background and geographical setting. Hence the need to take into account the cultural specifics of countries, or regions, when designing development plans.

Regardless of their diversity, cultures share general components (social, economic, political, and religious) which relate to their earlier stages of development or to foreign inputs, and show the ways in which they managed to interact with, and adapt to, their environment, both natural and cultural. Many clues to this understanding can be found in the cultural heritage in general, but particular aspects may actually lie buried in the archaeological heritage.

Since this book focuses on the practice of environmental management, and the cultural dimension therein is not currently taken into account, we shall divide this into a first part that gives some basic definitions, a second section with more practical points about cultural and archaeological heritage, environment and development, including examples in the form of case studies, and a final part suggesting some ideas for the future. Since the author's experience in this field mainly lies in South America, the topic under discussion is written against this background and with examples from Ecuador. When transposing the same problems to other regions, some degree of adjustment may be necessary.

First of all, we consider environmental management to be a means for sustainable development, not an end in itself. Sustainable development must be the objective for human society as a whole, be it in the developed world or in the developing world. The first needs to become a healthier society, while the latter must catch up in a sound way. As stated in the Brundtland report:

sustainable development is not a fixed state of harmony, but rather a process of change in which the exploitation of resources, the direction of investments, the orientation of technological development, and institutional change are made consistent with future as well as present needs.

This means that, for the time being, we must limit the use of the environment if we don't want to exhaust our natural resources. Simultaneously, we need to help poor countries develop in a sound way, which, in turn, demands an extra amount of resources. In order to resolve the apparent contradiction, we must combine environmental policy with development policy. In doing so, we should be able to reduce poverty, increase democracy and control consumption and demography.

However, care must be taken not to establish a one-sided, narrow-minded concept of sustainable development, which would then tend to impose itself in a rigid way everywhere. It would almost certainly be a western point of view, based on exclusively western assumptions about development and sustainability. This would only be a repetition of past errors and be doomed for quick failure. On the contrary, a lot of input is needed from the quiet majority, the ones that traditionally have been recipients and have been directed towards targets that were not their own. If we are serious about sustainable development, we need to accept that there is not one but several facets to sustainability, reflecting the many actors who will be participating in the drama of the future.

CULTURE AND SUSTAINABLE DEVELOPMENT

When speaking about development, culture usually is not an issue. When considering development assistance, cultural aspects are hardly ever included in plans, programmes or projects. A possible explanation is that development assistance has always been regarded as a purely technical matter, while culture has been viewed rather in the opposite way. A more important and, at the same time, more negative distinction between both has to do with feelings of solidarity with broad population levels when talking about development assistance while thinking in terms of distance, abstraction and being somehow elite-oriented when mentioning culture.

Culture can be defined as learned behaviour, transmitted from generation to generation, for coping with both the natural and the human environment. It is therefore based on tradition, but also on innovation, and is characteristic of a geographical region at a certain point in time. Cultures can be very long-lived, evolving slowly in one place, or expanding their influence in an imperialistic way. They can disappear suddenly, due to disaster, or be conquered and replaced by other human groups. Wherever cultures are located and whenever they existed, the natural environment has always been of key importance, by the mere fact that human development has been a process of progressive domination of nature in order to ensure survival. They have been managing their environment in their own right, in the same way as we are trying to do now. In this continuum, our ideas may replace earlier ones or combine past and present knowledge.

Although culture dynamics can ultimately teach us a lot about the success stories or failures of extant or extinct social systems, the careful observation of particular culture traits may give insights into their unique ways of adapting to specific environments. These ways often include ideal solutions to particular problems, examples of adapted technology that are generally more environment-friendly than present-day practices.

As states, indigenous people often have a unique knowledge of their environment and its natural characteristics. In combination with modern scientific research, this knowledge can produce new opportunities for sustainable development. Therefore, indigenous people should be given more rights of self-determination, should administer their own natural resources and participate in the decision-making. Finally, indigenous people should be protected against dominant societies that threaten their natural resources, culture, prosperity and way of life.

First, the many different, specific cultural answers to environmental conditions can form an inventory of possible alternatives for good environmental practices in development policy. Therefore, thought should always be given to local knowledge when planning development actions, seeking direct involvement of the local population. In this regard, recent trends in development assistance and environment, calling for more bottom-up and participatory approaches, must be warmly welcomed.

Second, it will soon become clear that not only cultural specifics, that are technical solutions, may play an important role in finding the right solutions, but the whole of society targeted by the development activities must have an input into the process. Only then can development be socially integrated, guaranteeing not only positive direct results, but also long-term improvements and multiplicator effects.

In the long run, repeating the exercise over and over again will enhance cultural sensitivity on both sides of the development co-operation, making for better results, closer relations and mutual understanding of each other's needs and deeds.

Cultural heritage

Cultural heritage encompasses all possible expressions of a society. We generally think of material phenomena such as art, technology, architecture, etc., but whatever particular cultural trait we look at, no abstraction can be made of the ideas and beliefs embedded in it. One of the main problems in the present-day cultural reality of certain societies is the degree to which the original traits have been altered by the importing of foreign ('modern and progress-oriented') elements, such as technology, economic systems, models and the like. A good example is South America, where Iberian conquest willingly changed all aspects of pre-Columbian society. By now, 500 years later, a lot of knowledge would have been lost forever, were it not that historical and archaeological research is recuperating it.

The developed countries also have an important share of the responsibility in the cultural realm. Haven't we imposed our culture on many societies in different latitudes, thereby inflicting serious damage or actually destroying unique local cultures? The principle of 'the polluter pays' may work in the material dimension, provided there is still a way to mend the damage and that nature can regenerate, but on the cultural level, being entirely man-made, the destruction may have been terminal. If a local population has been exterminated, who is going to bring it back to life? At most, it can be re-created to serve as a showcase in some ethnographic museum, but the living thing, the dynamic society, has stopped existing. Need it be said that the developed world was a cultural depredator long before turning to destroying nature? If the origins of the latter can be tracked back to the industrial revolution, did not the first start shortly after the Neolithic revolution, several millennia earlier?

As rich countries, with the extra resources and knowledge to take care of cultural heritage, it is our duty to be guardians not just of our own cultural heritage and that of the countries we are related to, but also of world heritage, so as to ensure that future generations can know and understand the rich cultural diversity on our planet. In order to do so we must decisively undertake actions to preserve and protect the cultural heritage. This means that we should invest in the safeguarding of culture, for we can only protect and preserve those cultural elements we know. Through anthropological research in the field, a lot can be learned about important aspects such as local political and social organisation. Present-day knowledge and technology can be studied through direct contact with people, but certain traditional features may be harder to detect by simple observation or interview. Some of them may actually be forgotten, buried in the minds and in the soil. Archaeological research may therefore not only recover the origins of the local population, explain the reason for their presence and actual situation, but additionally discover fine examples of ecologically well-adapted technology, dating from centuries ago.

Several other examples could be mentioned, but entering into the details would lead us too far. There are, however, interesting elements on the level of infrastructure, such as condensing water from daily mist and using it for irrigation in the desert west coast of South America, or increasing agricultural areas and preventing soil erosion by a wide array of terracing and channelling techniques, of which many good examples exist all over the world. On a smaller scale, and still awaiting further exploration, ancient technology continually startles researchers with many examples of simple and very logical technical solutions for a wide variety of problems in metallurgy, ceramics, architecture, food storage, etc. They may not serve industrial purposes, but they can still be applicable on the artisan level.

Recuperating Technology

In many regions of South America, a traditional agricultural system known as 'raised fields' has been reported since ancient times. It is composed of raised parcels of land, limited by small, shallow channels, which are interconnected and feed into bigger watercourses, while being interspersed with dammed areas for stocking water reserves. This way a dynamic system of drainage and irrigation is created. When located in tropical lowlands, this is its main function. However, identical agricultural systems also occur in the interandean valleys or high altitude plains of South America. Here, research has proven that during the dry period in the Andes the water in the channels creates a microclimate by absorbing sun heat during the day that is radiated at night, providing the extra degree or tenths of a degree Celsius that may make the difference between conserving the crop or losing it all by freezing. As these raised fields are located on the valley floor or lower slopes, drainage/ irrigation may also be a function.

Archaeological investigations of the raised field complex to the North of Guayaquil, Ecuador, have dated the earliest phase of this system as far back in time as 2000 BC, increasing its extension and complexity over time. During the last pre-Columbian period, that is AD 500-1500, vast areas of the Guayas plain were covered with raised fields, articulated around a hierarchy of settlements, providing the economic basis for chiefdoms that reigned over the tropical wetlands behind the pacific coastline.

Not only did the raised fields yield different kinds of crops, planted higher or lower on the slope of the field according to the need for more or less water, but the channels too provided an important part of the diet, through the fish and molluscs they contained, and the birds they attracted. Maintenance of the system required periodic cleaning of the channels by removing the deposits and spreading them on the fields, as a natural fertiliser. This way the raised field system became an interestingly diversified source for subsistence and surplus production.

Excavations of raised fields and settlements associated with them have given a clear picture of how adapted technology could sustain a large population and its social development for many centuries, failing only at the moment when the Spanish Conquest disrupted the indigenous society. Experiments with planting crops on selected fields have proven the potential of the system even today—an excellent example of lessons to be learned from the past and possibilities for applying them to the future.

Archaeology

Archaeology is the scientific discipline that studies past cultures, and their development, based on the material remains that these cultures have left behind. It does so through surveying the landscape, registering all kinds of visible remains and by excavating sites where those remains are buried. The remains of the past are not only limited to what we traditionally consider as such, that is objects and buildings, but include all things produced, used or slightly modified by man, comprising a variety of elements—bone, seeds, soils, stone, wood, shell, metal, ceramics, etc.

All these elements, together with the specific context in which they are encountered, and its structure, allow the archaeologist to build a sequence of cultural events, reconstruct the way of life at different points in time and infer the broad historical processes. In order to fulfil its objectives, archaeology seeks the help of many other disciplines: anthropology, history, geology, physics, chemistry, biology, etc. For the present publication the past is defined in a very broad way, be it fifty or a thousand years ago. Archaeology discerns many different periods, based on geographical, chronological, cultural or evolutionary parametres. There may be South American, prehistoric, Roman or Iron Age archaeology, each of them—and many more—with its own specifics.

They may be important at the time of actually conducting archaeological research, but not for this kind of general discussion. Age is not necessarily a factor in determining the importance of archaeological remains. The standing remains of the past may have a fair chance of surviving, at least partially, if the population is respectful of them, through identifying themselves with the ruins of their ancestors. Unfortunately, architectural remains often serve as quarries for cheap building materials. The finest Inca masonry embellishes modern chimneys in Peru, and Indian carpentry becomes incorporated as decorative elements of houses in the west. These are just two simple examples of a much wider problem. In a way, it may be a minor problem, because of the size, weight or visibility of the objects being moved. On the other hand, there are hundreds of thousands of less spectacular, though even more destructive, pillages going on. Most of these concentrate on the buried remains of the past, with a marked preference for ancient graves. Millions of funerary objects can be found on the shelves of museums and private collections, be they ceramic pots, textiles, basketry, metals or any other artefact that accompanied the dead in the afterlife.

The great majority is the product of illegal excavations and trade between developing countries and the rich nations. On both sides, unscrupulous people have established the necessary channels to plunder the archaeological heritage for the sole sake of economic profit, thereby destroying beyond repair what may be unique contexts. Although archaeological cemetreies may be particularly vulnerable to this greed, a lot of other situations are disastrous for the buried archaeological patrimony. Most big building projects, such as roads and dams, don't take into account the existence of archaeological sites, and numerous controversies have arisen where ancient remains have been detected in time, holding up progress and causing huge economic losses.

But a lot of damage can also occur on the level of the individual citizen. It covers the wide range from innocent sherd-picking on archaeological sites to organised treasure hunting, from souvenir buying to illegal traffic in antiquities. All these destructions seriously limit the potential for discovering lost knowledge that may be of use today. Quantifying the amount of trade in cultural heritage will always be difficult, since an important part of it occurs clandestinely. However, recent estimates speak of US$ 1 billion worth of commerce, a great part of it made up by archaeological patrimony. This makes it second only to drug trafficking on world level. Some figures may illustrate the seriousness of the situation:

- In 1973 some 1 per cent of the economically active population of Costa Rica was estimated to be involved in illegal excavation or commerce of the results of it, representing about US$ 0.5 million annually (Walden, 1991).
- Of all thefts of cultural property, and in the case of illegal excavation probably less, only 12 per cent is ever recovered, meaning that over 88 per cent enters the illegal trade network (ibid.).
- One of the incentives to loot and sell the products can be found in the dazzling increase in prices for art and cultural property. The most important auction houses report incredible growths in revenue over the last ten years. Sothebys increased 800 per cent, Christies 700 per cent.

Archaeological Heritage

We look at the archaeological heritage as an important resource for sustainable development, a resource that is both instructive and finite, and thus irreplaceable. We therefore urgently need to consider the cultural aspect of our environment as essential as the ecological one. We must work out ways to protect the cultural environment from becoming as deteriorated as the natural environment now is. We suggest that one way of doing this is to define our environment in an integrated way, meaning that we are talking of a cultural-ecological environment. A few general reasons underlie this thinking:

- The natural environment doesn't have a lot of meaning if it doesn't include all of its components, a key player being man. The mere fact that the human element is now jeopardising its natural environment, makes it all the more interesting to investigate how such a situation was arrived at and, more importantly, how it used to be, when man and nature had a more symbiotic way of life. Maybe history can show us similar problems in the past and teach us how they were solved.

- Ecological preservation has hit the news for decades now, but it used to be completely different. We remember the times when almost anything was allowed in order to attain a higher level of development, including destroying the natural environment, resulting in the situation we have now. So let us not commit the same error on the cultural level, as we need it for assuring the right quality of life of future generations.
- There is a perceived need for safeguarding biological diversity, the rich natural variety of living species, which should be transposed to the cultural level. The many different cultural expressions represent the variety of adaptive responses to equally different situations, both natural and social, that can, ultimately, teach us solutions to present-day problems. So preserving the remains that illustrate the cultural diversity can have modern applications.
- Cultural identity is a fundamental need of populations that are undergoing major processes of change, as is the case of developing countries trying to catch up. Their feeling of proper identity must be strong enough to assimilate foreign inputs and to retain their own, while being constantly influenced and measured by international, universal standards that have no meaning whatsoever in their native world-view. Historical background, reflected by the archaeological remains, represents a key factor in cultural identity.

These reasons notwithstanding, modern-day measures for protecting the archaeological heritage leave much to be desired. Although legislation exists in almost every country, enforcement is usually very low key on both sides of development. If Italy still struggles with its tombaroli grave looters, one can imagine what the situation is in developing countries. Alarming, and often very sad, reports come from everywhere: primarily Middle and South America and Africa, but also South-East Asia. In all these regions, countries are facing the ever-increasing pillaging of their archaeological sites. Manifestly the most efficient protection measure is expropriation of the archaeological site, turning it into an archaeological park with appropriate infrastructure for tourism or recreation. But only very few sites qualify for this kind of treatment, because of the high costs involved and the often very complicated legal aspects.

Levels of Decision-making

Once the importance of the cultural heritage in general, and the archaeological patrimony in particular, has been accepted, one must ensure that it will be taken into account when designing development plans. First of all, of course, the political will must exist to redefine the environment as a dual concept that comprises both natural and cultural aspects. This battle against traditional theories and conservative bureaucracies may not be easy, but the concept of sustainability in all its facets should be of paramount usefulness. Its emphasis on social and economic aspects, besides the ecological one, should allow for broadening the scope of the definition and, as a corollary, the scope of action.

We must beware of being overoptimistic: the systematic inclusion of cultural aspects, let alone the archaeological heritage, in the broad field of development planning will indeed be a very hard task. A comparison with ecological conservation can be instructive. Even now, after decades of warnings, the systematic screening of development projects on their environmental consequences is only slowly finding its way into the higher levels of decision-making. The discussion about extending the environmental impact assessment (EIA), on the project level, to the strategic environmental assessment (SEA) on the policy level, has only just been initiated and promises to be lengthy. We can only hope that the new ground being broken there will provide a path for our purposes.

At the highest level then, policy-makers need to be convinced, but regional authorities and local people are equally important. Indeed, many times already the initiatives that eventually lead towards the execution of development projects have originated within the population that, later, will become the target group of those projects. Development should always happen this way. Problems should be recognised by those who suffer their consequences, and be communicated to the next level of hierarchy, which should take action to solve the problems. Too many times in the past, and even now, existing problems were perceived at a high level of decision-makers who then turned to external sources for help, both economic and technical, without a thorough knowledge of all the aspects of the problem in question. As a result the solution offered often failed to meet the expectations and the real needs of the population involved.

The input of the local population is especially indispensable when considering cultural aspects and archaeological heritage. High-level policy-makers may belong to an entirely different cultural group, or may simply ignore the existence of archaeological remains. Many reasons may exist for not taking these elements into account, most commonly lack of interest or fear of complicating the action under consideration. This does not mean that the central authority cannot have good ideas for developing local groups; it does mean that close co-operation between the local population and the authorities at all levels, from the very beginning of development planning, will undoubtedly lead to easier execution and positive results. External donors should be very much aware of this mechanism and, without intending to dictate to the developing countries, should definitely try to promote local involvement in decision-making.

When speaking of local authorities, a wider range than the official authorities should be envisaged. Sometimes, government officials at the local level are people brought in from outside the region and may lack sympathy with the local group and its historical roots. In parallel, there may be an ethnic local government, according to traditional social organisation. It is not uncommon to have several tribal chiefs, ethnic lords, or whatever, living under the authority of a representative from the central government. These chiefs themselves head a complex social structure, not necessarily compatible with the official government structure, and are probably acting as buffers between the official and the ethnic sides. When it comes to implementing development plans successfully, the local ethnic players may prove to be of decisive importance. Their familiarity and identification with the region, both ecologically and historically, their knowledge of ancient technology and archaeological sites will all be assets in designing and implementing integrated development plans.

The intervention Cycle

If we are serious about giving consideration to the cultural aspects of a society, and among them the historical testimonies of its identity, then we need to do so from the outset. Any intervention in a country, region or human group should evaluate the possible consequences for the archaeological heritage of the involving people target population, in exactly the same way that the impact on the natural environment is being assessed.

The community of Agua Blanca, located in the valley of Rio Buena Vista, lies in the southern part of the Province of Manabi, on the coast of Ecuador. This small community, composed of some 40-odd families, living in a small hamlet and some scattered houses in the valley, subsisted traditionally on a mixed economy of fishing, some cattle-herding and limited agriculture.

Being situated in the heartland of the pre-Columbian Manteño culture (AD 500-1500), surrounded by a fair quantity of architectural remains, an important complementary income was generated by pot-hunting in the archaeological sites.

When the area was incorporated into the Machalilla National Park in 1979 and serious restrictions were imposed on the exploitation of natural resources, archaeological looting practically became the main revenue for the local population, in spite of the fact that one of the park's objectives was to preserve the archaeological resources. Regularly, recognisable Manteno objects from the region invaded the antiques market, a practice that continued for several years.

It wasn't until the 1980s, when a British archaeologist became interested in the area and started designing a research project that the local people became aware of the damage they were inflicting on their heritage. By explaining the importance of the ancient remains, showing their extension in the valley and beyond, and inferring the economic and social situation, he was able to raise the locals' interest in their 'ancestors'.

When starting his research, the archaeologist hired the local people to participate in the survey and excavations. During fieldwork frequent comments were heard about similar finds the locals had made during their looting campaigns and the archaeologist could gather a lot of additional information. He was even allowed to see several personal collections and learned about others.

Over time, becoming ever more acquainted with the local population and its problems, the archaeologist managed to finance certain improvements in the infrastructure of the valley and took effective steps to promote the archaeological heritage, so that tourism started to increase.

After the fieldwork and the processing of the archaeological finds, the local people became involved in the maintenance of the site and finally ended up attending the visitors. In order to present a better view of the history and the archaeological heritage of the region, a museum was built and was equipped with a few objects stemming from the excavations and...a lot of artefacts donated by the local people. Nowadays, the daily care of site and museum is in the hands of the community. The income from entrance fees and from the selling of handicrafts has completely replaced that from archaeological looting. Additionally, the Agua Blanca community is known as an important defender of the archaeological heritage, organising meetings with other communities in order to raise awareness through communicating their own experience.

This means that an archaeological impact assessment should be considered, as an integral part of EIA. Ideally, this exercise should begin as early as the identification phase of an intervention, but should continue throughout the rest of the cycle. Indeed, not everything can be foreseen when it comes to evaluating the archaeological heritage of an impact area, given that many elements may be buried, and trying to detect the totality of them beforehand may be beyond the overall scope of the intervention. Flexibility during the whole project cycle thus becomes a very important characteristic. Flexibility in general should always be a prime concern when designing and executing development plans.

The screening of interventions for their eventual archaeological impact should be integrated into the systematic environmental screening, by including specific questions that seek general information on visible or known remains from the past. Further key questions relate to the amount of subsurface intervention that is planned, as it may affect buried elements. The quantity and quality of the remains must then be evaluated and safeguarding priorities established. Not everything can be preserved but a representative sample should be protected by changing the intervention modalities or localities. A few exceptional sites may be worth saving from destructive large-scale projects in the way UNESCO did at the time of the building of the Aswan dam.

If, at an early stage, the projected activities of the intervention suggest that part of the archaeological heritage will be affected in a negative way, specific actions need to be taken in order to avoid or minimise impact. If no danger exists, the intervention can go forward. If there are uncertainties about the type and extent of the archaeological heritage that will be affected, then further study is warranted. Ultimately, an entire project could be cancelled because of unjustifiable destruction. Before such a harsh decision is taken, however, alternatives to the original project should be sought or redesigning of the project should be intended.

Impact Assessment

As soon as the archaeological elements of a region are considered to be an integral part of the environment, then any AIA should not be separated from the general EIA. It would just be another dimension of EIA, to be handled by an archaeologist within the EIA team, since only a professional can have the accurate knowledge of both the existing information and the techniques actively to discover ancient remains.

The first step is getting acquainted with the intervention area and the objectives of the project. This should give initial indications about a potential impact on the archaeological heritage. Many interventions may be rapidly qualified as non-destructive, so that no further action is required. Projects in sectors such as public health and education rarely jeopardise archaeological remains. In general, only interventions that modify the landscape, including any form of digging, should be closely watched.

During the second step, unless the archaeologist in charge is completely familiar with the region, time will be needed to study the specialised literature. Information may be found in old maps, travel accounts, early geographical descriptions, historical archives, former official documents, excavation reports, anthropological studies, etc. All elements thus discovered should be mapped provisionally and their existence and state of conservation verified in the field. Interviewing people who know the area and its history well may increase the preliminary inventory of archaeological remains. At this point, a better idea of the potential impact can emerge. Once the verification and final mapping is completed, certain patterns in the ancient remains, or the lack of them, may show up and a decision on the need for further research must be taken.

Up to this point the assessment may be considered as a standard screening and scoping procedure, identical to environmental screening and resulting in a broad classification of the kind 'no impact', 'low impact', 'high impact'. In addition, however, there may often be insufficient information available. Indeed, lack of information in archaeology doesn't automatically mean that there are no remains; usually it means that they haven't been found yet, mostly because they are buried and thus invisible to the naked eye. The decision on whether or not to continue investigating will be difficult, since any further research will be more specialised, longer term and more expensive.

The next step represents the active search for archaeological remains through a wide variety of surveying techniques. Where available and applicable, remote sensing is a great tool for having easy access to extended areas. Aerial photography, originally used for national cartographic purposes, is an important source for detecting monumental remains. Satellite images can do the same with an ever-increasing degree of detail and resolution. Low altitude aerial photography can even show buried remains through soil marks, crop marks or shadow marks. But no survey would be complete or accurate without a pedestrian phase, walking the area while scrutinising the surface for remains of buried sites. In order to limit time and expenses, several sampling techniques can be applied. If a realistic image of the archaeological heritage is being pursued, then test excavations must be conducted.

Only in this way can the depth and the characteristics of archaeological components of the region be established. Now the archaeological picture should be sufficiently clear to evaluate the real impact of the planned intervention. The archaeological impact assessment in itself can be considered to be finished, but mitigating actions may be warranted. Setting aside an eventual follow-up, it should be clear that, at this stage, already a lot of energy and resources will have been allocated while the possibility of cancelling the intervention still lures. This may result in very tough decisions to take, much in the same way as applies to the ecological environment, but sooner or later this is the point we should reach. If planning starts a long time ahead and if it is integral, that is integrating all aspects of sustainable development, then a lot of surprises can be avoided and enough time will remain to either conduct the necessary research or look for alternatives. Ultimately, the real anticipatory approach, as stipulated by SEA, should prevail, thereby transcending the narrow and restrictive project-by-project approach.

Once the archaeological picture is crystal clear, decisions with regard to the project must be taken. Several options may be present and we shall run through them briefly, from no special action required to project cancelled. After an exhaustive study of the project impact area there may be no evidence at all of standing or buried archaeological remains. Obviously no special action is then required and the planned project can go ahead unmodified. The archaeological study may have come across remains of the past that will be impacted by the project activities as originally set out. Different possibilities for the conservation of the cultural elements arise:

1. They may be left untouched by changing the project.
2. They may be safeguarded against the effects of the project.
3. They may be saved by removing them from their original location.
4. They may be destroyed.

In order to arrive at the best solution, many factors must be studied, compared and weighed for each option and a lot will depend on the kind of project activity and the type of archaeological remain. In order to illustrate these options let us suppose that a development project will inundate part of a valley with the aim of providing drinking water, irrigation and electric power to the populations downstream. After having studied the area archaeologically, the project may be approved on the condition that certain modifications be introduced and complementary activities be taken up. The modified version of the project may reduce the height of the dam, limiting the flooding so that archaeological sites may be left untouched (1). The most important remains may be surrounded by a protective wall, creating sunken islands (2), or they may be dismantled, transported to higher grounds and reassembled (3). A few sites, considered less important because they are repetitious or have been studied thoroughly, could be sacrificed (4).

However, a site should never be destroyed without being properly registered, meaning that its location and characteristics are carefully described. Because each archaeological site has a story to be told, destruction should be the last resort, conservation being the prime target. Nevertheless, trying to preserve every single testimony of the past is utopian and undesirable. It would turn the whole world into a showcase, denying the right to progress. The ultimate goal of conservation is sustainable development, not stagnation by exaltation of antiquity.

It should be clear by now that any form of AIA and its follow-up will inevitably cause additional time and money requirements on the part of the project. These incremental costs should be considered in the same way as the present environmental impact consequences of development projects. Funding facilities should be available for cultural/ archaeological impact mitigation, much in the manner they operate for the impact on the ecological environment.

In this sense it is a promising perspective that the World Bank encourages borrowers to incorporate into their environmental action plans any major cross-sectoral issue, including cultural and natural heritage. The World Bank considers the conservation of important cultural property to be part of the sustainable development process because the important cultural values of a society or social group are frequently reflected in cultural property. Also UNDP has expressed and practised the linkage between its global urban development co-operation strategy and the cultural preservation of historic cities, especially in Latin America and the Caribbean.

Protecting Sites for Conservation

Given the importance of the archaeological heritage as a key factor in the identity of people and as a potentially rich source for traditional knowledge and know-how, given also the possible omnipresence of the archaeological patrimony and therefore its proneness to destruction, given finally the ever-increasing lack of already scarce resources for research and *ad hoc* conservation, mechanisms should be developed to go beyond the project-oriented approach, that is to anticipate possible problems during project preparation, much in the way that the EIA approach is now trying to move towards an SEA approach.

The strategic approach in archaeological conservation would involve vast programmes of archaeological reconnaissance and survey, in order to establish the extension and characteristics of the heritage, followed by effective and efficient measures to assure its long-term conservation. Indeed, if we want to protect our common patrimony, we first need to know precisely where it is located and what the most immediate dangers are. We therefore suggest we start out around big cities or other places that are expanding rapidly so that once specific urbanisation plans appear we already know how to adapt them to the situation of the archaeological heritage.

Important archaeological sites or areas may eventually become real archaeological parks that are well-protected areas where any kind of disturbing activity is banned or controlled by law. The number of these parks, at any time, will probably be limited and reserved for very special monuments, but a fair amount of archaeological sites may be combined with existing ecological reserves or natural parks, thereby enhancing these with the human aspect, while profiting from the protective ruling. Where the previous solutions are not feasible, archaeological sites should be turned into green areas within the urban perimetre. The kind of activities allowed in these places will depend on the characteristics of the site. Standing remains should be protected against direct contact. Buried sites could serve as a recreation area as long as interference with the subsurface archaeological layers is avoided. Sometimes adding a protective cover of topsoil may create a perfect archaeological reserve, while allowing some social function.

Monitoring

Once a clear picture of the archaeological heritage exists and the different degrees of conservation categories, with their specific conservation measures, have been established, a matching system of monitoring should be devised. Monitoring is here understood to be the periodic evaluation of the state of conservation of an archaeological site.

According to the kind of site and the protection measures that apply to it, monitoring can range from a simple inspection visit in the case of public green areas, to a specialised and integral monitoring mission when checking on important monuments. It should be carried out by a specialised national institution, normally the same one that establishes and assigns the conservation categories.

In any case, special care must be given to an adequate level of reporting of the monitoring exercise, developing a standardised reporting system so that the information gathered over time may be comparable. That information should include aspects other than the mere physical condition of the site, covering its use and abuse, its social and economic functions or potentials, paying special attention to the informal economy that tends to build up around tourist places.

Quito, the capital of the Republic of Ecuador, is located on a step-like terrace of the interandean valley, that runs North-South along the Western Cordillera. A long-stretched city of a little over 30 km long by 5 or 6 km wide, at 2,800 m above sea level, and almost exactly on the Equator, it is endowed with year-round spring weather and a rich variety of ecological niches in the immediate surroundings.

No wonder human occupation in and around Quito is among the oldest in Ecuador, dating back as far as 7000 BC with well-established settlements in what is now the city from 1500 BC onwards. The Neolithic village of some 26 hectares and 700 inhabitants has now become a capital that occupies approximately 20,000 hectares and houses 1.1 million people, and is growing rapidly.

The Municipal Planning Unit has analysed the historical information on urban growth over the last 85 years, establishing a decreasing growing rate, but still projecting a doubling of the urban area to over 40,000 hectares by 2020, and a tripling of the population to almost 3.5 million. On the other hand, recent archaeological research in the Quito Valley by the Belgian Agency for Development Co-operation has established a density of one archaeological site per 2 km^2, based on a systematic regional survey by sampling.

The conclusion from both types of information can only be that over the next 20 years a total of 100 archaeological sites will be lost, due exclusively to the urban expansion of the capital. Therefore, a project was suggested, and will hopefully be implemented some day, that would develop the capacity of the municipal services to anticipate the emergency situations that will occur once effective urbanisation starts.

The project would basically aim at the organisation of a municipal archaeological service which, in close co-ordination with the office for urban planning, would design a survey programme systematically to cover all the areas that will eventually become incorporated into the city. The presence and characteristics of ancient sites would be registered and evaluated in order to assign conservation categories and priority degrees for their protection. According to this system, urbanisation plans will have to take into account the archaeological heritage and adapt to it. The project would also contemplate campaigns of awareness-raising in the other municipal services and at the level of the general public.

Although the basic research preceding this conservation classification, i.e. survey and excavations, will require specific human and financial resources, positive outputs may be expected in terms of understanding the region's archaeology, and in terms of significant economic gains at the time of urbanisation, by avoiding costly delays in work already started.

Awareness-raising and Capacity-building

In a field that is as new as environmental management and archaeology, much awareness-raising and capacity-building is required. In many developing countries a lot has still to be done on the level of basic archaeology teaching. Indeed, with a few notorious exceptions, professional training leaves much to be desired and when formal teaching exists, it is often concentrated on the theoretical level, leaving the students with hardly any field experience by the time they graduate. Whenever these young professionals get involved in emergency situations or regular research, their work clearly shows those training deficiencies.

This situation has originated a kind of intellectual or cultural colonialism on the part of foreign scholars or graduate students, who are eager to find new fields of study in the developing countries. They used to invest time and money to explore these lesser-known regions and become experts and founders of new archaeology departments at home. Fortunately, many of the early explorers have taught local people in the field or have provided grants to study abroad. However, even today we must ascertain that there still are, mostly at the doctoral dissertation level, European and American graduates who exploit intellectually the archaeological heritage of a developing country by conducting their research without feeding back its results to the country that generously hosted them.

In order to take up the archaeological heritage in the environmental management, capacity-building should be applied to different levels. At the highest level, political will must be created by informing the policy-makers about the importance of the cultural and archaeological heritage in identity-building and sustainable development, emphasising its educational role and taking into account its economic potential. Ministries of culture and education, national institutes for the cultural heritage or national museums for history and archaeology should take the lead in these awareness-building, seeking examples of proven good practices in other countries. Enhancing the capacity to cope with the more practical action plans on the national level may require specific assistance from outside.

In the professional realm, a quality basic training in archaeology at the national university level should be assured, complemented with specialisation possibilities abroad, through grant agreements with foreign academic or technical institutions. Emphasis should be put on the interdisciplinary approach of archaeological research and on the social function the discipline should pursue, beyond the pure scientific immediate results. General notions about the objectives and functions of archaeology should also be introduced in related disciplines, especially those that are frequently in the field that is natural sciences but also, and very importantly, urban planning and general development.

At the service level, much archaeological information is lost through lack of reporting or destruction by ignorance, due to the fact that fieldworkers of companies or institutions that take care of electricity and telephone distribution, of water or sewer infrastructure, etc. have not the slightest clue to the importance of the remains they come across. These people especially are in constant contact with subsurface layers in the urban and rural area, and countless stories have been heard of the many fortuitous finds they have discovered during work. Workers and field supervisors, as well as the higher administrative levels of these companies and institutions should therefore receive some basic knowledge of how the past may appear in their daily work, who they should report to and what emergency measures eventually could be taken.

Finally, at the level of general education, starting in primary school and from there up, the young should not only learn about their country's history on a textbook basis, but should be confronted directly with whatever remains of that history are left. Raising awareness about the importance of conserving the evidence of past cultures should be developed together with building up the ecological conscience. Basic education probably represents the most important level on which to work for this purpose, since it means both investing in the future—this youth will soon become the main actor in sustainable development—and creating a multiplicator effect through the influence youngsters exert on their parents.

International Co-operation

Our self-imposed programme for the future, Agenda 21, covers a wide array of hopes and aspirations for a better future, intrinsically relating the environment to the economics and social aspects of development. Several legally binding offsprings of the Rio Conference are well underway in taking effective and efficient measures to put ideas into action. However promising and necessary all this is, the cultural dimension of development is still missing.

Little regard is given to the uniqueness of the social systems that managed the environment in ways that were much more sustainable than our 'modern' alternatives. At the most, brief references are made to the need for recuperating local know-how, but only very rarely is mention made of the preservation of indigenous culture. Since no precise definitions are usually given, the question of how culture in this context is exactly conceived remains wide open. One strongly senses that it is rather limited to folk culture, the present 'exotic' aspects of foreign people, not the rich totality of traditional beliefs, knowledge, art, technology, etc. that has its most genuine expression in the archaeological heritage.

One of the reasons for this lack of cultural dimension may be due to the fact that other bodies have been involved in these problems at an earlier stage and, at the same time, from a more technical point of view. The international organisation that first comes to mind is UNESCO, which adopted the World Heritage

Convention in 1972—the same year of the Stockholm Conference on the Environment—in order to protect the *natural and cultural* heritage against increasing threats of destruction by natural and human causes. Earlier conventions deal with the protection of cultural heritage in armed conflict and with the measures to prevent illegal import, export and transfer of cultural heritage. So, apparently, several international agreements are taking care of the cultural and archaeological heritage. In effect, a lot has been done, but past and present efforts were not able to, and still can't, keep up with the ever-increasing pace of development and the subsequent destruction of ancient remains. UNESCO alone can't handle the situation, although it has been building partnerships on a regional or national basis everywhere.

Clearly, synergy must be developed if we want sustainable development to become a truly integral approach. In the same way that the mixed sites, that is natural and cultural heritage sites, on the World Heritage List make up only 3.86 per cent of the total, cultural considerations within the purely environmental realm are equally insignificant. However, neither Agenda 21 nor the ILO Convention contain any direct reference to the safeguarding of the indigenous cultural heritage, although both admit the importance of traditional knowledge and know-how concerning the management of natural resources. The same recognition of local knowledge, and appeal to use it, can be seen in the Convention to Combat Desertification, while the Convention on Biological Diversity shows only very indirect reference.

It seems then that a better co-ordination between the existing international agreements is warranted. Probably a combination of environmental conventions and cultural agreements, as a legally binding mechanism, could do the job. The right formal framework and practical organisation of such a co-operative effort should be established as soon as possible. The conclusions and guidelines that might result from this negotiating process should be incorporated into the overall sustainable development policy. Only if there is a concerted exercise at the international level with enough technical and moral authority can we expect the individual countries to start effective actions on behalf of the cultural and archaeological heritage. The environment will then have broadened its definition, beyond the aspect of mere natural resources, to the integral concept of environment with an emphasis on the interaction of man and his natural environment through time, the historical experiences of this relationship and lessons learned therefrom for their application in the future.

Environmental management, as a means for attaining sustainable development, must encompass all aspects of the human environment, including natural and cultural elements. When this objective is clear to all stakeholders, recognising the fact that certain cultural elements and archaeological remains contain knowledge and know-how that is applicable today as an alternative to current, negative practices regarding the natural environment, then the cultural/archaeological heritage should become an integral part of any form of environmental management. Consideration of this heritage should become fully integrated into the initial screening and scoping of development projects on their environmental effects and, if necessary, an archaeological impact assessment (AIA) should be fully incorporated into the EIA procedure.

As a result mitigating actions or simple disapproval of a project may occur, but monitoring should be ongoing. Needless to say, for this suggested course of action awareness must be raised at all levels and local capacities must be systematically increased. It seems logical that this objective could best be reached within the framework of existing, international and legally binding environmental agreements, but if this proves to become difficult, then a special convention may be warranted. The concept of global benefit also applies to the archaeological aspect of the environment, since this heritage represents our collective memory, locally but also universally, and the loss of any culture, past or present, is tantamount to the loss of a biological species. It would be ridiculous to preserve biological diversity while disregarding the diversity of our own species.

Index

N

O

P

Q

R

S

T

U